Live Poetry
An Integrated Approach to Poetry in Performance

| 153 | Internationale Forschungen zur
Allgemeinen und
Vergleichenden Literaturwissenschaft

Begründet von Alberto Martino und in Verbindung mit

Francis Claudon (Université Paris-Est Créteil Val de Marne) – Rüdiger Görner (Queen Mary, University of London) – Achim Hölter (Universität Wien) – Klaus Ley (Johannes Gutenberg-Universität Mainz) – John A. McCarthy (Vanderbilt University) – Alfred Noe (Universität Wien) – Manfred Pfister (Freie Universität Berlin) – Sven H. Rossel (Universität Wien)

herausgegeben von

Norbert Bachleitner
(Universität Wien)

Redaktion: Paul Ferstl und Rudolf Pölzer

Anschrift der Redaktion:
Institut für Vergleichende Literaturwissenschaft, Sensengasse 3A, A-1090 Wien

Live Poetry
An Integrated Approach to Poetry in Performance

Julia Novak

Amsterdam - New York, NY 2011

Gefördert durch das DOC-Stipendium der Österreichischen Akademie der Wissenschaften und den Theodor Körner Preis.

Gedruckt mit Unterstützung des Bundesministeriums für Wissenschaft und Forschung in Wien und mit Unterstützung durch die Österreichische Forschungsgemeinschaft.

Cover design: Pier Post

Le papier sur lequel le présent ouvrage est imprimé remplit les prescriptions de "ISO 9706:1994, Information et documentation - Papier pour documents - Prescriptions pour la permanence".

The paper on which this book is printed meets the requirements of " ISO 9706:1994, Information and documentation - Paper for documents - Requirements for permanence".

Die Reihe "Internationale Forschungen zur Allgemeinen und Vergleichenden Literaturwissenschaft" wird ab dem Jahr 2005 gemeinsam von Editions Rodopi, Amsterdam – New York und dem Weidler Buchverlag, Berlin herausgegeben. Die Veröffentlichungen in deutscher Sprache erscheinen im Weidler Buchverlag, alle anderen bei Editions Rodopi.

From 2005 onward, the series "Internationale Forschungen zur Allgemeinen und Vergleichenden Literaturwissenschaft" will appear as a joint publication by Editions Rodopi, Amsterdam – New York and Weidler Buchverlag, Berlin. The German editions will be published by Weidler Buchverlag, all other publications by Editions Rodopi.

ISBN: 978-90-420-3405-1
E-Book ISBN: 978-94-012-0692-1
© Editions Rodopi B.V., Amsterdam - New York, NY 2011
Printed in The Netherlands

Acknowledgements

"Ladies and Gentlemen, please give it up for ..."

Several people have made important contributions to the development of my PhD project. I am grateful to my supervisors Prof. Eva Müller-Zettelmann and Prof. Werner Huber for assisting so competently at the birth of the complicated brainchild that is my thesis, and for providing invaluable advice and feedback. During the last three years, Prof. Huber has supported me in the two-fold role of co-supervisor and employer, and it is not least because of his commitment that I have been able to complete my project within a reasonable time span.

I wish to thank Elisabeth Siegel, my fellow doctoral candidate and colleague of several years, whose constructive criticism and encouragement I much appreciate: she has tirelessly read all the chapters in this book, some in multiple versions. Many thanks also to my other colleagues at the English Department – Elke, Susi, Sandra, Dieter, Johnny, Paul, and Stephen – who have variously provided critical feedback, strategic and stylistic advice, encouragement, tea and sweets. I further owe thanks to Karin Lach, who for many months gave me a quiet place to work in the English Studies Library, and to Henry Widdowson, who shed light on some of the linguistic issues that my work raised.

I am indebted to all the poets and live literature practitioners who permitted me to record their performances and patiently answered my questions about their work in interviews, thus helping me gain a better insight into the nits and grits of live poetry. Special thanks go to Melanie Abrahams of 'Renaissance One' and to Maggie Pinhorn and Liz Weston of 'Alternative Arts', who mentored my first professional steps in the live literature sector, making them an enjoyable and formative experience.

Furthermore, this is the place to thank Margit Ötting, my former English teacher at school, whose excellent, inspiring lessons over four years gave me a head start at university, and, of course, my parents: for taking me to the UK on holiday countless times and encouraging my interest in British culture and the English language. I guess that's how it all started.

Finally, I cannot thank my husband Jakob enough for sending me off to the library to find definitions of "live" and "poetry" when I was unsure how to get started, for keeping me alive with countless lunches and dinners over the past years, for tolerating my sloppy, workaholic ways, for cheering me up in times of doctoral crisis, and for generally being the best thing that has happened to me yet.

Thanks to all of you.

Table of Contents

Introduction — 11

Part One: Theorising Live Poetry — 15

1. Key Challenges for the Scholar of Live Poetry — 15
- 1.1 Neglected History / a History of Neglect — 15
- 1.2 Like So Much Hot Air? Live Poetry and the Discourse of Orality — 18
  - 1.2.1 Orality versus Literacy: The Great Divide — 19
  - 1.2.2 From Orality to Literacy: The Evolutionist Model — 22
  - 1.2.3 Performance Poetry: A Controversial Form of Live Poetry — 29
- 1.3 Literature Review — 33

2. Towards a Definition of Live Poetry — 49
- 2.1 Poetry as a Bi-Medial Art Form — 49
- 2.2 Live Poetry and Theatre — 56
- 2.3 A Definition of Live Poetry — 62

Part Two: Analysing Live Poetry — 63

3. Comparing the Written Poem and the Performed Poem — 65

4. Audiotext — 75
- 4.1 Audiotext and Paralanguage: Experiential Meaning Potential, Provenance, Voice Set and Voice Action — 75
- 4.2 Non-Verbal Sounds — 80
- 4.3 Articulatory Parameters — 85
  - 4.3.1 Rhythm — 86
  - 4.3.2 Pitch — 99
  - 4.3.3 Volume — 109
  - 4.3.4 Articulation — 115
  - 4.3.5 Timbre — 120
- 4.4 Notation — 125
- 4.5 Composite Parameters: Tone of Voice, Accent — 132
- 4.6 Paratext — 138

5. Body Communication	145
5.1 Kinesics: Studying Body Communication	145
5.2 Functions of Body Communication	151
5.3 Elements of Body Communication	158
5.3.1 Gesture and Posture	158
5.3.2 Facial Communication	164
5.3.3 Artefactual Communication	168
5.4 Notating Body Communication	170
6. Contextualising the Performance	173
6.1 A Communication Model for Live Poetry	176
6.2 Participants	178
6.2.1 The Poet-Performer	179
6.2.2 The Audience	194
6.2.3 The MC	200
6.2.4 The Producer	202
6.2.5 Aims and Format	204
6.3 Spatio-Temporal Situation	207
6.3.1 Localised Audiences in 'Borrowed Spaces'	207
6.3.2 The Performance Space	209
6.3.3 Place of Performance and Fictive Space	214
6.3.4 Time of Performance and Act Sequence	216
7. Jackie Hagan's "Coffee or Tea?": A Sample Analysis	221
8. Checklist for the Analysis of Live Poetry Performances	233
Conclusion	237
Bibliography	239
Table of Figures	263
Index	265

"And the willingness to expose the poem to aural reception is not, as I see it, of a different order from the willingness to print it."

Denise Levertov

Introduction

> Listening to 'live' poetry, from being the peculiarity of an odd few, has come to be accepted (as it was long ago) as an unsurprising thing to do, and one which a good many people have increasing opportunities to experience. [...] In the big cities there is not a month in the year when the poetry buff can't find some reading to go to. (Levertov 46)

Published in 1981, US-American poet Denise Levertov's assessment of the popularity of live poetry – poetry performed or 'read' by the poet in front of a live audience – holds true for the beginning of the twenty-first century. Although poetry has long been pronounced a dying literary genre in terms of the publishing market,[1] it is experiencing a renaissance through the spoken word. The UK, like the US, has recently seen the development of a dedicated live poetry scene consisting of organisations, festivals, and agencies that organise poetry events all over the country and are fully committed to the spoken word. What is new about these developments – after all, poetry readings and performances have existed for a long time – is the willingness to concede to live poetry an aesthetic value independent of print. With the spread of specialised live poetry events such as the open mic and the popular poetry slam, the English-speaking world has become increasingly aware of the aesthetic and social potential of poetry in its spoken form.

Literary critics, however, have barely taken notice of the activities of the new live poetry scenes: unlike printed collections, poetry performances are hardly ever reviewed. "This absence of documentation," Charles Bernstein notes, "together with the tendency among critics and scholars to value the written word over the performed text, has resulted in a remarkable lack of attention given to the poetry reading as a medium in its own right" (22). This neglect may be due in part to the fact that live poetry bears not only literary but also musical (speech melody, rhythm, etc.) and theatrical (mimic, gesture, etc.) features, which complicate its unambiguous allocation to traditional research disciplines and review categories. Live poetry would thus appear to be situated in an undefined, liminal zone, with the result that few people feel competent or responsible for its critical examination. Although poetry has long been an object of literary studies, the discipline offers no systematic methodology, no analytical 'toolkit,' with which to address the distinctive characteristics of *live* poetry. The aim of this study is to close this methodological gap by developing a systematic approach to live poetry that is suitable for the study of contemporary popular forms such as 'perform-

---

[1] See for instance Neil Astley's statement, "all the talk in poetry publishing is of crisis," in his article "Give Poetry Back to People."

ance poetry' as well as more traditional poetry 'readings.' The proposed mode of analysis is based on a conception of oral performance as a basic realisation mode of the art of poetry, which is a parallel to, rather than a mere derivative 'version' of, the written mode. Live poetry is thus defined as a specific manifestation of poetry's oral mode of realisation that is characterised by the direct encounter of the poet with a live audience.

I start out from the assumption that means of describing and analysing live poetry already exist in some form and that suitable methods can be found in various disciplines that can be made applicable to the study of live poetry.

Part One, "Theorising Live Poetry," lays the theoretical foundation for an academic study of poetry performances. Chapter 1 outlines the key challenges of scholarly occupation with live poetry, namely the lack of historical documentation and of a critical language. Twentieth century developments in literary studies and theatre studies are scrutinised with regard to their relation to live poetry and the value judgments surrounding it as an oral art form. In the light of a notional 'Great Divide' between orality and literacy, live poetry is often represented as a derivative practice in opposition to a stable written 'original,' and thus the diverse and complex relations existing between poetic writing and speech are often obscured. The literature review, finally, sketches out major areas of research which have demonstrated an interest in various aspects of live poetry. The review highlights the findings that this study can build on and points out shortcomings in terms of a coherent methodology for the study of poetry in performance.

Chapter 2 examines the materiality of live poetry as an artistic medium, identifying it as a basic realisation mode of the art of poetry rather than as a mere oral presentation of a printed work. The chapter reviews the quasi-acoustic terminology applied in literary studies to discuss the 'evoked' sound of (written) poetry and reveals its shortcomings for analysing the real, physical sounds of live poetry. In order to arrive at a definition and clear profile for 'poetry in performance' as an artistic medium in its own right, live poetry's relation to the medium of theatre is explored in view of its distinguishing features.

Part Two, "Analysing Live Poetry," presents the 'method proper': a broad range of analytical criteria drawn from various disciplines. Many of the examples discussed can be viewed as video files on www.livepoetry.net – the companion website to this book. After some preliminary thoughts on methodology and corpus, Chapter 3 charts the possible contrastive relationships between written and performed poetry, demonstrating how such a comparison of the two modes reveals the aesthetic characteristics and possibilities of live poetry.

The audiotext chapter focuses on the acoustic dimension of live poetry, with special emphasis on the concept of paralanguage. It broadly distinguishes between (segmental) non-verbal sounds and (supra-segmental) articulatory parameters. The discussion of the latter – incorporating aspects of rhythm, pitch, volume, articulation, and timbre – stresses their interrelatedness as aspects of an integrated acoustic performance and reveals the inadequacies of page-bound concepts (such as metre) for the analysis of live poetry. The chapter then devotes a separate section to different possibilities of notating audiotextual features, before introducing the composite parameters of tone of voice and accent and investigating the applicability of Genette's concept of 'paratext' to live poetry performances.

The subsequent chapter on body communication tackles the visual aspects of live poetry, identifying different functions of body behaviour – from expressing emotions to regulating interpersonal interaction – and demonstrating how the visible body can add another layer of meaning to the performed poem. The rubrics of gesture and posture, facial communication, and artefactual communication direct the researcher's attention towards different elements of body communication, pointing towards their role in live poetry by way of kinesic concepts and illustrated examples.

Chapter 6 – "Contextualising the Performance" – recognises live poetry as a strongly context-dependent art, the production and reception of which coincide in a common effort of various participants in a specific time and place. This section offers a communication model for live poetry that recognises that a poem's fictive speech situation is brought forth through an actual speech situation. The individual roles and aims of the poet-performer, audience, MC, and producer are then examined so that the interrelatedness of these participants, their spatio-temporal situation, and the larger aims and format of a performance can be analysed in greater detail.

Chapter 7 constitutes a sample analysis of a live poetry performance which implements many of the critical criteria introduced in order to demonstrate how they can be integrated meaningfully. Chapter 8, finally, provides a checklist for the analysis of live poetry that is intended as a practical aid for the researcher: essentially an analytical grid based on the aspects of live poetry performance discussed in Part Two.

This project was born out of a keen interest in live poetry which was instilled by my own professional experience in the UK literature scene. A declared aim of devising an approach to live poetry was to reflect current practices in live poetry: the study thus incorporates findings from personal interviews with poets and other practitioners. This endeavour to engage with the actual workings of a flourishing live literature scene will, I hope, render my approach all the more relevant. Ultimately, this approach may also help to achieve a concomitant long-term objective of this project: to bring live poetry into the mainstream of literary research and criticism.

Part One: Theorising Live Poetry

1. Key Challenges for the Scholar of Live Poetry

The key challenges any current scholar of live poetry needs to address are the neglect of live poetry as a subject worthy of academic study – and the resulting lack of historical documentation and a critical language – and the value judgements of live poetry and scholarly occupation with it in the light of the traditional literacy/orality dichotomy.

1.1 Neglected History / a History of Neglect

> How is it that poetry readings have come to be an essential part of the writing and distribution of poetry over the past 40 years? The interrelation of campus readings, avant-garde performances, poetry slams, ethnic performance, religious arts, and the heritage poetries of minority languages has not yet been researched, and we know almost nothing about how specific poems, poets, and types of poetry have been shaped by expectations of performance. [...] In our view, histories of English-language poetry of the past 60 years are so much based on the study of printed texts that they miss one of the most important forces at work in the shaping of poetry at all levels of its form, meaning, and genre. (Marsh, Middleton, and Sheppard 46)

The focussed interest among academics in the oral performance of poetry is a relatively recent phenomenon, noticeable for instance in funding initiatives such as the British Arts and Humanities Research Council's "Beyond Text" programme, which supports, among others, a research project on "British Poetry in Performance, 1960-2008" (see http://www.beyondtext.ac.uk). For the most part, however, the scholar of live poetry is dealing with a subject whose history is, as yet, mostly unwritten. To give an impression of the richness and complexity of this history it suffices to mention some of the poets and literary currents in the second half of the twentieth century who clearly regarded performance as a crucial aspect of their art:

The early 1950s saw Dylan Thomas's famous reading tours through the United States, increasing the popularity of poetry readings at a time when Charles Olson propagated his notion of 'projectivism' (51-62). Olson's insistence on the essential connection between verse and the human breath would influence the Beat Poets and their practice of "writing for the *voice*" (Cusic 80), which was underlined by frequent live performances. Harry Lewis writes of a "growing sense," generally felt in the New York of the late

1950s, "that poetry was not an art experienced best in print" (85), and the Black Arts movement of the 1960s and 70s embraced live poetry performances particularly as a means of political self-assertion.

Similarly, Jamaican dub poets in Britain voiced their political concerns and demands for social justice in their live performances in the late 1970s and 1980s, writing poetry for the express purpose of moving live audiences. Another notable performance-oriented group in England were the Liverpool Poets, who appeared on the scene in the 1960s. Their lively performances were influenced by American Beat poetry, which is another example of the cross-fertilisation of live poetry between continents. In the 1980s, British punk poets such as John Cooper Clarke and Attila the Stockbroker came to fame, frequently performing with punk bands.

In the late 1980s a new poetic mass phenomenon, the poetry slam, was born in the US and spread to many parts of the world over subsequent decades. The popularity of this democratic competition format – with poet-performers judged by the audience – led to the development of a large spoken word scene in the US and the rise of 'performance poetry' in the UK in the 1990s, which today incorporates such diverse practices as the hip hop poetry of Jonzi D or the humorous work of John Hegley, influenced by stand-up comedy. Together, they form part of what Dana Gioia terms "the wide-scale and unexpected reemergence of popular poetry" (*Disappearing Ink* 7), which has amazingly "thrived without the support of the university or the literary establishment" (7). These recent developments have led to the postulation of 'live literature' or 'spoken word' as an art form in its own right. They point towards a renewed interest in the oral delivery of poetry which also extends to the more traditional poetry 'readings' that often seem to be staged as a means of marketing the written word rather than advancing a distinct performance aesthetic.

Despite the conspicuous new interest in orality in the literary world, which is also manifest in the proliferation of literary festivals over the past decades, the trend has not caught on in academia. Introductions to the study of poetry still largely ignore the oral realisation mode (see Chapter 2.1). Neither literary studies nor theatre studies – a neighbouring discipline that seems well suited to shed light on the performative aspects and the 'liveness' factor – have so far undertaken systematic attempts to charter the uncertain territory of live poetry in its past and present. This twofold neglect has itself a history.

The literary scholar's prioritisation of the book as his/her central focus of interest originates in the pre-eminence of scripture and print when literary studies established itself as an academic discipline (Hiebler 474). In the twentieth century it was particularly the rise of New Criticism that led to a conception of text as an autonomous object which ought to be studied independently of cultural context – "*sub specie aeternitatis*" (Brooks x) – to emphasise its universal artistic value rather than its historical contingency. Kenneth Sherwood, reflecting on the "emergent" dimensions of live poetry, concedes that the second half of the twentieth century brought about new currents of critical thinking which "have opened certain contextual or extratextual spheres and showed the text itself to be less than stable and determinate," from "Structuralism, Psychoanalysis, and Marxist criticism to Feminism, Deconstruction, New Historicism and gender and ethnicity theory" (120). With regard to performance, however, they "have effectively left the published text firmly anchored as the object of literary study" (120). Ruth Finnegan observes that one may frequently encounter references to performance as conceptualised in J. L. Austin's theory of "performative utterances" or in postmodern "discussions about 'performativity' or 'performing' gender" (165), but these "seem to follow up rather different issues" ("The How of Literature" 165) than the oral realisation of literature in a live performance. This disregard of oral performance, its dismissal as a mere "vehicle for textual distribution" (Marsh, Middleton, and Sheppard 46), is epitomised by the very term 'poetry reading,' which conflates the two modes of realisation – the acoustic live event and the silent reading of written text – describing the former in terms of the latter.

Conversely, the history of theatre studies represents a continuous move away from the authority of the written text towards the live performance on stage as its primary concern and the acknowledgement of theatre's essential plurimediality. Theatre studies have, in fact, developed in opposition to literary studies and its traditional treatment of theatre as textual artefact (Fischer-Lichte, *Ästhetik* 42f), which would explain why live poetry with its strong focus on the verbal, albeit orally performed text, has so far been of little interest to the field.

Subsequently, the twofold neglect of live poetry by scholars of literature and theatre is reflected in the lack of a "critical language for performance-based critique," as deplored by writer Ruth Harrison (Breeze et al. 31).[1] Ian Ferrier strikes a similar note with both his contention that "the best poets on the page are no more or less powerful than the best onstage. What's changed is the toolset" (36) and his advocation of "a vocabulary that defines the toolkit a performer is using and then engages the performance on its own terms" (37).

---

1   In a 'roundtable discussion' with Harrison in 1999, dub poet Jean 'Binta' Breeze complains that critics do not "come to a performance and critique the performance, like how you critique a play," and is answered: "They don't really know what they're doing, do they?" (Breeze et al. 31).

While the absence of a 'critical language' poses obvious problems for live poetry scholarship it may, by extension, hamper the progress of the art form as such, as Tom Chivers demurs:

> I do think it's important that with any emerging art form that there is a large degree of critical engagement because, for me, one of the scariest things is that this whole scene will explode. There will be tons of people excited by spoken word and ready to go to events because they've heard so much about it and then they turn up at some dreadful open mic night, where there's no production values, the poets are rubbish, the MC is some stuttering fool [...]. What critical engagement will do is to create a sense of what's good, what's not and equally a sense of pathways between what's not and what is. (Chivers interview)

Finally, Fortner Anderson makes an important point regarding the absence of rigorous methodology for a scholarly occupation with live poetry in view of its future:

> Without a critical discourse, there is also no history. [...] once all the sound of the words and performances has faded away, all of it slips quickly and irrevocably from memory. Without comment, analysis, interpretation and judgement, both masters and poetasters have been forgotten. (46)

If literary scholars today continue to sideline live poetry as an inconsequential by-product of printed poetry, as lying outside their academic domain, future scholars will find no documentation and prior critical engagement from which to reconstruct a history of live poetry that will enable them to engage with new developments in the light of their historical context. It is exactly this lack of a critical 'toolkit' to guide and facilitate criticism of, and reflection on, poetry in performance that the current study aims to redress.

1.2 Like So Much Hot Air? Live Poetry and the Discourse of Orality

We encounter poetry as written or spoken word. These two medial possibilities – orality and literacy – are frequently conceived in opposition to each other and are not always ascribed equal artistic value. For decades scholars from different fields have engaged in a discourse around the orality/literacy dichotomy and revealed the set ideas held about these two modes of verbal communication. While this debate is now regarded as largely historical, traces of the traditional dichotomy remain observable in poetic practice and criticism even today.

An awareness of the evaluative force of the concepts of orality and literacy and of live poetry's position in this discursive field is thus crucial for deciding on a methodological approach for its study. Acknowledging the artistry of a poetry performance – its specific aesthetic as one valid manifestation of the art of poetry – will, for example, lead to an approach that pays heed to its poetic form and performative aesthetic, while the negation of its artistic merit may suggest an approach that examines live poetry exclusively in terms of its sociological significance. The following is an outline of the orality/literacy debate as it applies to live poetry and the value judgements it elicits, which affects the evaluation of entire sub-genres such as performance poetry.

1.2.1 Orality versus Literacy: The Great Divide

In his introduction to *The Poet as Performer*, Don Cusic notes that "[i]n the end, the poet will be judged by his poetry and not by his performances" (8). In his view, the live performance of poetry apparently has little to do with 'poetry itself,' which is obviously envisioned as writing. The written word will endure "in the end," when the poet is no more and the oral performance – which for Cusic is something *other* than poetry – has evaporated like so much hot air.

Orality and literacy are frequently conceived of as two forms of cultural expression that stand in stark opposition to each other, as indicated in the above quotation. This notion of a Great Divide[2] is manifest, for instance, in the idea that the written poem is a stable, tangible, and timeless artefact that exists independently of situational context. Performance is envisaged as unstable by contrast, a transient process that depends on its occurrence and disappearance in time and is therefore often regarded as a mere variant of the printed 'original.' Such set ideas of an opposition between the two modes have often obscured the diverse and complex relations that may exist between writing and speech. Charles Bernstein counters, for instance, that

> there is often no one original written version of a poem. Even leaving aside the status of the manuscript, there often exist various and discrepant printings – I should like to say textual performances – in magazines and books, with changes in wording but also in spacing, font, paper, and, moreover, contexts of reader-

---

2   For a discussion of the Great Divide model, see Graham Furniss 131ff and J. M. Foley 36ff.

ship; making for a plurality of versions, none of which can claim sole authority. (8)

Moreover, Ruth Finnegan points out that the reception of poetry in a silent reading is a process located in time just as much as a live performance: she calls this the "enperformancing of a written text" by the reader, "the 'now' when the reader personally encounters and recreates" the poem ("The How of Literature" 176). Thus, from the recipient's point of view the original/variant dichotomy of the relation between print and performance may be reversed easily. Another example is when the recipient experiences the performance before the silent reading. An audience member who attended the book signing after Anthony Joseph's performance at the Vienna Lit Festival in 2006 expressed his enthusiasm for the performance and sighed that a silent reading could never be the same, whereupon Joseph answered, "You will hear my voice in your head man." This possible role of print as a reminder of a concrete experience of live poetry is contemplated by Finnegan:

> Print too may carry the sonic echoes of a sung acoustic performance. Someone who has once heard a poem performed by the Jamaican dub poet Lillian Allen, for example, [...] will surely always hear it in the printed book too: the performance in the text. ("The How of Literature" 177)

Another angle from which to investigate the relationship between written text and orally performed text is to examine a poet's compositional practice, as some poets' writing habits naturally include an oral element. Adrian Mitchell, for instance, mentions in an interview that he performs his poems out loud as he is writing. "I walk around to get the rhythm" (qtd. in Hardy 7), he adds, describing poetic composition as a rather physical process. Patience Agbabi also speaks the words to herself as she is writing: "That's part of my creative process. It often helps me if I get stuck, you know, to try to get to the next line" (Agbabi interview). Anthony Joseph reveals that "when I'm writing I'm singing the words back to myself to see how they sound, so, you know, it's a very integrated process. [...] I want to create sculpture in the air" (Joseph personal interview). If poetic composition is in part an oral process the original/variant dichotomy could again be turned on its head in this respect, with the writing becoming a 'mere transcript' of a prior oral 'original.'

Significantly, some poets relate that their public performances may impact back on the writing. Lucy English describes her compositional practice as a two-way process:

> To me – okay, it may start as an idea – but I write it first on the page and it's there and I will edit it and work it. Then, when I start to perform it, what sometimes happens is that it changes because it needs a few performances to sort of settle. (English interview)

Similarly, Allen Fisher notes, "My poems are never complete until I've read them to somebody. If there's any rewriting it takes place after the first reading. ... Public might only be two people, but it would need to be public" (Marsh, Middleton, & Sheppard 60). Thus, a written poem is by no means 'carved in stone,' the words may still be altered if a live performance uncovers some hidden flaw: the live poem can serve as a measure for the print poem. Automatically assigning an oral performance the status of a mere 'interpretation' of the seemingly immovable original of the printed poem, to which it stands in opposition, would thus be a gross misrepresentation of the complex relations that may develop between writing and speech in the processes of poetic composition and reception.

Finally, the conception of speech and writing as two opposed forms of cultural expression is refuted by the numerous poets who view book publication and live performance as integrated practices which together make up the artistic activity of poetry. British poet Rommi Smith, who was the UK's first parliamentary writer in residence and performed on many occasions to a public, invokes performance skills as a basic requirement of her vocation. In an interview, she expresses her admiration for Patience Agbabi's second collection *Transformatrix* in view of Agbabi's skills as a writer *and* performer, noting that "*Transformatrix* for me is a benchmark about how you craft on the page but also you are a really sharp performer of your work, and I think that's incredibly important" (Smith interview). She also points to the economic aspect of performance, responding to the question whether she ever rehearses for a live performance as follows:

> Of course. And that's because if you are going to communicate with an audience ... I mean it's fine if you just want to publish your work, you don't want to present it ... which is a very rare thing, I mean poetry is one of the poorest sellers in bookshops, we know that. So we know that most poets, even when it's just that they have a book launch or a book tour, they are going to have to be fairly competent presenters of their work. (Smith interview)

For Smith, being a "sharp performer" and being able to "communicate with an audience" are indispensible skills for a poet.

Similarly, Anthony Joseph stresses the communicative aspect of poetry and the essential dual nature of the poet's craft. When asked about 'spoken word' and 'performance poetry' as potential labels for his work, he explains:

> I think it's "poetry." [...] I think essentially I consider myself a poet first and foremost. I think as a poet, to be a really good poet one of the abilities you need is to translate your work live. You know, and some people can do it really well, some people can do it ... not that well, but it's a skill that as a poet you should have. Because poetry for me is [...] about communication. (Joseph personal interview)

Thus, many poets regard live performance as a generic aspect of the poet's trade and effective communication with their audience as an important dimension of poetry itself rather than merely an economic necessity.

To sum up, a general opposition of 'the written poem' as a stable artefact to the variable 'versions' of oral performance is unjustified. A poet's writing process often involves elements of performance: during the first conception of a text as well as at a later stage, where oral performance may function as a corrective device. Poetic composition is an integrated process and many written poems exist in several versions, meaning that any manifestation of a poem ought to be regarded as a 'version' in the absence of a stable original. Furthermore, silent reading can be regarded as a 'performance in the head' of the written text: just as live poetry must be 'processed' by the audience, silent reading is a process with a temporal dimension, which renders the stable/unstable division meaningless. Finally, the activity of poetry comprises both writing and performing, as emerges from poets' accounts of their vocation. Communicating effectively with their audience is a central concern for many poets, as they view their craft as a form of communication. Moreover, performance skills are an economic asset, generating income directly and through increased book sales. Writing and speech are therefore not opposed to each other along the lines of a 'Great Divide' but are integrated processes of the art of poetry.

1.2.2 From Orality to Literacy: The Evolutionist Model

> [A] poem – no matter how dramatic its language and content – is an object that should be contemplated more than it should be declaimed. We can enhance our appreciation of a poem by hearing it performed by a reader, but the performance of the poem, *in itself*, is not fundamentally artistic. (Wojahn 268)

David Wojahn's conception of the poem as an "object" that should be "contemplated" continues the idea of the 'Great Divide' in that it limits the art of poetry to the written mode and dismisses live performance as an activity quite apart from poetry. Wojahn goes beyond simply opposing the two modes, however: he actually devalues live poetry by characterising it as a non-artistic practice. His statement is a telling example of the kind of views that have long defined orality and literacy as poetic media. They can be understood as a continuation into the poetic realm of the evolutionist[3] notion of orality as a primitive form of communication which the 'sophisticated Western world' has long left behind – an idea that cultural anthropologists investigating a diverse range of verbal art in different cultures have been fighting for some time now.[4] How live poetry is affected by the evolutionist stance that pervades the orality/literacy discourse shall be explored in the following section.

The term orality is often "used to denote an extended complex of elements associated with oral CULTURES – that is, cultures either unaffected by literacy and the written word or only marginally affected by them" (Hawthorn). The term 'orature,' referring to the vast field of oral verbal traditions in these cultures, was coined by anthropologists in order to avoid the inherent etymological incompatibility of 'oral literature' and also to provide "a positive term in its own right" for the diverse forms of verbal art researched under this label, as Ruth Finnegan explains (*Oral Traditions* 16). Her statement already hints at the habitual sidelining of oral traditions as primitive and inferior to the literary practices of the 'civilised' Western world. 'Oral poetry,' then, refers to a poetry that "essentially circulates by oral rather than by written means" and whose "distribution, composition or performance are by word of mouth and not through reliance on the written or printed word" (Finnegan *Oral Poetry* 16). It is generally characterised by a textual variability and fluidity (Lord 863) and often composed in a special technique that draws on "formulae" and "themes."[5] Walter Ong even suggests that oral poetry reflects the different mindset or thought patterns of the oral cultures in which it originates, contrasting them to highly literate cultures as "[a]dditive rather than subordinative" (37), "[a]ggregative rather than analytic" (38), "[e]mphatic and participatory rather than objectively

---

3   Ruth Finnegan terms this the "evolutionist model of one-way progress" (*Oral Traditions* 27).
4   See, for example, Richard Bauman, *Story, Performance, and Event*, 7-8.
5   The exact manner of composition and circulation varies, of course, from culture to culture. For an introduction to oral poetry see Ruth Finnegan, *Oral Poetry: Its Nature, Significance and Social Context*. The most famous exponent of the oral-formulaic theory is Albert B. Lord, whose groundbreaking study *The Singer of Tales* links the compositional practices of Serbo-Croatian bards to the oral-formulaic design of Homer's epics.

distanced" (45) and thus provides an example of the discourse of primitivism that still seems to pervade the research of oral traditions.[6]

Live poetry, as defined in this study, is not usually subsumed under oral poetry as its manner of composition involves writing, which makes it a case of "medial orality" – meaning that it is realised in the medium of speech – while oral poetry is marked by "conceptional orality" (Bakker 8).[7] Live poetry does, however, partake in the struggle of oral poetry to assert its value in the face of the continuous privileging of written literature as the more 'progressive' medium, implying 'civilised,' 'cultured,' 'refined' etc. The following statement points to the long history of the appreciation of speech, by contrast, as the more natural, original and vital medium for the communication of poetry. While the evaluative outcome differs, it has the same argumentative basis, attributing particular qualities to the oral medium:

> To most simple communities poetry is the gift of the gods which fills out and makes radiant this life of ours. When I think of *primitive* men, or, indeed, of any *simple* community, I think of men sitting about a poet, enjoying poetry. [...] And yet to the men in our communities poetry has fallen from her estate. (9, my emphasis)

This quotation is an excerpt from John Masefield's speech to the Scottish Association For the Speaking of Verse, given at its first general meeting in 1924, in which Masefield continues to deplore the "separation of the artist from his audience" and the fact that "[l]istening to poetry is not a national pastime at present either here or in any of the *complex* communities known to me" (11, my emphasis). In his nostalgic account of the poetic practices of "primitive men" and "simple communities" speech emerges as the genuine, the direct, the *ur*-medium of poetry which prevents the separation of art and life that he observes in the cold detachment of the "complex" civilised communities and their unhealthy fixation on the written word.

Jacques Derrida detects this evaluative opposition of speech and writing in the very foundation of Western thought, tracing it back to the work of Aristotle.[8] His critique of 'phonocentrism' is directed, for instance, against the linguistic theories of Ferdinand de Saussure, who made the following claims in his seminal *Course in General Linguistics*:

---

[6] See also Furniss 133, Bauman, *Story, Performance, and Event* 7f. and Bernstein 20 on the 'primitive versus civilised' debate.

[7] John Miles Foley calls poetry which is composed in writing but delivered orally "Voiced Text." Cf. Foley 39.

[8] Cf. Jacques Derrida. *Of Grammatology* 27ff. See also Peter Middleton, *Distant Reading* 53-54 for a discussion of Derrida's critique of phonocentrism.

> Language and writing are two distinct systems of signs; the second exists for the sole purpose of representing the first. (23)
>
> Though it creates a purely *fictitious* unity, the superficial bond of writing is much easier to grasp than the only *true* bond, the bond of sound. (25, my emphasis)

For de Saussure, as for Masefield, speech constitutes the more 'natural,' original and direct mode of communication. Derrida criticises de Saussure's treatment of speech as a pure and direct manifestation of thought marked by 'self-presence' (30), with writing being envisioned as a supplementary mode of language use which, in the absence of the speaker, represents speech as the "sign of a sign" (39ff). He deconstructs this opposition of speech and writing, pointing out that in view of de Saussure's proposition of the arbitrariness of the sign, "one must exclude any relationship of natural subordination, any natural hierarchy among signifiers or orders of signifiers" (44).

If the spoken word is frequently associated with nature, primitivity, presence, and authenticity, writing, conversely, has often come to be considered more artificial; yet it is privileged as the more advanced, cultured, and refined means of communication. Peter M. Boenisch argues that the primacy of writing has shaped the "cognitive principles at the heart of Western cultural ideology," which "is dominated by visual perception subsuming all other senses" and "favours passive consumption from a distance" ("Aesthetic Art to Aisthetic Act" 107).

The pre-eminence of writing has thus led to a prioritisation of visuality and the ordering principles it admits, which has also affected the valuation of poetry. In literary criticism, this is reflected in the analytical practices of New Criticism, for instance, which looks "for juxtaposition rather than sequence, and for spatial rather than temporal relationships, which may be appropriate for a poem by T.S. Eliot, but not for one by Chaucer," as Balz Engler (14) notes. The literary text comes to be regarded as a stable, tangible object that can be scrutinised independently of its maker and the context of its composition, very much like a visual artefact.

This conception of text as an autonomous object of study[9] later finds its most radical manifestation in Roland Barthes' notion of "The Death of the

---

[9] The conception of the literary text as an autonomous artefact was embraced in the 20th century not only by New Criticism and its insistence on the universal artistic value of literary texts but also underlies the French formalist practice of *explication de texte* (which bears similarities to 'close reading,' cf. Gudas 396) as well as the Russian Formalists' view of "the Word [...][as] an object in its own right, an autonomous source of pleasure" (Erlich 1101).

Author." In this seminal essay, Barthes advocates the free interplay of meaning in any literary text. A literary text, for Barthes is a "tissue of quotations" which "has no other origin than language itself" (146). "To give a text an Author," he claims, "is to impose a limit on that text, to furnish it with a final signified, to close the *writing*" (147, emphasis added). The 'death of the author' and its central claim that "it is language which speaks, not the author" (143) implicitly preclude the oral realisation of a poem by the poet. Since Barthes rejects the notion of originality, of the author as the source of meaning, he would most likely object to the author's presence in live poetry, regarding it as an undesirable restriction on, and channelling of, meaning through the force of his/her poetic 'authority.' His argument leaves no room, however, to even contemplate the possibility of oral realisation by the poet. Like the New Critics, Barthes – and deconstruction in general – has firmly laid the focus on writing as the one true medium of literature. Barthes's principles of criticism do not simply devalue live poetry as an insignificant literary practice – they extinguish the very possibility of oral performance as an alternative to the written word.

The evolutionist notion of linear progress from speech to writing is thus perpetuated, which is also noticeable among poets. In 1983, Vernon Scannell typically declared the poetry reading to be at best an "enjoyable and instructive adjunct" but certainly no "substitute for reading poetry on the page" (121). Decades earlier Wallace Stevens refused to read his work in public with the words "I am not a troubadour and I think the public reading of poetry is something particularly ghastly" (qtd. in Robinson 10), and very recently British novelist Martin Amis has declared poetry dead, claiming that it has "a ghoulish afterlife in readings and poetry slams" (Hart) – a view of live poetry that is far from complimentary.

One area where these evolutionist tendencies come to the fore is in the evaluation of poetry on the basis of its effectiveness in different media. This point is illustrated by Tom Schmidt's recounting of the story that poet and literary critic Yvor Winters "thought a poem should be read aloud as badly as possible. If it could survive such verbal butchering it proved, yes, that the poem was a good one" (134). The effect and aesthetic value of a live performance are thus completely discounted as, at best, irrelevant: they can be no measure for the quality of a poem – only the printed word can be. Even today, critics such as Steven Z. Athanases, who argue for "a place in a revised canon for the literary work whose value is contingent upon the interpretative strategy of performance" (117), are the exception rather than the norm. Athanases cites Gwendolyn Brooks's work as exemplary of this principle, noting that when I had first read selections of Brooks's poetry, I had found the works at times overly alliterative, joining words in ways that at moments seemed forced or showcased, draining energy from the sweep of the work. Yet later, when I would hear each poem in Brooks's voice, the cadence, the surprising intonation, the syllables held for multiple counts, I knew that in each case she had written it right or, rather had somehow composed it. [...] Brooks's poems are not *in* her books. (118)

More often than not, poetry that is apparently more effective in performance than on the page is vilified, even today. American writer David Groff, for instance, depicts live poetry as the ultimate ruin of the genre in his essay "The Peril of the Poetry Reading," warning that "[t]he prospect of eventually reading a poem aloud can also affect a poet's creative process." He claims, "looking to please the madding crowd, poets can unconsciously take aesthetic shortcuts that can damage a poem; the effects that work so well in performance are often the kind of schtick that deadens a written poem" (Groff). The effects that "work so well in performance" will "damage a poem" – that is to say, of course, "a written poem."[10] By contrast, to claim that the value of Paul Muldoon's work, for instance, is lessened because the majority of it is more effective 'on the page' would seem quite absurd. Arguably, the opposition of speech and writing, and the subsequent undervaluing of oral performance, thus continue the notion of writing as a more advanced and sophisticated medium.

These evolutionist ideas have been criticised from several quarters. An obvious argument against the primitive/sophisticated divide in the orality debate is the fact that much contemporary (written) poetry bears features of 'orature.' As Alfred B. Lord notes, orality

> gave us anaphora, the use of the same word at the end of a series of lines, alliteration, assonance, rhyme, both internal, medial and final, and the sense of balanced structure as typified by parallelism in sentences and other forms of parataxis. In short, our poetics is derived from the world of orality, with some later additions and modifications introduced by the world of literacy. (qtd. in Pfeiler, *Sounds of Poetry* 14)

Features such as anaphora and various types of rhymes are frequently found in the verbal art of 'oral cultures,' where they are employed to aid memorisation. Not only are they often encountered in the poetry of Western 'literate' cultures, they are also explicitly sought for by literary scholars, who are trained to analyse the workings of anaphora, alliteration, assonance etc. as

---

[10] In the same vein, Maya Angelou's work, which is very much written for the voice, is derided by Dan Schneider as "doggerel" ("This Old Poem").

part of their standard toolkit for the interpretation of poetry. Thus, rather than regarding contemporary 'literary' poetry as having overcome orality in its progressive development towards a more advanced form of literary expression one must recognise its continuous indebtedness to typically oral forms, which heighten, of course, its potential and suitability for oral performance.

Furthermore, Graham Furniss insists that orality lies "at the heart of *all* societies" (17), not only those commonly referred to as oral cultures. "With all the communications technology at our fingertips, why do business people fly halfway round the world to look each other in the eye as they make arrangements?" (1), he asks perceptively. Politicians, too, tend to meet up in person to carry out negotiations of national or international import rather than rely exclusively on written presentations of their arguments. In the age of television, radio, and live-stream internet broadcasts one could in fact argue that orality – and with it, personality and presence – have become more important than ever as channels of (re)presentation.[11] Politicians are increasingly trained to use their voice effectively, to mind their posture and body language and to produce quotable sound bites for the mass media.

The world of literature has, of course, been affected by this new focus on orality. More and more poetry books are published with an accompanying audio CD, or even DVD,[12] and poets have long discovered the opportunities that web platforms such as Myspace and YouTube afford for audio or video publication. Marie-Luise Egbert points out how the renewed interest in the "subliminal appeal" of the spoken word has led to the rise of the audiobook as a popular medium for literary texts of all kinds (63). Similarly, the upsurge of literary festivals over the past few decades may be regarded as a tribute to the revaluation of orality, especially in its focus on presence and the staging of personality. The great popularity of poetry slams in the USA, and, to a lesser extent, in the UK, can be cited as a further example. The 1998 independent feature film *Slam* (Trimark Pictures, USA) demonstrates poetry's potential as an audio-visual media spectacle, serving

---

[11] Walter Ong has coined the term "secondary orality" (136) for the post-literate revaluation of certain features of orality caused by recent technological developments, which is nevertheless rooted in literacy. Internet blogs and chatrooms, in this sense, are a product of secondary orality: while they are based on writing they are characterised by the fluidity, instantaneous communication and focus on community that generally pertain to primary orality (Cf. Ong 136f).

[12] E.g. Jackie Kay's collection *Red, Cherry Red* (Bloomsbury 2007) was published together with an audio recording of the poet reading her own work. Further examples are Rommi Smith's collection *Moveable Type* (Route 2000) that came out with a CD, and Bloodaxe's DVD-anthology *In Person: 30 Poets* (2008), edited by Neil Astley.

as a stage for the performance of cultural identity. Thus, orality surrounds us everywhere: in politics, in our everyday-lives, and increasingly, also, in literature.

1.2.3 Performance Poetry: A Controversial Form of Live Poetry

What is true for live poetry as a whole – the continuing dispute about artistic value against the backdrop of the orality/literacy divide – becomes all the more obvious in the case of 'performance poetry': a variety of live poetry at the extreme end of its spectrum which, as the name indicates, is entirely conceived in relation to oral performance.

What Dana Gioia terms "the wide-scale and unexpected reemergence of popular poetry" (*Disappearing Ink* 7) – under which term he includes rap, cowboy poetry, poetry slams, and performance poetry – in the USA has also taken hold in the UK. These forms of 'popular poetry' are all realised in performance and depend on orality for their materialisation. On the live poetry spectrum they are situated at the opposite pole from 'flat' poetry *readings* that make no attempt at developing a distinct performance aesthetic but are understood rather as a way of acquainting the audience with a book. Over the last two decades, performance poets in Britain have conquered pubs, small theatres, bars, radio programmes, literary festivals, and the internet. They form part of a general renewed interest in orality, as discussed above. For Neil Astley, editor of Bloodaxe Books, the rise of performance poetry has had a positive impact on the entire live poetry scene in the UK:

> [T]he flourishing of performance poetry has encouraged poets who might see themselves as writing more for the page to become better readers of their own work, and that has improved the standard of poetry readings and meant audiences have become more excited about all kinds of poetry. (Evaristo and Astley 17)

While Astley underlines the positive aspects of the popularity of performance poetry, Bernadine Evaristo points to what she sees as its negative consequences:

> I think performance poetry has become synonymous with poetry from Black writers, and that has been to the detriment of poetry that has the complexity, nuance and texture required to withstand scrutiny on the page. [...] I am not objecting to performance poetry per se, which I see as a literature/performance genre with its own specialised craft and production values, but I do object to the fact that it has taken precedence over poetry not written for performance. (Evaristo and Astley 16-17)

Evaristo refers to the fact that Black performance poets today are "among the most celebrated and visible poets in this country" (17) and have become role models for younger poets, many of whom also "aspire to become performance poets" (17) rather than to write for the page. The point is, though, that she opposes "performance poetry" to "poetry that has the complexity, nuance and texture required to withstand scrutiny on the page," while conceding that performance poetry may be "a genre with its own specialised craft and production values" that has, after all, brought success to many of "the most celebrated and visible poets in this country." In its review of various definitions of 'performance poetry' the following section will probe the value judgements pertaining to a form of live poetry that can be regarded as one of the most significant developments in English-language poetry over the last two decades.

A basic problem one encounters in the attempt to define performance poetry becomes clear in a comparison of the following two statements. Russell Thompson of the poetry organisation "Apples & Snakes" sees a gradual distinction between a "reading" and "performance poetry":

> The definition of performance poetry, as I see it, is declaiming your poetry in public in such a way that you acknowledge that there is an audience there. I think if somebody gets up on stage and [...] reads all their poems with their head buried in their book ... I don't really think that's performance poetry. Not because they're reading it but because they're not acknowledging that there is an audience there. (Thompson interview 2006)

Lucy English, by contrast, who introduces herself as a performance poet, provides a very different definition:

> To me, a performance poem is a poem that has been written for a live audience like a play is a piece of drama that has been written for a live audience. [...] I would say that when I'm writing a performance piece, I would predominantly always write with an eye to how the audience are going to interpret it. (English interview)

Thus, while Russell Thompson seems to regard performance poetry as a specific manner of presenting poetry that "acknowledges that there is an audience there," Lucy English describes it as a literary genre written specifically for live performance, which is then performed to a live audience in a manner that is not "flat, dull, unanimated" (English interview). The former view conceives of performance poetry as contextually determined by the performer's efforts to communicate with his/her live audience, the latter defines it as a text-immanent generic quality that marks a poem as being destined for performance. Both of these competing definitions have their followers. Nathan Penlington would appear to be a proponent of the 'literary genre' definition when he characterises performance poetry as

> A form of poetry that's performed, that might not necessarily work on the page I think is fair to say ... you could say that poetry that is less difficult and moves towards stand-up ... in a way, is performance poetry. (Penlington interview)

While Penlington's statement remains neutral as to the quality of "a form of poetry that's performed, that might not necessarily work on the page," Keith Jebb, in his article on the poet Michael Horovitz, reveals the negative image of performance poetry as a genre, claiming that "[y]ou can't *dismiss* Horovitz as a performance poet in the sense that he doesn't work on the page" (17, my emphasis). John Siddique, finally, expresses a thoroughly derogatory view:

> judging by the practitioners who use the words 'performance poetry' it means somebody who wants to express themselves, wants to express their emotions, ... who has probably ... never read a book since they have left school, who wants to kind of have it all their way and wants to be adored. And they use forms which they learned in primary school, saying that they're not influenced by anybody ... and they make blanket abstract noun statements that amount to nothing. [...] Like ... drugs are bad, racism is bad. [...] No subtlety, no ... no craft, no art, no literature, you know ... everything that poetry isn't, quite honestly. (Siddique interview)[13]

Siddique's statement again hints at the problematic racial connotations the term 'performance poetry' entails: often it does not simply connote 'bad writing,' but more specifically, has come to stand for "poetry from Black writers" (Evaristo and Astley 17). Patience Agbabi, a black British poet, is mindful of these clichés and attaches great importance to the quality of the writing, confirming that "we had that accusation fired at us years and years ago [...] about the writing, [...] you know, it's just masking bad writing" (Agbabi interview).

While Agbabi is generally comfortable with the label "performance poet," she does not specifically write for performance, as a definition of performance poetry as a literary genre intended for performance would suggest. This brings us to the second definition of performance poetry as a manner of presentation. For Russell Thompson, it means "declaiming your

---

[13] While Siddique generally associates performance poetry with "bad writing" he is careful to concede that there are "exceptions" such as performance poet Zena Edwards, who, as Siddique knows, "sits up all night crafting her work" (Siddique interview).

poetry in public in such a way that you acknowledge that there is an audience there," as quoted above, and he further notes,

> that can often be down to things like the occasional bit of eye contact. Or it could be down to introducing your poem in such a way so as to involve the audience and not exclude the audience. (Thompson interview 2006)

Such a broad definition would certainly apply to Patience Agbabi's performances, and it would also be an apt description of the poetry readings of John Siddique, an engaging performer of his own work who, as demonstrated above, has a fairly low opinion of performance poetry, or of whatever the term denotes to him.

Thus, a definition of performance poetry as a literary genre, i.e. poetry written specifically for performance, would exclude the performances of artists such as Patience Agbabi (who sometimes calls herself "performance poet" although she does not write specifically for performance) and Anthony Joseph (a renowned performer of his own poetry who rejects the label performance poetry for his work as he does not write for performance). On the other hand, defining it loosely as a mode of presentation that acknowledges the presence of the audience would again not only include those artists who regard themselves as performance poets but also a range of artists who, like John Siddique, are competent performers of their own work but would under no circumstances label themselves performance poets.

What emerges quite clearly from these difficulties of defining performance poetry, however, is the discomfort the term causes when it is read as a prioritisation of orality over the written word. John Siddique distinguishes between "performance poetry" (bad writing) and "poetry in performance," which is poetry that "has been written, crafted, edited, worked on and then, whilst living on the page, is given further life by being given voice to" (Siddique interview). He demands that a poem be "living on the page" in order to be classified a 'good poem': if a poem is effective primarily in oral performance it is therefore 'bad poetry' – or perhaps not poetry at all. Similarly, Rommi Smith, who has made a remarkable career as a writer *and* performer of poetry, rejects the label 'performance poet': although she notes that there is a "performability" about her work, she insists that "everything stems from the written word" (Smith interview). Thus, when Nathan Penlington, a performance poet and ardent producer of live poetry events, defines performance poetry as poetry that is effective in its oral realisation on stage though it "might not necessarily work on the page" and is "less difficult" (Penlington interview) he cites exactly those qualities that debase it to the status of 'bad poetry' in the eyes of many poets and critics who regard the written poem as the ultimate measure of poetic quality. Some of their experience of performance poetry can perhaps be compared with a visit to the local theatre when one expects an operatic performance of *The Magic Flute* and is served a non-vocal production by a contemporary dance theatre company – an entirely different experience, of course, and one whose particular aesthetic qualities the audience will miss if it continues to evaluate the performance as an opera.[14] The bias against the oral realisation mode arguably applies to performance poetry more than to works labelled as 'spoken word' (a broader concept which may include prose, poetry, and even storytelling or stand-up comedy) because it contains the word 'poetry' and thus easily provokes judgement based on the criteria applied to poetry books.

To conclude, the numerous debates in the poetry world about the merits and pitfalls of performance poetry must be read in light of the traditional orality/literacy dichotomy and the aesthetic priorities it has borne: they spell out a tension between conflicting values that applies, often in a more subtle manner, to the whole of live poetry, although it is particularly conspicuous in its subgenre of performance poetry.

1.3 Literature Review

Although there are signs that a renewed interest in the mediality of text and its impact on poetry is emerging, there are at present few critical works available that specifically concern themselves with live poetry and even fewer that attempt to develop a systematic methodology for its analysis and interpretation. The literature reviewed in the following section has been selected for its merit regarding an explicit methodology proposed for the study of live poetry, or its application of an implicit approach.

The sections of this chapter will provide overviews of critical studies and articles grouped together according to their thematic focus and theoretical outlook. Thus, this report first discusses literature revolving around 'oral poetry' and 'verbal art.' Most of the forms of oral performance studied in this field are not, strictly speaking, classifiable as live poetry. However, critical engagement with them has yielded insights that are also relevant for a discussion and analysis of live poetry. The second section focuses on poetry as an acoustic event, followed by a section with a broader focus on poetry in performance. After that, some of the literature dealing with the popular

---

14 Which is not to say that all performance poetry will always be an eye-opening, enlightening experience: performance poetry can be trite, unimaginative, clichéd – just as 'page poetry' can.

forms of 'performance poetry,' 'spoken word,' and poetry slam is reviewed, and the final section is dedicated to biographical and historical studies on live poetry.

Oral Poetry, Verbal Art

Some methods applicable to the study of the live performance of poetry have been developed in the fields of anthropology, ethnopoetics, and folklore studies. They generally share a relatively broad concept of 'oral poetry' or 'verbal art,' realised in a diverse range of cultural practices and geographical areas, as well as a move away from the textual artefact towards performance as a mode of aesthetic (inter-)action.

Richard Bauman's definition of verbal art as "a mode of language use, a way of speaking" (*Verbal Art* 11) that may comprise "both myth narration and the speech expected of certain members of society whenever they open their mouths" (*Verbal Art* 5) is typical of this area of research. The objects of inquiry focussed on by linguistic anthropologists and folklorists range from the telling of jokes and Malagasy oratorical marriage negotiations (*Verbal Art* 12) to Mayan verse (Tedlock 216) and the songs of the Mandinka griots.[15]

Rather than just pursuing a close analysis of the verbal 'artefact' (of 'text' in its abstract sense), the work of anthropologists and scholars of ethnopoetics/folklore often displays a more holistic approach, examining verbal performance within its medial and social contexts. Dennis Tedlock's *The Spoken Word and the Work of Interpretation* (1983), for instance, takes into account the varied acoustic nature of oral performance, the features of which are lost in a mere verbal transcript. His transcription suggestions for 'reperformance' in the "Guide to Reading Aloud" (20) include a system for the representation of paralinguistic features, such as relative volume and pitch, based on standard typography. These suggestions have since been taken up by many other scholars and have also proved of some value to the present study (see Chapter 4.4).

While Dennis Tedlock is concerned with transcribing paralinguistic features of what is referred to in this study as 'audiotext,' Elizabeth Fine takes into account the additional aspects of body communication. Her book *The Folklore Text* (1984) serves as a useful starting point for a consideration of paralinguistic and kinesic performance features, as it includes a survey of the

---

[15] West African poets and praise singers: the 'guardians' of verbal art traditions. See Bauman, *Verbal Art* 21.

methodologies developed in these fields and an evaluation of their practicability for the description and analysis of verbal art. Fine defines verbal art as an aesthetic mode of communication the particularities of which need to be captured by a 'performance record.' Furthermore, she stipulates the need to provide a 'performance report' to accompany the 'record.' This report is to account for the contextual 'situatedness' of a performance, thus textualising folklore performance so as to attain Fine's declared aim of generating "a systematic record of a performance" that "includes nonverbal and contextual features" (preface). Similarly, John Miles Foley, in his guide *How to Read an Oral Poem* (2002), stresses the need to "read" (understand) oral poetry in context.

Oral performance as process is thus considered on its own aesthetic terms in linguistic anthropology and folklore studies, rather than as a derivative practice based on a stable textual artefact — a stance which has been amply theorised in the field. Ruth Finnegan, for example, reflects on the diverse relations between written and oral texts in "The How of Literature" (*Oral Tradition*, 2005) and offers a lucid critique of the traditional literacy/orality dichotomy.

While the critical studies considered in this rubric have inspired the present study's conception of live poetry as a medium in its own right, their frequent emphasis on 'foreignness,' on working in widely differing cultural contexts, renders their approaches and findings applicable to the study of live poetry only to a very limited extent. Thus, in his examination of Zuni stories and Mayan verse, for instance, Dennis Tedlock copiously reflects on the methodological challenges of translation. Ruth Finnegan's *Oral Traditions and the Verbal Arts* (1992) similarly operates with a broad concept of verbal art that seems, to a large degree, to be based on working in a foreign language in 'oral cultures.' She includes chapters on translation and 'Ethics' and conceives of the researcher as a 'fieldworker.' Richard Bauman's influential study *Verbal Art as Performance* (1977) draws up an elaborate typology of performance "keys" or framing signals: "explicit or implicit messages which carry instructions on how to interpret the other message(s) being communicated" (15). As they vary widely across cultures, it is crucial for the scholar of indigenous verbal art to be aware of these keys when studying alien cultures, for instance in order to know when a performance is about to begin in the first place. However, while the paratext chapter of the present study gives some thought to the framing of live poetry, linguistic and cultural translation is not a central concern.

In their attempt to cover a diverse range of different phenomena in various cultural and geographical contexts, anthropologists and ethnopoeticists largely embrace a broad conception of verbal art, which results in a rather unspecific methodology. A case in point is Ruth Finnegan's *Oral Traditions and the Verbal Arts* (1992), which is designed as "A Guide to Research Practices," as the subtitle explains. True to form as a 'research guide,' *Oral Traditions* surveys a broad range of general aspects of, and issues related to, the study of verbal art. Such aspects include the challenges faced by the 'field-worker,' as well as theoretical perspectives on orality and verbal art, the roles of audience and performers, the technicalities of recording equipment, practices of collecting, recording and creating texts, and the pitfalls of translation and transcription. In view of its broad scope Finnegan's study must necessarily remain on the level of 'survey' and is consequently lacking in depth: the chapter on "Observing and analysing performance" spans merely twenty pages, for instance. The book is a useful introduction to the research of verbal art, however, and each chapter refers the reader to a wealth of literature by other scholars working in the respective fields.

John Miles Foley's *How to Read an Oral Poem* (2002) can be criticised on similar grounds. Foley identifies four categories of oral poetry: "oral performance" (e.g. Tibetan paper-singers), "voiced text" (e.g. slam poetry), "voices from the past" (e.g. Homer's *Odyssey*), and "written oral poems" (e.g. the work of Bishop Njegoš), and presents three methods for their study: "Performance Theory," which is a reworking of Richard Bauman's keys to performance, "Ethnopoetics," defined through its "three-part agenda" of reading, representing, and reperforming (95), and "Immanent Art," an application of 'oral-formulaic theory' and the concept of register. Due to its broad conception of 'oral poetry,' the suitability of Foley's triple methodology for the analysis of live poetry is limited – a trait his study shares with many other works from the fields of anthropology and ethnopoetics.

While many forms of oral poetry and verbal art depend to a large degree on improvisation, the following sections review literature which is devoted to aspects of live poetry in the narrower sense, i.e. poetry which has been composed prior to its performance, whose text is relatively stable and which usually has a parallel existence in writing.

Poetry as an Acoustic Event

Another category of works that deal explicitly or implicitly with means of analysing poetry in performance is focusing on the aspect of sound. A basic distinction must be drawn here between studies limited to a discussion of the 'inscribed' or 'evoked' sound of written poetry and its meaning potential – of which there are many – and those concerned with poetry as an actual acoustic event. A prime example of the former is Francis Berry's *Poetry and the Physical Voice* (1962), which defines poetry "as essentially a phenomenon of sound," mentioning the factors of pitch, duration, timbre, volume, etc., but then conceives of it "in terms of the 'writer's' voice, which is recreated in the 'reader's' inner ear when he experiences verse" (18). This and similar works[16] have little to offer in terms of a methodology for analysing live poetry. An early example of a work dealing with actual sound, Yvor Winters's essay "The Audible Reading of Poetry" (1951) lays down rules for the correct manner of declamation: to "render the rhythm with precision" (436) rather than "descend to the practice of the actor" (437), for the reading must effect an "impersonal illumination" (447) through a "restrained but formal chant" (435). While Winters's essay is narrowly prescriptive and does not distinguish between audible reading as reception (by the reader) and audible reading as publication (by the author), it has served as a significant point of departure for later critical works on the sounding of poetry (cf. e.g. Engler 42), of which there are still few. In the following, a number of works drawn from literary studies, musicology, and communication theory will be discussed for the useful criteria or points of departure they provide for the present study's analysis of different aspects of actual sound.

In *Reading and Listening: The Modes of Communicating Poetry and their Influence on the Texts* (1982), Balz Engler makes a claim for the importance of "experiencing a poem adequately," in "the way it was intended" (22). He postulates reading and listening as two profoundly different modes of communication with a text and strives to uncover the signals each written poem contains to indicate its optimal mode of reception. Such signals may be found in a poem's "length" (24), "complexity" (26), "spelling," "punctuation," and "typography" (27). The "five types of relationships between the aural and the visual elements in a poetic text" (36) which Engler identifies – namely score, comment, complement, contrast, and contradiction – provide a useful starting point for Chapter 3 of this study, which discusses relationships between the poem written and the poem performed. Engler claims to start out from the 'event' of listening to poetry and reflects on the manner in which the effect of a performance is determined by various types of audience-text and audience-performer relationships. However, his rather narrow focus on the written text as an indicator and reflector of particular reception situations limits the usefulness of his approach for an analysis of live poetry.

In *Poetry into Song: Performance and Analysis of Lieder* (1996), Deborah Stein and Robert Spillman's main concern is with German art song. The authors propose an approach to the study of Lied performance that integrates poetic

---

[16] See also, for instance, Perrine's *Sound and Sense*, Matterson and Jones's *Studying Poetry*, or Eagleton's *How to Read a Poem*.

and musical analysis and "models how [the authors] believe performers need to study a Lied in performance preparation" (xiii). They demonstrate how musicological concepts such as dynamics and timbre can be applied to poetry and thus provide useful parameters for the study of poetry as an acoustic phenomenon. While their approach focuses on 'how to best study Lieder for performance' rather than how to analyse actual performances, they nevertheless manage to draw significant parallels between poetry and music – the two acoustic modes of expression combined in the Lied.

Although Theo Van Leeuwen's work *Speech, Music, Sound* (1999) is also not specifically geared towards an analysis of poetry, it deserves to be mentioned here since it proposes a quasi-semiotic classification of sonoric 'choices' that the production of speech, music, and other kinds of sounds affords, which are analysed on a common basis as acoustic phenomena. Thus, Van Leeuwen provides parameters for an elaborate categorisation of speech (and musical) rhythm, voice quality and timbre, for instance, and presents thoughtful reflections on the workings of contextual soundscapes and the use of different voice qualities for the creation or reduction of "social distance" (12-14), much of which can be applied to live poetry. He also elaborates on the semantic potential of sound, discussing 'experiential meaning potential' and 'provenance' as two central meaning-making principles. The articulatory parameters introduced in the 'audiotext' chapter of the present study are based on Van Leeuwen's classification in *Speech, Music, Sound*, although they have been partly modified to better suit the specific characteristics of the sound of live poetry.

Finally, another work from the field of literary studies shall be introduced here: Martina Pfeiler's *Sounds of Poetry: Contemporary American Performance Poets* (2003). *Sounds of Poetry* could also be grouped with the body of critical texts reviewed in the following category ('poetry in performance'), as it partly treats aspects of performance beyond the acoustic dimension, or with the works discussed in the rubric "performance poetry / spoken word / slam," as its subject matter is American performance poetry. However, in view of its declared focus on "poetry as verbal art performed by the poet, whose main artistic tools are real sounds of spoken language" (9) it is best discussed at this point, where it also constitutes a suitable transition to the next section.

After an initial review of poetry's oral "roots" Pfeiler discusses the "performing voices of poetry" (narrative, dramatic, lyric; 39ff) and lists sound effects such as cacophony, rhyme, phonetic intensifiers, and rhythmic devices as "the performing sounds of poetry" (51ff). She then proceeds to classify poets according to their performance and/or writing practice as "Pagers," "Page-Stagers," "Stagers," and "On-Stagers" (performance poets), before she discusses the work of a range of American poets in a performance context. While Pfeiler demonstrates her broad knowledge and experience of American performance poetry throughout the book, she often fails to adhere to her own principle of analysing the "real sounds of spoken language." She cites an audio CD for her discussion of Gwendolyn Brooks' dramatic poem "The Mother" (44), for instance, though she never really engages with the poem's audible qualities. Her use of the concept of "voice" is often ambiguous – sometimes referring to the actual sound production of human vocal cords, sometimes to the fictive lyric or dramatic speaker inherent in a written poem. Similarly, her classification of "performing sounds" remains mostly on the abstract level of 'evoked' sound (the phonetic value of words), although early on in the book she stresses the "different texture and quality" (39) of an oral performance in contrast to a silent reading. The inconsistencies noticeable in Pfeiler's approach exemplify the insecurity about the concept of poetic sound still pervading literary studies.

When she does engage with actual performance, however, as in her discussion of the functions and effects of the pause (69ff), Pfeiler's reflections are well-observed and to the point, and one of the chief strengths of her study are the numerous analyses of orally delivered poems (either in live performance or audio recordings). While her methodology is mostly intuitive, she often takes into account important aspects such as the shape of the performance space (31), the ad lib and its effect (31), the use of gestures (37), and the general choreography of an event (31), and demonstrates the meaning potential of particular voice qualities (71).

In conclusion, the discipline of literary studies evinces a certain awkwardness in engaging with the actual sounds of a performed poem rather than with the evoked sound of its words on the page. Even such studies as Balz Engler's *Reading and Listening* or Martina Pfeiler's *Sounds of Poetry*, which insist on the difference between a silent reading and an audible performance and claim to be concerned with the latter, fall short of developing a consistent methodology for the analysis of performed sound. The critical criteria they propose, or the implicit methodology they apply, are helpful only to the extent that they provide starting points for the discussion of some individual aspects of oral performance. By contrast, studies from musicology or communication theory which also set out to theorise vocal/verbal sound production have a different focus or are too unspecific in terms of their methodology to be directly applicable to the study of live poetry: the criteria they propose must first be adapted to the task at hand.

Sound is, however, not the only aspect that distinguishes live poetry from writing. While the works discussed thus far focus on various acoustic aspects of poetry performance, the essays and essay collections introduced in the following section offer a more inclusive view of orally performed poetry.

Poetry in Performance

A number of essays and studies examine poetry in performance through the institution of what is mostly called the 'poetry reading,' where 'reading' refers to the author's audible voicing of his/her own poetry. Several strands of criticism can be identified within this area.

Firstly, there are works that are concerned with the status and value of poetry performances in a general sense. One example is Donald Hall's essay "The Poetry Reading: Public Performance/Private Art" (1985), which revolves around the history of the poetry reading – which he defines as "publication by the body" (77) – and its typical forms in the USA. While Hall deplores the one-sided focus of poetry criticism on writing, he is critical of the 'entertainment factor' of the public poetry reading, which links his essay to Yvor Winters's critique of poets' attempts at 'acting.' David Wojahn strikes a similarly ambivalent note in his article "A Kind of Vaudeville: Appraising the Age of the Poetry Reading" (1985). He recognises the crucial role of poetry readings as a manner of publication while insisting "the performance of the poem, *in itself*, is not fundamentally artistic" (268). These essays are interesting on account of their reflections on the value of oral performance as both a form of art and a form of publication. Their scepticism vis-à-vis live poetry's potential for entertainment sheds light on the orality/literacy controversy in poetry, as discussed in detail in Chapter 1.2.

Steven Athanases' article "When Print Alone Fails Poetry: Performance as a Contingency of Literary Value" (1991) takes a more positive stance towards performance. Athanases criticises the constant privileging of the written mode in literary studies and argues convincingly that the literary canon should be extended to include poetry that depends on performance for its full effect, citing some of Gwendolyn Brooks's poetry to illustrate his point. Similarly, Peter Middleton's *Distant Reading: Performance, Readership, and Consumption in Contemporary Poetry* (2005) contains a chapter on "Poetry's Oral Stage." Rather than relegating 'orality' to distant cultures or past historical epochs, Middleton makes the general claim for oral performance to "make possible an extended semantic repertoire in which poetry fulfils more of its potentialities" (59). *Distant Reading* also sheds light on such seminal concepts as phonocentrism, sound symbolism, and "projected space" (32), and reflects on the unity of author and performer in live poetry (33-34). As such, like Athanases, Middleton points to the potential of performance to signify in its own right, recognising its artistic value. While the works in this strand of criticism offer no methods for the study of live poetry as such, they variously reflect on its status, which is fundamental for the development of any methodology.

The following group of essays and essay collections approach poetry from a more practical perspective. Notable examples are Stephen Vincent and Ellen Zweig's *The Poetry Reading: A Contemporary Compendium of Language & Performance* (1981), David Kennedy and Keith Tuma's *Additional Apparitions: Poetry, Performance and Site Specificity* (2002), and Mark Robinson's *Words Out Loud: Ten Essays about Poetry Readings* (2002). These works are mostly rooted in particular live poetry scenes (Vincent and Zweig in the USA, Kennedy, Tuma, and Robinson in the UK) and depart from the concrete experience of performance. They bring together ideas and reports from diverse quarters – many of them contributed by poets themselves – and comment on a broad range of aspects of live poetry. Thus, they comprise personal performance histories and accounts of poetry readings, essays on specific performance spaces or reflections on the status of the poet-performer vis-à-vis his/her text. As collections, they share a measure of heterogeneity and lack a coherent approach. Individual contributions are often anecdotal and their length does not allow for extended analyses. However, some of the essays, such as Barry Eisenberg's "Getting There a Little Late" (*The Poetry Reading* 64-67), display a holistic take on poetry readings that is interesting for the choice of aspects included,[17] conveying a sense of 'what matters' in live poetry. Frederick C. Stern's essay "The Formal Poetry Reading" (*The Drama Review*, 1991) also fits this category, as it describes a number of college readings by way of a "performance report" (cf. Fine 94) and discusses the presence of the poet as an emblem of his/her work or political stance, and how this presence affects different kinds of

---

[17] In Eisenberg's case these are the poets' style, audience reactions, atmosphere, as well as an evaluation of the strengths of the event. Other notable essays include Peter Middleton's "Performing An Experiment, Performing A Poem," which stipulates the dependence of the production of meaning on "the performance ecology of place, self, sound, and interaction" (*Additional Apparitions* 33); Mark Robinson's essay "In the Familiar Space of the Voice" (*Words Out Loud* 37-42), which points towards the significance of audience size and performer-audience interaction for the shaping of a live poetry event, and links the popularity of poetry readings to a "poet as personality cult" (40); and Laura Severin's chapter on Jackie Kay and Liz Lochhead in *Poetry Off the Page: Twentieth-Century British Women Poets in Performance* (2004), which offers a feminist take on the performance practice of these poets, examining their revitalisation of the dramatic monologue genre as a way of "avoiding author identification" (74).

poetic meaning. Notwithstanding their lack of theoretical depth, the strength of these projects is the authors' proximity to, and intimate knowledge of, specific live poetry scenes and their motivation to report from their first-hand experience.

By contrast, the following collections of essays, which also deal with performance, centre on more abstract concerns: Charles Bernstein's *Close Listening: Poetry and the Performed Word* (1998), Adalaide K. Morris's *Sound States: Innovative Poetics and Acoustical Technologies* (1997), and Brandon LaBelle and Christof Migone's essay collection *Writing Aloud: The Sonics of Language* (2001). *Close Listening* is a theoretically challenging work, which is mentioned by Kenneth Sherwood together with *Sound States* as one of "several critical texts [to] have initiated a discourse about sound and performance in literature," though they are limited "to more marginal avant-garde or intermedia contexts" (120). Most essays in *Close Listening* discuss different facets of poetry performance – such as sound symbolism, the 'talk poem,' or the potential of performance for "direct intervention in and commentary on public affairs" (Damon 332) – without concerning themselves with actual performances or drawing a methodological distinction between potential and actual sound (with the exception of Bernstein's introductory essay). Morris' collection *Sound States* focuses on the relationship between acoustic technologies and avant-garde experimental poetics. Similarly, LaBelle and Migone's essay collection *Writing Aloud* investigates avant-garde phenomena, such as synthesizer speech performance, and includes contributions such as a rather abstract "taxonomy of the stutter" (176), most of which have little to offer for a discussion of live poetry and its critical analysis.

However, as a rare attempt at listing relevant performance-related criteria for the analysis of live poetry Charles Bernstein's introduction to *Close Listening* is an explicit reflection on a suitable methodology. Bernstein discusses such central notions as "audiotext" (12) and its determining parameters, the social character of the poetry reading, and the "framing" activities observable in any poetry performance (5). While he touches upon numerous important aspects of live poetry, the nature of his introductory essay does not, of course, permit him to go into depth about any of them. This is a trait shared by Peter Middleton's essay "How to Read a Reading of a Written Poem" (*Oral Tradition*, 2005), which has also been a source of inspiration for the present study. Middleton calls for a "revision of the standard picture of texts as objects ready for interpretation" (8) and briefly outlines "the key factors at work in the production of meaning during a contemporary Anglophone poetry reading" (9), such as the role of the audience or the performance of "authorship" (22).[18] Kenneth Sherwood's essay "Elaborate Versionings: Characteristics of Emergent Performance in Three Print/Oral/Aural Poets" (*Oral Tradition,* 2006) also belongs to this set of methodologically conscious articles as it stresses the emergent quality of performance, provides some innovative sample analyses, and presents modes of transcription that take into account different dimensions of oral performance, such as paratextual introductions and certain paralinguistic features. These essays collectively call for a methodology for the study of live poetry that covers non-verbal and contextual performance features and hint at specific challenges encountered. Even though they are restricted in scope to a cursory mentioning of relevant performance aspects or a partial demonstration of selected critical criteria, they have been elemental to the conception of the approach introduced in the present study.

Performance Poetry / Spoken Word / Slam

Dana Gioia's essay "The New Oral Poetry" in *Disappearing Ink* (2004) discusses the recent rise of popular oral forms such as performance poetry, spoken word, cowboy poetry and rap in the United States, noting that

> [t]he limited commentary on the new popular poetry provided in the mass media by intellectuals has habitually focused on ideological issues, especially in the case of rap, which has been examined almost entirely for its subject matter or sociological significance. (8)

Interestingly, while Gioia praises the healthy self-reliance of the "new popular poetry" he also separates it from artistic literary production in his essay,

---

[18] Middleton's article further points to the historical contingency of performance styles (24) and is also interesting for the sample analyses it contains, which take account of acoustic features such as phrasing and audible pauses. However, the "four subcategories of the ordinary poetry reading" Middleton identifies in his essay seem somewhat arbitrary: he distinguishes between the "institutionally organised poetry reading (often at a university or college) that is fairly formal," the "poetry reading series that mainly presents poets whose work is based on a communicative, even conversational, use of language," "the more avant-garde poetry reading series where the poet rarely speaks autobiographically and instead presents vocalized artifices of language," and "the arena like Apples and Snakes in London or the Nuyorican Poets Café in New York," which is curtly classified as "politically aware entertainment" (22) – the word 'poetry' being omitted from its description. Thus, his classification is based on an uneven mix of event formats and frames ("university"), text styles ("conversational use of language"), and motives ("politically aware entertainment").

claiming that "like virtually everything else in contemporary mass culture, the new popular poetry resembles entertainment more than art. It courts its audience too assiduously" (*Disappearing Ink* 19). Approaching the issue from another angle, yet arriving at a similar conclusion, Kenneth Sherwood insists on the difference between a performance proper and a poetry reading or "recitation" (127), claiming that the former must be characterised by an improvisational element.

In the critical literature on poetry in performance a rift is indeed observable between work that engages with the "popular" forms of spoken word,[19] performance poetry, and poetry slam on the one hand, and studies of the "poetry reading" on the other. This division is also "broadly apparent in the critical apparatus for contemporary British poetry," as pointed out by Nicky Marsh, Peter Middleton, and Victoria Sheppard (48), who researched "two different constituencies" of poets in the UK: avant-garde writers who have "always valued performance" and "a highly successful network of younger poets, often associated with an Afro-Caribbean community, for whom stage performance is an explicit goal" (48). The authors note that the existing critical literature "made much of the allegedly persistent demarcations between the political, aesthetic, and social ambitions of these two groups of poets" (48).

The present study does not assume a fundamental opposition between the traditional 'poetry reading' and 'performance poetry.' The problematic implications of such a distinction have already been pointed out in Chapter 1.2.3, where 'performance poetry' has been revealed as a controversial concept, sometimes implying a mode of presentation, at other times a genre of writing. The clichés of the quiet, static, 'literary' poetry reading with no entertainment value on the one hand and the flashy, overly dramatic presentation of the performance poet (possibly compensating for 'non-literary' writing) on the other can at best be regarded as two extreme poles of a continuum that encompasses a wealth of different styles and text types, all of which can be encountered in live poetry. Similarly, 'slam' is an event format that potentially attracts many different types of writers, texts, and modes of presentation. Furthermore, the two allegedly separate scenes – the 'popular'

---

[19] "Spoken word" is a broad and 'trendy' term that encompasses various forms of performance. Poet-performer and producer Nathan Penlington explains the term thus: "And spoken word ... I quite like as a term, more than performance poetry, because [...] it's a lot freer and can cover all sorts of forms, literary poets who are purely page-based and just come out and read ... traditional readings basically ... And it can cover ... comedians telling stories, ... all sorts of poetry. Yeah, and storytelling ... which isn't poetry ... can come in spoken word" (Penlington interview).

and the 'literary' – are, in fact, marked by considerable overlaps and an active exchange. For instance, John Agard, the winner of a Paul Hamlyn Award for his poetry in 1997, has also performed for the UK live poetry organisation "Apples & Snakes" – the country's "leading organisation for performance poetry" ("About") – as have other noted 'literary' poets, such as Choman Hardi and Daljit Nagra.

Interestingly, although the critical literature on live poetry can be divided into titles dedicated to performance poetry / spoken word / slam and those dealing mostly with 'poetry reading,' similar tendencies can be observed in both strands of criticism. Thus, there are also essay collections on the 'popular' forms of live poetry which cover a broad range of topics and whose individual contributions often stem from poets themselves or revolve around personal observations, accounts of concrete performances, or portraits of specific artists. Examples include Stephen Wade and Paul Munden's essay collection *Reading the Applause: Reflections on Performance Poetry by Various Artists* (1999), Gary Glazner's *Poetry Slam: The Competitive Art of Performance Poetry* (2000), Mark Eleveld's anthology *The Spoken Word Revolution* (2007), which has been published with an accompanying audio CD, and issue 130 of the *Canadian Theatre Review* (2007), a rare attempt on the part of theatre studies to engage critically with spoken word. While these works can be recommended for the variety of interesting aspects they address – from the relationship between slam and the academy (McDaniel) and the pedagogic potential of performance poetry (Millum), to the rhythmic particularities of rap poems (Gioia, "The New Oral Poetry") – they are generally lacking in coherence of approach, methodological foundation, and theoretical depth.

Three monographs are noteworthy for their treatment of culturally specific forms of live poetry. Christian Habekost's *Verbal Riddim: The Politics and Aesthetics of African-Caribbean Dub Poetry* (1993) is a seminal study on the historical development of Caribbean dub poetry and its political impetus. Habekost defines a number of parameters that need to be taken into account in an analysis of dub poetry performance, such as its reggae-based 'riddim,' and the specific medium of the performance (a cappella recital, recording, concert performance, etc.). While each analysis undertaken in the last section of *Verbal Riddim* includes "performance aspects," which are often quite illuminating, his analytical 'toolkit' lacks precision and is, of course, geared specifically towards an analysis of dub poetry. His study's general applicability to live poetry is therefore very limited.

In *Contemporary English Performance Poetry in Canada and South Africa: A Comparative Study of the Main Motifs and Poetic Techniques* (1997), Pamela Dube defines performance poetry as a genre characterised by oral mnemonic techniques (such as alliteration and assonance), the "mission" of which is determined solely in political terms as "an active struggle against diverse forms of institutional and ideological domination" (200). Her study provides interesting insights into South African live poetry practices – such as contemporary 'worker praise poetry' – in a post-colonial context, but falls short of introducing a consistent methodology for their discussion and analysis, and – like so many other critical works – pays only lip service to the central role of body language and the live voice (37).

In her doctoral dissertation *Authenticating Voices: Performance, Black Identity, and Slam Poetry* (2003), Susan Somers-Willett gives an insightful account of slam poetry as a 'counter-cultural' phenomenon in the USA, focusing on "the mass media's commodification of urban blackness at poetry slams" (vi). After a survey of some influential currents in US poetry regarding performance practice (e.g. Beat poetry, the Black Arts Movement), Somers-Willett discusses slam poetry as a "real-time discursive critical act" (85) in which cultural identity is performed via the staging of 'authenticity.' She makes a number of interesting points about the identity of author, performer, and fictive speaker in poetry slams. However, like Habekost's and Dube's studies, *Authenticating Voices* focuses on a small and culturally specific segment of the live poetry spectrum from a highly selective point of view, which renders her approach only partly useful for the development of a larger methodology with which to study live poetry.

Biographical / Historical Studies

A number of studies approach poetry in performance primarily from a historical/biographical point of view. They include interviews with, and portraits of, poets, touching on matters such as their performance practice and attitudes towards performance, details of compositional practice, and questions of models and traditions of writing and performing.

Poets on Stage: The Some Symposium on Poetry Readings (1978) was edited by Allen Ginsberg and contains interviews with such renowned poet-performers as Denise Levertov, Audre Lorde, and Allen Ginsberg himself on their experiences of, and thoughts on, live performance. Don Cusic's study *The Poet as Performer* (1991) surveys a number of poet-performers of the twentieth century – among them Vachel Lindsay, Robert Frost, Dylan Thomas, and Allen Ginsberg – in terms of their performance activities and how these shaped their careers. Nathan Penlington provides a distinctly British perspective in *Don't Need English Lessons to Learn our Lines: The Unspoken History of Performance Poetry* (2000), a comprehensive collection of material on performance poetry – the 'popular' end of the British live poetry spectrum – since the 1960s, including promotional flyers, newspaper clippings, and numerous quotations by, and interviews with, well-known poet-performers such as the Liverpool Poets, John Cooper Clarke, and Patience Agbabi.[20] In "'Blasts of Language': Changes in Oral Poetics in Britain since 1965" (*Oral Tradition,* 2006) Nicky Marsh, Peter Middleton, and Victoria Sheppard's discussion of the role of performance in British poetry over the last few decades is based on a series of interviews with poet-performers from various styles and genres, such as Patience Agbabi, Peter Finch, Cris Cheek, and Allen Fisher. Lesley Wheeler's study *Voicing American Poetry: Sound and Performance from the 1920s to the Present* (2008) sketches the history of live poetry in the USA in the twentieth century, including university readings, Beat poetry, and poetry slams, as well as a "selected list of public poetry soundings" in the United States since 1950 (169).[21]

Although the few biographical and historical studies available are not concerned with techniques of a 'close listening' or a 'close viewing' of live poetry, they provide contextual information on various poet-performers and demonstrate the historical contingency of performance practices.

What emerges clearly from the above review of critical works on poetry performance is the persistent absence of a systematic methodology for the analysis and interpretation of live poetry that takes into account the aesthetic and contextual particularities of live performance. While an increasing awareness of this 'other' mode of realising poetic text is noticeable in literary studies, and while there have been numerous calls for a 'toolkit' for performance analysis,[22] no attempt has, as yet, been made to develop a comprehensive approach to live poetry that would draw together all the individual aspects and fragmentary attempts at defining criteria for its analysis. Furthermore, there is a conspicuous divide between works dealing with poetry 'readings' on the one hand, and those with an interest in performance poetry, spoken word, and slam on the other. This dichotomy is less than helpful – not only considering that the great variety of contemporary performance practices hardly allows for a clear-cut distinction between 'literary' and 'popular' factions. It is also problematic in so far as it impedes the consolidation of the critical approaches and methods of analysis developed in

---

[20] Asher and Martin Hoyles' poetry collection *Moving Voices: Black Performance Poetry* (2002), which has been published together with an audio-CD, is also relevant in this context for its detailed introduction to the roots of Black performance poetry in African and Caribbean oral traditions.

[21] However, a good part of the book "addresses textual voice," as Wheeler admits, meaning "voice as a metaphor in literary texts" (23).

[22] See, for example, Anderson 46, Ferrier 37, Breeze et al. 31.

either strand of criticism, which could, in fact, usefully complement each other.

The present study aims to close this gap by introducing a methodology for the study of live poetry that will enable researchers to engage with the aesthetics of poetry in performance regardless of whether it is presented at a poetry slam or in a university lecture hall, whether it is noisily 'ranted' or quietly 'read' from the page. This report on previous research has demonstrated that suitable methods do exist and that selected analytical criteria can indeed be found scattered across the critical literature on poetry in performance. The task before us now will be to integrate and complement existing methods and criteria so as to arrive at a coherent approach to live poetry.

2. Towards a Definition of Live Poetry

2.1 Poetry as a Bi-Medial Art Form

In order to provide a more exact delineation of the term "live poetry," a closer examination of its two components is necessary:

Defining the qualifier 'live' in our context is, for now, relatively simple: it is best understood as indicating a performance that is "given in front of an audience, rather than being recorded and then broadcast or shown in a film" ("live").[1] Thus, the 'live' in 'live poetry' denotes an author's recitation of poetry for an audience that is physically present.

Defining 'poetry' is, however, somewhat more challenging. For J. A. Cuddon, the term "can be taken to cover any kind of metrical composition" (726). Cuddon further characterises a 'poem' as "[a] composition, a work of verse, which may be in rhyme [...] or may be blank verse [...] or a combination of the two. Or it may depend on having a fixed number of syllables, like the *haiku*," before apparently giving up on outlining distinctive features of 'poem,' concluding instead that

> [i]n the final analysis what makes a poem different from any other kind of composition is a species of magic, the secret to which lies in the way the words lean upon each other, are linked and interlocked in sense and rhythm, and thus elicit from each other's syllables a kind of tune whose beat and melody varies subtly and which is different from that of prose. (721)

The first definition – "any kind of metrical composition" – is as narrow as the second is vague, and one could enlist numerous other attempts to produce sets of supposedly essential features, most of which would rule out a substantial proportion of the works commonly labelled 'poetry.' As one of the three basic genres of literature, poetry is notoriously difficult to delimit.

In *Lyrik und Metalyrik*, Eva Müller-Zettelmann overcomes this difficulty by basing her theory of the genre on the very impossibility of capturing poetry as a fixed set of essential criteria, and invoking Wittgenstein's concept of 'family resemblance,' according to which elements of a 'family' resemble each other by a set of overlapping features none of which is necessarily common to all. Thus, Müller-Zettelmann cites criteria such as relative brev-

---

[1] Philip Auslander, criticising the frequently cited "binary opposition of the live and the mediatized" as "reductive" (3), points out that "live performance now often incorporates mediatization to the degree that the live event itself is a product of media technologies [...]: as soon as electric amplification is used, one might say that an event is mediatized" (25).

ity, aesthetic self-referentiality, and heightened epistemologic subjectivity, while pointing out that a literary text may not fulfil all of these and still be recognised as a poem. Her theory is a useful starting point for this study, especially in view of the diverse corpus of works selected.

For our present purpose, however, the question "What is poetry?" shall be reformulated once more: What is the materiality of poetry? How does it communicate, i.e. what sensory channels does it activate? What we seek to determine here is the specific 'mediality' of poetry, with media functioning as a "conventionally distinct means of communicating cultural contents," as Werner Wolf explains:

> Media in this sense are specified principally by the nature of their underlying semiotic systems (involving verbal language, pictorial signs, music, etc., or, in cases of 'composite media' such as film, a combination of several semiotic systems), and only in the second place by technical or institutional channels. ("Intermediality" 253)

Poetry would thus be primarily characterised by 'verbal language' (the underlying semiotic system) and further differentiated according to the way in which language is transmitted. Hence, it can be experienced as written or

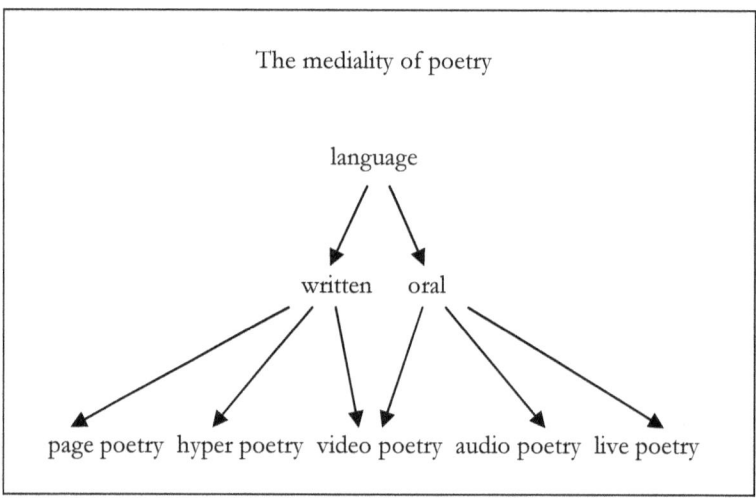

Fig. 1: The mediality of poetry.

spoken language and further divided into *page poetry* (print) and *hyper poetry* in its written mode, for instance, and into (recorded) *audio poetry* and *live poetry* in its spoken form, with hybrid media such as *video poetry* bridging the gap between written and spoken language.[2]

The question of mediality is crucial for the art of poetry, as, indeed, for any other art. Ever since Marshall McLuhan's famous dictum that "the medium is the message" (7) scholars have considered the vital symbiotic relationship between media and the artistic (or other) content they carry. Artistic communication is inconceivable without media, just as media cannot be experienced in isolation from the message or content they transport. Thus, it will be of no small relevance whether poetry is experienced on paper or in performance.

In this context, it is interesting to observe that the Latin origin of the word 'literature' – 'littera' meaning letter – etymologically binds 'literature' to writing, while no such restriction applies to its subgenre 'poetry,' which derives from the Greek word 'poieo': "to make, to produce" (Klarer 1, 28). As a term, poetry specifies no medial predilection, and Chris Baldick's definition of poetry as "[l]anguage *sung, chanted, spoken,* or *written* according to some pattern of recurrence that emphasizes the relationships between words on the basis of sound as well as sense" (*Concise Oxford Dictionary*, my emphasis) indicates its dualistic nature as an art: it may exist in oral performance and as written text. T. V. F. Brogan elaborates on this notion in the *New Princeton Encyclopedia of Poetry and Poetics*: "It is the point of view taken here that these two representational modes are not entirely congruent and that, more centrally, the visual text is not a mere transcript or notation-system for the oral text" (940). Neither is the performance of a poem "to be viewed as an implementation of the written record," he goes on to say. "Rather, they are two versions of the prior, originary, abstract entity called 'the poem.' Neither has ontological precedence" (940).

A poem, to Brogan, is an abstract entity that is only made accessible to experience in one of two distinct modes of representation. Consequently, the term 'live poetry' denotes a medial realisation that is already contained in the concept of poetry and which is to be regarded as more or less independent of the written representational mode. Such a view is in line with the practice of most poet-performers introduced in this study: while they see live performance and the direct encounter with an audience as an important part of their work they also strive to have their texts published. As such, most poets operate in two distinct media. This view, however, remains in-

---

[2] Hyper poetry is produced digitally, often exploring the possibilities of word animation and reader interaction on the internet. For examples see www.wordcircuits.com. For a discussion of more detailed classifications of poetry according to media technologies see Pfeiler, *Poetry Goes Intermedia* 108-116.

congruous with the current practices of literary criticism, which clearly give precedence to one realisation mode only.

One need only browse at random through a number of introductory works to discover a palpable imbalance at work: a distinct bias towards the written. Such a discovery may seem neither surprising nor remarkable after the discussion of value judgments pertaining to orality and literacy in Chapter 1, if it were not for the fact that many critics initially stress the sensual, oral or performative nature of poetry only to ignore it altogether in the methodology they subsequently propose for its analysis. A fine example in point is Laurence Perrine's advice to students in *Sound and Sense: An Introduction to Poetry*: "Poetry is written to be heard: its meanings are conveyed through sound as well as through print. [...] Practice reading poems aloud. When you find one you especially like, make friends listen to it" (17f). The above statement seems to suggest that an audible performance of a poem is at least as important as a silent reading of it. However, this thought is not followed up: the rest of the book embraces an idea of poetry that limits its existence to the page. It even denies the possibility of experiencing a poem in a live performance, as the following remark on poetic 'tone' demonstrates: "But the correct determination of tone in literature is a much more delicate matter than it is with spoken language, for we do not have the speaker's voice to guide us" (Perrine 138). Similarly, Michael Meyer mentions the crucial role of mediality in *English and American Literatures*, claiming that

> [t]he function of the medium cannot be reduced to the mere material form of literature because it is closely related to the ways of communication. Orality (*Mündlichkeit*) is based on contact, participation and community. Oral literature or orature takes place in face-to-face interaction and therefore includes voice, facial expression, gesture and movement to support understanding. [...] Poetry slams revive the communal experience of oral tradition. (8)

Despite this claim that medial specificity cannot simply be reduced to "the mere material form" but that this form impacts considerably on the whole process of literary communication, Meyer's introduction does not go beyond merely mentioning this 'other,' oral realisation of poetry that entails a "communal experience." His work is based on the experience of poetry on the page, in a silent reading, and his methodology takes no account of oral delivery and performance or the communal aspect he points out.

This one-sidedness often appears grounded in the idea that sound, as a quality inherent to the written word, can be found on the page, and thus can be analysed as the sound caught by 'the mind's ear' in a silent reading rather than any actual sound produced in a recital.³ This widespread approach to the acoustic dimension of poetry is often reflected in the terminology of literary studies. In Barnet et al.'s *Introduction to Literature*, for instance, students are encouraged to:

1. Read the poem aloud, or, if you can't bring yourself to read aloud, at least
2. *sound* the poem in your mind's ear. Try to catch the *speaker*'s *tone* of *voice*. (501, my emphasis)

The following example from *Studying Poetry*, in which Matterson and Jones discuss a poem by Linton Kwesi Johnson, reveals a similar application of quasi-acoustic terminology. After mentioning that Johnson comes from a tradition of oral performance they claim that

> [a] significant dimension of the rhymes in the poem is that to *hear* them as full rhymes we have to *hear* the *voice* of the *speaker* (or singer) rather than standard English. An obvious example is the first rhyme, Poelan/oweshan. In standard English 'Poland' and 'Ocean' might be considered a half-rhyme but certainly not a full rhyme. Yet here the representation of the words to reflect the speech of a British Caribbean speaker indicates that there is a full rhyme. (153, my emphasis)

Again, to "*hear* the *voice* of the *speaker*" neither refers to an actual act of hearing (which would be induced by airwaves vibrating on the eardrum) nor to an actual voice (the physical organ that produces these vibrations, and by extension, the sound produced), and certainly not to a real-life speaker. Matterson and Jones are not concerned with actual poetic speech, with the recitation of a poem by a British Caribbean poet, they are interested instead in "the *representation* of the words to *reflect* the speech of a British Caribbean speaker." Thus, not only do they ignore the fact that Linton Kwesi Johnson's live poetry performances are considered artistically outstanding and well worth analysis on their own terms, they also disregard the crucial role these performances play in Johnson's work as a dub poet.

Numerous other critical instruments are employed to produce analyses of poetry that are geared exclusively towards an experience of text on the page, although they principally carry the potential to account for phenomena in both written and performed work. In his chapter on rhetorical form, Michael Meyer defines "emphasis" as an effect "highlighted by an unusual position of a word in the line" (Meyer 37), neglecting to mention how em-

---

3   Garrett Stewart distinguishes between "a merely evoked aurality and an oral vocalizing" (5), referring to the "silent textual sounding" as "evolcaliz[ing]" (1).

phasis may be achieved in the concrete manner of delivery.[4] Similarly, Meyer points out that "[a] comma, colon or full stop within a line of verse indicates a pause (caesura, *Zäsur*)" (42), but not that a pause in live poetry may occur as a moment of deliberate silence that has nothing to do with commas, colons or full stops. Even 'tone' and 'sound' only ever seem to be produced by "choosing certain words in a line or stanza" (Klarer 38), and are rarely regarded as physical qualities that emerge from a poet's particular 'sounding' of these words in performance. The most striking example of this tendency to restrict potentially bivalent terms of analysis to the written mode of realisation can perhaps be found in Terry Eagleton's guide *How to Read a Poem*, where the author claims that "[w]e can speak, too, of the pitch of a poetic voice, meaning whether it sounds high, low or middle-ranging" (116). Again the 'pitch of a poetic voice' is related to the choice of words, the "sense we make of the words" (116) – anything but the actual pitch of a physical voice heard in a live poetry performance.

This limitation in the analysis of poetry, which has been identified as the current *modus operandi* of literary criticism, is further confirmed by the typical answers critics will provide to the very basic question of how we can recognise a text as poetry in the first place. There are two criteria which several of the works quoted above invoke as essential markers of poetry, the first being the specific lineation of poetic texts, their conspicuous use of space, with lines often starting on the left side of the page and being deliberately brought to terminate before the end of the page on the right (cf. e.g. Bode 13, Furniss and Bath 12). The second refers to the context in which a poem is encountered and which identifies it as poetry by embedding it in a particular frame of reference. For Christoph Bode, for instance, it is the text's being "located in a volume of poetry or an anthology" (14, my translation) that enables readers to recognise it as a poem. Similarly, Jonathan Culler notes that texts are treated as poetry when they are found "in a book of poems or a section of a magazine, library, or bookstore" (18). Both these criteria – lineation and a text's location in an "anthology," "library," "bookstore" etc – are frequently cited in introductory works and obviously apply to poetry in its written mode only.

From this evidence we can conclude that regardless of its affirmations of the bivalent mediality of poetry, its sensual dimensions, its origin in oral performance and the importance thereof, literary criticism continues to

---

4   Interestingly, Meyer offers the German equivalent "Betonung" in brackets. This word choice is telling, as it contains the word "Ton," which translates as tone, sound, or even musical note and is therefore clearly linked to the acoustic realm.

sideline or outright ignore live poetry as a subject for academic study.[5] It provides a plethora of analytical instruments geared towards extracting the potential, 'imagined' sound that is 'built into the written poem' but no critical tools with which to attend to the spoken word, to the actual physical sound that creates the poem in performance.

Furthermore, sound is, of course, only one dimension in which the notable differences between written poetry and live poetry come to the fore. The physical co-presence of poet and audience in a live poetry performance allows for a range of other sense perceptions (facial expression, body communication, audience interaction etc.) that considerably impact on the impression the audience has of the performance and thus on the meaning-making process. While the concept of sound is treated in a one-sided manner by contemporary literary criticism, these other aspects relevant to live poetry tend to be absent from most analyses of poetry altogether, although critics such as Meyer correctly observe that poetry also exists as a way of literary communication that is based on "contact, participation and community" (8). Once again this near-total omission is closely connected to the methodological principles at work. If we ask for the source of the poetic "sound" so many critics write about, the answers to be deduced from their writings will be either "the text," as it contains representations of sound, or, as a logical consequence, "the reader," who creates "imagined" sound in his or her mind on the basis of these representations. The answer will never be "the poet," since the fixation on the potential sound of poetry experienced in silent readings of written text precludes any encounter between poet and audience in a live poetry performance. Taking aspects such as body language or audience interaction into account would therefore require a paradigmatic shift in poetry criticism from a system of thought that privileges the written mode as it purports to provide methods for an analysis of poetry's sensual acoustic aspects, to an approach that fully acknowledges live performance as an alternative realisation mode and thus directs the critic's attention to a range of novel criteria that have hitherto been dismissed as lying outside the domain of literary criticism.

This neglect on the part of literary scholars may, to some extent, be attributable to the medial specificity of live poetry. Answering the question "What is live poetry?" is also significant for determining the academic discipline(s) that will consequently recognise live poetry as a legitimate object of

---

[5] In his study of song lyrics, Lars Eckstein similarly points to a "stubborn bias towards the written word and a persistent refusal to work with a concept of 'embodied' language" in literary studies (Eckstein 14).

study. As a definition of live poetry as "poetry in performance" may suggest that it falls into the domain of theatre studies, its relation to theatre shall need to be briefly explored.

2.2 Live Poetry and Theatre

Following Chiel Kattenbelt's broad conception of theatre as "the art of physical presence (face-to-face communication in a situation of here and now) and of expression in words, gestures/movements and sounds" (32), live poetry could indeed be considered as a form of theatre. It is obviously related to text-based theatre, with which it shares an oral delivery of the text and the simultaneity of production and reception. As live poetry generally does not make use of props or elaborate stage scenery, it could perhaps most easily be classified as "Poor Theatre,"[6] as defined by Jerzy Grotowski. Grotowski explained the essence of theatre as follows:

> By gradually eliminating whatever proved superfluous, we found that theatre can exist without make-up, without autonomic costume and scenography, without a separate performance area (stage), without lighting and sound effects, etc. It cannot exist without the actor-spectator relationship of perceptual, direct, 'live' communion. (23)

It is this element of 'liveness,' of being in the moment, that is most evidently shared by the two art forms, and while live poetry can be demarcated quite easily from certain theatrical forms such as Pina Bausch's dance theatre, its distinction from text-based theatre is far less obvious. This section will introduce a range of criteria that help to distinguish live poetry from theatre and thus contribute towards the delineation of a clear profile for live poetry as an art form in its own right.

A first step is the comparison of the *relationship drama text/theatrical performance to that of the written poem with its performed counterpart.* Theatre scholar Erika Fischer-Lichte criticises the frequent depiction of the text-performance relationship in theatre as that of score to realisation, or deep structure to surface structure, pointing towards the fundamental role of the medium as not just a carrier of a pre-defined artistic content but as a shaper of that content (Fischer-Lichte, "Die Zeichensprache des Theaters" 251). She proposes to conceive of both drama text and performance as a work "sui generis" (252), which seems to echo T.V.F. Brogan's claim for written

---

[6] Cf. also Bernstein 10 for the idea of the poetry reading as 'poor theatre.'

poetry and live poetry as two different manifestations of an "abstract entity called 'the poem,'" neither of which "has ontological precedence" (940).

The written text in theatre is, however, "radically conditioned by its performability," as Keir Elam (191) notes:

> The written text, in other words, is determined by its very need for stage contextualization, and indicates throughout its allegiance to the physical conditions of performance, above all to the actor's body and its ability to materialize discourse within the space of the stage. (191)

Drama as a literary genre is specifically written to be performed in theatre, which renders "performability" an absolute requirement. The drama text contains references to the physical world of the stage, as when Lady Macbeth scolds her murderous husband with the words "Infirm of purpose! Give me the daggers" *(Macbeth* II.2.53-54). These two short phrases indicate the presence of two characters on stage (the speaker Lady M and the addressee Macbeth) who are related to each other through a common 'purpose,' which is connected to the physical transfer of two solid objects (props) between them. The need for stage contextualisation becomes even clearer in the case of stage directions. The playwright may give instructions for a scene to be set in a "forest in winter," for instance, which will be indicated by the stage design in which the characters are moving and to which they may deictically refer.

Poetry, by contrast, often allows for its realisation as live poetry but is not generically geared towards performance, i.e. it is not defined as 'written text serving as a basis for stage performance.'[7] Rather, performability in poetry must be envisioned as a continuum ranging from 'unperformable' (e.g. visual poetry) to 'highly suitable for performance' (e.g. performance poetry, which is often explicitly written to be spoken to an audience). Thus, live poetry is a possible parallel, rather than a generically intended manifesttation, of the written poetic text. A poem that is performed will, of course, display a minimum degree of performability in its parallel written mode[8]: not

---

[7]   Even in drama there are, of course, exceptions in the form of plays that range nearer the pole of "unperformable" – one need only think of some of the work of Tristan Tzara and Alfred Jarry. However, these are still considered drama in so far as their central conceit is that they are ostensibly 'written for performance.'

[8]   That live poetry generally has a parallel existence in writing is confirmed by empirical evidence: at 'poetry readings' poet-performers present their work orally whilst relying on a written text, while 'performance poets' often confront their audience without a book in hand but still commit their poems to paper beforehand in the process of composition, and will often publish the writing in some form, too. This practice is in line with poetry's generic focus on form and verbal density (cf. p. 61), which can

by indicating an allegiance to physical stage conditions but in the sense that it is at least 'speakable.'

Another feature that distinguishes live poetry from theatre is the fact that in live poetry *the presence of the audience is directly acknowledged* by the poet-performer, in contrast to classic "fourth-wall" theatre as originally defined by Denis Diderot in his *Discourse on Dramatic Poetry* (1758).[9] This latter tradition is based on the idea of an invisible wall that separates stage and auditorium and allows for the actors/characters to act as if no audience were present, turning the spectator into a *voyeur*. Even if poets do not openly address their audience they will generally face them in performance and thus recite their poetry directly to the audience and acknowledge their presence.

A related criterion for distinguishing between the two art forms may be found in what Werner Wolf calls *"aesthetic illusion"* ("Illusion, ästhetische" 310). This principle concerns the fact that theatre has a performative as well as a referential function, as pointed out by Fischer-Lichte ("Grenzgänge und Tauschhandel" 279). The body of actor Toby Stephens in the Donmar Warehouse production of Harold Pinter's *Betrayal* (London 2007), for example, *refers to* the fictive character Jerry as he enacts his role on stage, leading the audience to suspend disbelief for the duration of the play and accept the conceit that it really is Jerry they see. Theatrical tools such as props, costumes and stage scenery encourage and strengthen the identification of actor and character and the wilful plunge into the fictitious world. Strong aesthetic illusion such as this is rarely generated by poetry, as Müller-Zettelmann (125ff) notes, partly due to textual factors such as the relative brevity of poems, which would not allow for an extended illusion to arise, or their tendency to draw attention to their own formal make-up and thus demand a more distant manner of reception (97f). With regard to the role of the performer, it must be noted that in a live performance of poetry, the poet-performer *presents* him or herself rather than *representing* a fictitious character. Even in dramatic monologues – the poetic genre most closely associated with theatrical speech and the formation of a fictitious character –

---

hardly be achieved in spontaneous oral composition, and also helps to distinguish live poetry from related art forms such as 'oral poetry' and its comparatively loose manner of composition (cf. Chapter 1.2.2), or David Antin's spontaneous 'talk poems' (cf. Perelman 203f).

[9] Cf. Diderot's *Discours sur la poésie dramatique* (1758): "Imaginez sur le bord du théâtre un grand mur qui vous sépare du parterre. Jouez comme si la toile ne se levait pas" (339; "Imagine a great wall at the front of the stage that separates you from the audience. Act as though the curtain had not risen," my translation).

the poet will not be collapsed with the "character" (speaker) of the poem to the same degree as a theatre actor with his/her character.[10]

This idea of embodiment in theatre leads us to another crucial difference to live poetry: the principle of *ostension*. "The story on stage is not told but shown and the audience looks directly at the action," Peter Eversmann explains in his essay on "The Experience of the Theatrical Event" (143). He refers to the fact that although theatre may rely heavily on the dramatic text, it can systematically activate a range of other means to 'tell the story' and create meaning. If the stage character Kate is supposed to eat her dinner in *The Taming of the Shrew* it suffices for the actress to physically complete or at least indicate the action – there is no need to verbalise it. Live poetry, on the other hand, depends to a much higher degree on the spoken word to convey its story or images. Theatre commonly employs the effect of props, costumes, scenery, additional sound and light effects to function as parallel systems of meaning (often to represent a fictive character or world), which may be of equal or even greater importance than the dramatic text. In live poetry, the verbal element is not simply one component of several: it is at the very core of the art form.

Furthermore, Wolf's definition of media as a *"conventionally* distinct means of communicating cultural contents" ("Intermediality" 253, my emphasis) stresses the importance of conventions in the delimitation of different art forms. While Wolf's 'conventions' refer primarily to the demarcation of ideal aesthetic categories, they may be applied to characteristic features of performance practice. One such pragmatic convention that helps distinguish live poetry from traditional theatre is summed up in Naila Keleta Mae's impressions that "[i]n Canadian theatre, playwrights and actors were cogs in the wheel; in spoken word, the writer/performer was the wheel" (102). While a theatrical performance is generally shaped collectively by the playwright, director and leading actors – with the director often holding a prominent role as decision maker – *live poetry will predominantly be performed by the writer* him- or herself,[11] who is thus cast in a triple role of writer, actor,

---

[10] A reversed process of identification can sometimes be observed in performances of lyric poetry, however: while in theatre the material body of the performer is conventionally 'read' as referring to a fictitious character and thus understood as a fiction, it is the poem's fictive speaker and the experience s/he expresses that is frequently mistaken as referring back to the poet-performer and his/her real life experience and therefore read as autobiographical. On the performance of identity in live poetry, see chapter 6.2.1.

[11] The author-as-performer criterion has an empirical basis in so far as it applies to an overwhelming part of contemporary live poetry performances. Its aesthetic implications are discussed in Chapter 6.2.1.

and director of their own performance. The tripartite nature of this role helps to classify Vanessa Redgrave's minimalist one-woman performance in Joan Didion's stage adaptation of *The Year of Magical Thinking* (London, National Theatre 2008) as theatre rather than live literature, although the focus is placed heavily on Redgrave's verbalisation of the script, while Rommi Smith's 'theatrical' stage performance of her poems from *Mornings & Midnights* is deemed live poetry, not theatre.[12]

The importance of the author-as-performer criterion is underlined by the surprising amount of resistance with which the presentation of poetry by actors is met in the poetry world. Charles Bernstein relates this "common dislike, among poets, of actors' readings of poems" to a

> style of acting that frames the performance in terms of character, personality, setting, gesture, development, or drama, even though these may be extrinsic to the text at hand. That is, the "acting" takes precedence over letting the words speak for themselves (or worse, eloquence compromises, not to say eclipses, the ragged music of the poem). (11)

Equally, John Whitworth claims that

> [a]ctors have all sorts of ways of making poetry awful. They read with insufficient attention to the FORM, they read as if it were prose. [...] Or they read to draw attention to themselves rather than the poem. (19)

Russell Thompson strikes a similar note when he comments on poet Abe Gibson's performance at London's Soho Theatre in early 2007:

> Yeah, there's a lot of theatre in there. I think he stopped short of sort of overdoing it. He had that one for two voices that he finished on, but I was never in any doubt that the words were the main thing, that the voice was the main thing. He was doing his usual facial expressions, but I never felt as though facial expressions and the gestures were getting in the way of the words. (Interview 2007)

Ensuring that the "acting" component does not "get in the way of the words" would appear to be a crucial requirement for live poetry perform-

---

[12] As the live poetry scene is a living conglomerate of creative minds who often embrace deviance rather than a static set of rules, certain hybrid forms may occasionally be encountered as a way of sounding out the boundaries between live poetry and theatre, such as spoken word shows where the poet-performer is assisted by a director (e.g. Lemn Sissay, "Something Dark," Contact Theatre, Manchester 2004), or poetry performed by hired actors (e.g. Jonathan Davidson's "Being Alive" tour, UK 2006).

ances, once again demonstrating that the text and its formal make-up remain the main focus rather than notions of dramatic character.

This insistence on paying close attention to the verbal element and its patterning is corroborated by genre theory. Poetry tends towards a greater artificiality and density in the use of language than other literary genres, Müller-Zettelmann notes. Its characteristic density[13] is related to the relative brevity (73) of individual poems and the consequent reduction (76) of their subject matter, inherent communicative functions (speaker and addressee), and setting (77). The genre's tendency towards an enhanced artificiality figures as a network of internal correlations of structure, sound and sense (84ff). Rhyme, for instance, as a pattern of phonetic values, and rhythm (as a pattern of syllabic stress), mark poetry off from prose or ordinary speech. Thus, what poetry lacks in epic breadth it makes up for in the depth and density of its semantic structure, a network of correlations in which every word carries its weight towards the meaning-making process. At the same time, this linguistic artificiality leads to the genre's aesthetic self-referentiality as poetry draws attention to its own form (Müller-Zettelmann 97ff) rather than rendering its discourse transparent for an aesthetic illusion of, for instance, a perfectly rounded fictitious character to arise.

Significantly, for Müller-Zettelmann the concept of genre is not restricted to the level of text but also manifests itself in the *reader's expectations* of a text (16), and consequently in the attention brought to the reception process. Accordingly, in the case of poetry concepts of genre would entail a heightened focus on form in expectation of a certain density and enhanced artificiality which demand a high level of attention. Thus, while live literature generally focuses on the orally delivered text more than theatre, live *poetry* demands an even higher degree of concentration on the performer's words, which no misguided attempts at "acting" should "get in the way of."[14]

---

[13] The German word 'Dichtung' for the high art of poetry derives from 'dicht,' meaning 'dense.'

[14] Upholding a firm distinction between theatre and live poetry may also be crucial with regard to the allocation of public resources, as Jonathan Davidson notes. When asked about the usefulness of a term such as 'live literature' he points out that it is invaluable as a label and category for funding applications, for instance to the Arts Council of England: "I'd rather be up against other live literature projects when it comes to funding than up against the theatre world, which is massive and will trample all over us. [...] It's important to acknowledge that some art forms have particular requirements and situations [...] and we need to be, to some extent, guarded from that market [...] to allow ourselves to develop ("What is live literature?"). As such, it is not only factors such as aesthetic criteria and conventions of performance

2.3 A Definition of Live Poetry

To sum up, live poetry can be defined as emerging from the fundamental bi-mediality of the genre of poetry – i.e. its potential realisation as spoken or written word – as a specific manifestation of poetry's oral mode of realisation, which is a parallel to, rather than a mere derivative 'version' of, the written mode. As such, live poetry is characterised by the direct encounter and physical co-presence of the poet with a live audience. The poet will predominantly perform his/her own poetry and is thus cast in the double role of 'poet-performer.' The story and images of the poem are conveyed through the spoken word rather than through theatrical ostension, as focus is placed on the oral verbalisation of the poetic text.

Live poetry thus comprises presentations of 'performance poetry' as well as the more traditional 'poetry readings.' It may be encountered in a wide variety of settings: poetry slams, large public demonstrations such as anti-war gatherings, formal readings (for instance at universities), literature festivals and small open mics, to name just a few.

This definition will serve as a basis for the methodological approach to live poetry introduced in this study.

practice that may play a role in the classification of different art forms but also customs of institutional support which may require drawing a line between related fields.

Part Two: Analysing Live Poetry

In the following, a comprehensive approach to live poetry will be introduced which reflects the medial characteristics of poetry performances. Part Two presents a range of analytical criteria: of questions that can be asked of a live poetry performance, and of possible ways of answering them. Chapter 3, "Comparing the Written Poem and the Performed Poem," states some general observations on the possible relations between these two parallel modes of realisation and points out how a systematic comparison may yield interesting results about the nature of the live poem. Chapters 4 and 5, on audio-text and body communication respectively, demonstrate ways of a 'close reading' – and 'close listening' – of live poetry. They constitute guidelines for what Elizabeth Fine has termed a "performance record" (95), which focuses on the formal features of the poet-performer's aesthetic activity. The performance record must, however, be accompanied by a 'performance report' to account for the contextual situatedness of a live performance (Fine 94). Chapter 6, "Contextualising the Performance," therefore revolves around those additional factors that ought to be taken into account in an analysis of live poetry as a strongly context-dependent artistic practice. Part Two is completed by a sample analysis of Jackie Hagan's performance of "Coffee or Tea?" and a checklist for the analysis of live poetry.

The individual aspects of live poetry discussed in Part Two are illustrated by way of a range of different examples which together make up the corpus of audio and video recordings of live poetry performances underlying the present study. They have been selected according to the principles of diversity of gender, ethnicity, theme, and performance style. Following the definition of live poetry proposed in Chapter 2, they may all be classified as what John Miles Foley terms "voiced text" (39), i.e. text that is performed orally and received aurally, while it has been composed prior to the time of performance. These texts are relatively stable and usually have a parallel existence in print. The present corpus thus excludes 'oral poetry' in the narrower sense of poetry composed spontaneously or poetry depending to a high degree on verbal improvisation.

I have striven to do justice to the definition of 'liveness' as a physical co-presence of poet-performer and audience and to witness as many live poetry events as possible in person. The video and audio recordings referred to in this study serve as prompts to remembering the attended events, and many of them can be found on www.livepoetry.net – the companion website to this book. Recordings thus form the basis of the analysis of an art that is essentially ephemeral. Video camcorders are widely available today and have proved invaluable in terms of the density of information they record. However, their use is at the same time problematic in view of what they *cannot* record, as their perspective is limited.[1] It is often advisable, therefore, to take notes as well during a live performance, for which purpose the checklist in Chapter 8 may serve as an aid. Thus, while the ephemeral nature of live performance renders recording a necessity, it must not be forgotten that the performance and its recording are never the same thing.

Finally, the following chapters amount to a separate discussion of various aspects of live poetry which are, in fact, interconnected and occur simultaneously in performance. Elizabeth Fine rightly observes that

> a performance is much more than a simple sum of codes. Each of the linguistic, paralinguistic, and kinesic elements in a performance interact with, combine, and modify each other, and all of them influence and are influenced by aesthetic field elements, such as the physical and psychological setting and cultural norms of interaction and interpretation. (146)

Ideally, then, the aspects isolated here for the sake of clarity should be integrated and related to each other in an analysis of live poetry.

---

[1] For a discussion of the role of video recordings in the analysis of theatrical performances, see Hiß 126-7.

3. Comparing the Written Poem and the Performed Poem

Having defined live poetry and written poetry as two parallel modes of realising the poetic text, both of which are amenable to practices of 'reading,' a comparison of the performed poem and its written counterpart will yield interesting insights into the possible relationships between the two modes and, more importantly, into the widely differing aesthetic experiences live poetry affords.

Balz Engler's study *Reading and Listening: The Modes of Communicating Poetry and their Influence on the Texts* constitutes a rare attempt at classifying the relationships between the aural and the visual experience of poetry based on the assumption that reading and listening are two profoundly different modes of communication with a text. It shall serve as a starting point for the following discussion of how a live performance of poetry compares with its written counterpart. Taking the written text as his point of departure, Engler proposes a typology of five possible relationships ranging from [1] "score" – i.e. where the writing "indicates how the poem is supposed to sound" and "does not, ideally, contain any shapes that cannot be translated into sound" (29) – to [5] "contradiction," a relationship of incompatibility (34), as is the case with eye rhymes, for instance, which can be experienced only visually. Between the two poles, the written text may be [2] a "comment" on the aural elements, as in the case of capital letters at the beginning of lines that help to "characterize the text as a poem, in a way that can only indirectly be communicated to a listener" (31); the visual elements may [3] "complement" the aural ones, as for example in emblems and pattern poems (32), or they may stand in [4] "contrast" and thus "suggest an experience conflicting with the one indicated by the text as score" (33). Engler quotes enjambement as a case in point here: "While the sequence of spoken language, reflected by the syntax of the text, suggests continuity, the eye is forced to stop at the end of the line, and to move back to the left margin of the text" (33). Engler's claim that "the written text tends to indicate if a poem is meant to be listened to or read visually" (20), although "the evidence is often conflicting, some suggesting an aural experience, some a visual one" (29) indicates that his typology is, in fact, geared towards written text and its *potential* for translation into aural text, as do the examples chosen. In order to account for live poetry and its relationship with written text the priorities will have to be partially reversed. Nevertheless, Engler's categories provide a useful point of departure for examining different ways in which written text and audiotext may relate to each other.

The notion of "*complement*" can be applied to elements in the oral performance of a text that are not represented in the written text and thus add to it. An example is Shortman's piece "Beautifully Hectic," which the spoken-word artist performed at one of the bi-weekly open mics at London's Theatre Royal Stratford East in May 2005. "Beautifully Hectic" revolves around the hectic everyday life of a spoken-word artist and was recited by Shortman at an impressive pace in a regular rhythm. The words were interspersed with audible intakes of breath that reminded one of the gasps of a drowning man. They are represented here by the ↑ sign, which does not, of course, appear in his chapbook:

> Get that done call him
> Call her ↑
> Text him that phone number sooner
>
> Post that ↑ Deadlines
> Red light ↑
> Rushing its rush hour hurry I'm running late
>
> Invoice them
> Send in that demo tape
> Mailing list email ↑
>
> Sis grab some selotape
> Attention ↑ to detail […]
>
> ("Beautifully Hectic")

This rhythmic, audible inhaling is incorporated seamlessly into the audiotext and seems very much a meaningful part of it. In a comparison with the printed poem it thus emerges as an oral element that complements the written text.[1]

---

[1] On a practical note: this kind of complementary relationship, like all of Engler's five categories, can only be experienced directly if the printed text is familiar to the audience or available during the performance. While it is entirely possible in performances of well-known poets with a long publishing record to have a large number of the audience bring along the books in order to see them 'sanctified' in the subsequent book signing, it is far less likely if the poet-performer is not as advanced in his/her career and has perhaps not published his/her work yet.
Peter Middleton points out, however, that to follow the written text in a live performance could certainly "help with recognition of exactly what words and phrases are uttered, but for most people the division of attention would come at a high price – the loss of many of the nuances of the performer's soundings and embodiment of the text. Attempts to project poems on the wall run into similar difficulties" ("How to Read a Reading of a Written Poem" 10). A close comparison of written text and

"*Contradiction*" as a relationship of incompatible elements in the written poem and the live poem can, for example, be observed when a poet-performer departs from the written text in oral delivery, be it because s/he makes a mistake or because s/he adapts the live performance to the particular situation in which it takes place. An example is Patience Agbabi's performance of her mirror poem "Josephine Baker finds herself" at an "Apples & Snakes" event at London's Soho Theatre (28 Feb. 2007). Agbabi missed out a line by accident, a departure from the script that attentive listeners could have recognised as the poet had introduced the piece as a mirror poem, whose second part is the symmetrical opposite of the first, i.e. a duplicate in reverse order.

Another example of this kind of contradiction between written and aural text is Adrian Mitchell's performance of his famous poem "To Whom it May Concern" at a large anti-war demonstration at Hyde Park, London, in February 2003. Mitchell changed the chorus line "Tell me lies about Vietnam" into "Tell me lies about Iraq" to suit the theme of the demonstration. In this case it is quite possible that some of the audience recognised the alteration since Mitchell had performed the poem on numerous occasions before. The intentional contradiction between the written and performed versions is of great significance here, as not only does it alter the chief reference of the poem to a particular political situation and thus make an implicit point about the universality of anti-war sentiments, it also questions the idea of the poem as a fixed, stable entity. "I do change poems, particularly when I'm performing them," Mitchell notes, pointing towards the great flexibility of live performance as a poetic medium. "If it doesn't seem right on the night, I'll leave something out, change a verse, for example" (Hardy 6).

To apply Engler's categories of "comment," "contrast," and "score" to live poetry is somewhat more problematic and reveals the one-sidedness of his approach. As an example of "visual elements [...] that make a *comment* on the aural ones, without directly contributing to the meaning of the text" (31), Engler cites the capitalised line beginnings, which communicate a kind of meta-message about the text's genre, characterising it as a poem. In an oral delivery such a comment may perhaps be produced by the poet-performer's tone of voice, if it marks his/her speech as somehow out-of-the-ordinary: a way of speaking reserved for the special occasion of a poetry recital. It seems rather difficult, however, to decide which elements "contribute directly to the meaning of the text" (and can therefore not be classi-

audiotext is therefore best carried out in a post-performance analysis of video or audio recordings, where the performance text can be studied alongside the page at leisure.

fied as a "comment" according to Engler's definition) and which do not. For Engler, the 'meaning' of a poem seems to be located exclusively in the semantic content of the text substratum, whereas in live poetry, tone of voice may in fact form an important part of the aural experience of a poem and may well contribute to its meaning, as I shall argue later.

"*Contrast*" seems an obvious category to describe the relationship between visual text and live performance; and many instances of the kind of discrepancy between "line division" and "syntax and rhyme" (33) that Engler cites can be found in live poetry, where a tension may arise between line breaks and speech pauses. Peter Middleton notices this kind of contrast in Jackie Kay's recital of her poem "Brendan Gallacher," which was recorded on tape by the BBC in 1998. The line division of a passage of the printed version can be represented as follows:

> He'd get his mum out of Glasgow when he got older.
> A wee holiday someplace nice. Some place far.
> I'd tell my mum about my Brendan Gallacher
> How his mum drank and his daddy was a cat burglar.
> (Armitage and Crawford, 407)

Middleton notes that "if the spoken version were printed to indicate the breaks in her utterance it would look something like this:

> He'd get his mum out of Glasgow when he got older.
> A wee holiday
> someplace nice.
> Some place far.
>
> I'd tell my mum about my Brendan Gallacher How his mum drank and his daddy was a cat burglar."
> ("How to Read a Reading of a Written Poem" 12)

The problem one encounters in applying Engler's notion of contrast to live poetry, however, is that it cannot be regarded as one possible relationship between elements of the written and oral realisations of a poem: it is, rather, a general condition that will emerge to a greater or lesser degree in any comparison between the two modes. Any juxtaposition of a poem in print and a live performance will yield instances of contrast and surprise, where the oral realisation does not correspond to the expectation raised by the print version. If this were not the case, it should be possible to predict from the written text exactly what an oral performance would sound like.

This leads us to Engler's fifth category of possible written-aural relations: the "score." His claim that "the text as a score for performance indicates how the poem is supposed to sound" (29) must be put into perspective before we apply it to live poetry. In music, a score serves as a basis for performance that provides guidelines to the realisation of a piece in terms of melody, harmony, metre, tempo, and dynamics. As a piece of music will in most cases be performed by someone other than the composer, it is hardly surprising to note the considerable differences between various musicians' interpretations of the same score. Divergences are common even between different performances by the same artist. By analogy, Engler's "score" will be an approximate indication of the way a poem "is supposed to sound" only to the extent that printed letters and words can be understood as encoded sounds that can be turned into language which is recognisable as such. Supposing that a poetic "score" provides more detailed information on the speech melody of a performed poem, for instance, amounts to making a claim for Douglas Oliver's idea of the "neutral tune" to which a poem can be read. This "neutral" or "unmarked" tune is, according to Oliver,

> that which the words would assume for an average voice in a given dialect when no special emphasis (for example, dramatic or syntactic) is given to the line, providing there were absolute agreement between different readers about the semantic, emotional and syntactical interpretation. (x)

Apart from the conundrum of the "average voice" it seems highly unlikely to ever achieve "absolute agreement" between (how many?) "different readers about the semantic, emotional and syntactical interpretation" of a poem. The idea of the neutral tune seems to suggest that each poem possesses a natural, inherent melody and that it must consequently be the task of the performer to bring it out so as to present the poem to best effect. However, unlike the musical score, the written poem provides no explicit indication of an intended melody or tempo for instance, since many features of spoken language simply remain unrepresented in writing. Ian Davidson makes this clear in his account of a poetry reading he attended:

> Once one has heard a poet like Tom Raworth read, his voice skating across the surface as he spits out the words at a speed way beyond what is expected, it is difficult to hear the poems in another way. Yet the lines of two or three words could either be a clue to race through, or indicate a desire to linger over individual words or groups of words. (135)

The tempo in which the poet delivered his 'lines' clearly came as a surprise to Davidson, who found no reliable indication for it on the page. The notion of the score as specifying "how the poem is supposed to sound" (Engler 29) is therefore of little use for the present purpose.

Furthermore, the sole stipulation that a "score" will "not, ideally, contain any shapes that cannot be translated into sound" (Engler 29) considerably limits its operational value as a category for the classification of the relationship of written text and oral text. A quotation from Russell Thompson illustrates this:

> Certain literary poets whose poems are very densely written and may be relying heavily on lots of references or lots of very intricate uses of thought association maybe ... I'm thinking possibly here of somebody like Paul Muldoon, who I like very much as a literary poet and I have actually gone to hear him reading his stuff live, but I know that hearing him reading his stuff live you're probably missing out on maybe 75 percent of what the poem is actually dealing with. (Thompson interview 2006)

Sound-wise, Paul Muldoon's poetry can be (and has been) performed to a live audience, which would apparently suffice to classify his writing as a "score" for performance, despite the fact that a silent reading may actually be more conducive to appreciating much of his work, as Thompson points out. However, the idea of a score, in music for instance, entails performance as its chief purpose: a score is generally written so that a piece of music can be sounded out in performance. As a label for poetry that characterises a particular kind of relationship between written text and oral text it will thus imply an element of authorial intention, which can be problematic as the following statement by Patience Agbabi, who was asked whether she sometimes writes explicitly for performance, will demonstrate:

> Not any more. [...] I don't sort of sit down and think oh I specifically want to perform this. However, some pieces, of the pieces I write, just naturally lend themselves to performance because I use a lot of repetition, I like monologues, so ... For the Soho theatre gig, for example, I decided to just do monologues. And a monologue – of course it's somebody speaking to someone else, of course all monologues are going to work in performance. (Agbabi interview)

Although Patience Agbabi frequently performs her work she denies that her poetry is in any way written specifically for performance, as the notion of 'score' would suggest. The term *'performability'* seems more appropriate to describe the potential of a poem to be realised in performance, as it does not refer to authorial intention but rather specifies the poem's suitability for oral performance, which may depend on such factors as the configuration of the 'speaker' (as in monologues), for instance, and can be conceived of as a continuum ranging from "unperformable" (e.g. visual poetry) to "highly suitable for oral performance." It should not be forgotten, however, that the written text on its own is, of course, no indicator of the effectiveness of a live poetry performance.

Since 'performability' denotes an inherent 'potential' of the written text rather than emerging from an actual comparison of the two modes, it should be exempted from a typology of relationships between written text and audiotext, which leaves us with the following classification:

Contrast

Every comparison of a written poem and its corresponding oral performance will reveal a certain amount of contrast: instances where the oral realisation does not correspond to the print version or the expectations raised by the printed poem, and vice versa. Contrast is thus to be regarded as a general condition that will emerge to a greater or lesser degree in any comparison of the two modes. The dissimilarities between the two realisations of a poem can take on three forms, two of which are based on Engler's typology:

Complement

Just as there are emblem poems, whose visual images cannot be realised in an oral performance, the poet-performer may introduce distinct acoustic elements into his/her poems (such as rhythmic intakes of breath, sighs, whistling etc.) which are not represented in the printed poem. The audiotext opens up possibilities which have no correspondence in the written text.

Contradiction

Certain elements of the written poem and the live poem may be incompatible and thus stand in a relationship of contradiction to each other, as caused by a change of word order in performance, for instance. This kind of contradiction is often tied to the great flexibility of live poetry as a medium for publication.

Disambiguation

Each mode of realising poetry allows for certain ambiguities to arise that may be dissolved by the other mode, which leads to a contrast of determined/undetermined. Engler disregards this ability of one medium to disambiguate, or 'interpret,' the other as his categorisation is based on potential rather than actual sound. Disambiguation is, however, a crucial relation of written poem and audiotext, and one that is directly related to the different aesthetic possibilities the two medial realisations afford. A line of poetry on the page remains ambiguous as to its melody, for example, and while a silent reading as a way of "enperformancing" the written text (see Finnegan, "The How of Literature" 176) allows for a number of different 'virtual' intonations, it will generally sustain this ambiguity of the written text, as Peter Quartermain points out:

> But the more any of us reads a given poem, silently or aloud, the more established becomes an inward notional neutral tune that persists from reading to reading, familiar but *elusive* in its fine detail. [...] The difficulty of voicing the poem, though it has something to do with our understanding of the work, may also have to do with a kind of *tentative polyvocality*, a simultaneity of possible tones and interpretations, possible (at least in a gestural way) inside the head but impossible of public performance – a kind of *undecidable* music or tune [...] (221, my emphasis)

Quartermain makes an important point about the imprecision of the 'mind's ear': the potential, 'imagined' sound it 'hears,' which is often (implicitly) referred to in the literature on poetry, is essentially vague as to its exact pitch curve. Thus, while the written text remains ambiguous, allowing for several possible intonations to co-occur in a silent reading, the audiotext disambiguates the mind's 'tentative polyvocality' by presenting one particular intonational choice.

Similarly, the printed poem may resolve ambiguities perceived in the audiotext, as the following account of a 'mishearing' by Nathaniel Mackey demonstrates:

> I recall a Robert Duncan reading in 1979 which at one point conjured an image of a stairway beneath eyelids, a stairway a star ascended. It was an image I found startling, arrestingly so. [...] I'd read this poem a number of times in the years prior to attending the reading but I'd evidently forgotten that the word was "stare." I heard it as "stair." To hear it so was to "mishear" it – in quotes because to hear it so was to be true to the passage's play on the fact that a stare under closed lids is no stare, an eclipsed or suspended stare if not the inversely capable, inner sight or ascent suggested by "stair," the mind's eye the passage both advocates and opens. (96)

While the audiotext here creates a pair of homophones that allow for two differing images to arise, the written poem fixates a word so as to connect it to a definite semantic field.

Mackey's is another telling example of how the two media of sound and scripture can communicate different kinds of 'meaning' and may therefore lead to widely different experiences of the 'same' poem. If this is true for the relation of written text and audiotext, it is even more striking when live poetry is considered in its entirety: as a performance that involves verbal and non-verbal sounds, facial expressions, and other levels of communication the visible human body activates and for which no representation whatsoever exists in the written text. The following sections will provide an overview of the instruments a poet-performer has at his/her disposal to give shape to the poetic text in an audio-visual performance.

4. Audiotext

4.1 Audiotext and Paralanguage: Experiential Meaning Potential, Provenance, Voice Set and Voice Action

At the centre of a live poetry performance lies what Charles Bernstein calls the "audiotext" of the poem and which he defines as "the poet's acoustic performance" (13). It denotes an "audible acoustic text" (12) rather than the "evoked aurality" (Stewart 1) often referred to in discussions of the 'inherent' sound of the written word and thus acknowledges the essential transience of sound: the audiotext is communicated through vibrations of a certain frequency – oscillations per second – which makes its occurrence and disappearance dependent on the passing of time.[1]

As in theatrical performances, poet-performers bring forth their audiotext through (mostly) vocal production at a specific place and time. However, while few people in theatre would undertake a 'close listening'[2] of an entire night's performance, or even an act, the audiotext is the undeniable focus of live poetry, or, in Russell Thompson's diction: "words" and "voice" are "the main thing" (interview 2007), which renders close listening a crucial task. Incidentally, Thompson's statement draws an important distinction within the domain of audiotext: that between *verbal* and *non-verbal* elements. A plethora of literature is available on the verbal aspects of poetry (often equated with written text), and it cannot be the aim of this study to recapitulate techniques of analysing syntax, rhetorical figures, rhyme schemes, diction and so forth, most of which may be applied to written and sounded text alike. An exception will be made for the notion of paratext, a part of the verbal audiotext that accompanies the 'poem proper' in the form of introductions, comments, etc., and which shall be examined in terms of its specific forms and functions in live poetry.

The non-verbal elements of audiotext, by contrast, are scarcely dealt with and barely even acknowledged in the literature on poetry, as pointed out in Chapter 2.1. Charles Bernstein characterises audiotext as "a semantically

---

[1] The audiotext of a live poetry performance can, of course, be recorded, and although audio recordings lose the liveness factor, they may serve as an aid to memory and close analysis of live poetry. Conversely, most of the analytical criteria introduced in this chapter can also be applied to 'audio poetry' produced in professional recording studios. Charles Bernstein suggests that in fact, audio reproduction as a means of publication does more justice to the medium of live poetry than video recordings, which tend to be rather static (12).

[2] A term proposed by Charles Bernstein in analogy to close reading, see Bernstein 1998.

denser field of linguistic activity than can be charted by means of meter, assonance, alliteration, rhyme, and the like" (13), i.e. by means of the traditional analytical tools literary studies provides. A poet may shout or whisper, race through a text or drawl each vowel, deliver his/her 'lines' in a sing-song interspersed with rhythmic laughter or recite them in a monotonous drone like a liturgical incantation, all of which generally remains unaccounted for in conventional analyses of poetry. These non-verbal vocal features can be discussed under the heading of '*paralanguage*,' which Fernando Poyatos defines as "the nonverbal voice qualities, modifiers and independent sounds and silences with which we support or contradict the simultaneous or alternating linguistic and kinesic structures" (Poyatos 130). Paralanguage comprises "any aspect of vocal behaviour which can be seen as meaningful but is not described as part of the language system," including "aspects of voice quality; of the speed, loudness, and overall pitch of speech; of the use of hesitation" and "intonation to the extent that it is not covered by an account of phonology" ("Paralanguage"[3]). Although they do not form part of the 'language system,' i.e. they cannot be accounted for by a systematic 'grammar' of paralanguage, these features are recognised as 'meaningful': speakers apply them "for pragmatic, emotional and stylistic reasons" and "to meet the requirements of genre," as Ann Wennerstrom (60) observes.

However, there is no dictionary of non-verbal sounds: their meaning is often strongly context-dependent, which renders an analysis more difficult. No tangible 'grammar' exists to regulate paralanguage, and paralinguistic features of the supra-segmental order pose an additional problem in so far as they do "not always offer a 'unit' analogous to the phoneme, susceptible to being built up into larger structures," as Fernando Poyatos (130) observes: they are mostly gradual phenomena operating along continuums of

---

[3] The same article points out that "by the nature of this definition, the boundaries of paralanguage are (unavoidably) imprecise" ("Paralanguage"), which is also reflected in the discrepancy between different definitions in various publications. David Crystal's *Dictionary of Linguistics and Phonetics*, for instance, restricts the term 'paralanguage' to "variations in tone of voice which seem to be less systematic than prosodic features (especially intonation and stress)," such as "the controlled use of breathy or creaky voice" (349). While the term 'prosody' in linguistics may encompass "intonation, rhythm, tempo, loudness, and pauses, as these interact with syntax, lexical meaning, and segmental phonology in spoken texts" (Wennerstrom 4) and thus seems to overlap to a high degree with certain definitions of paralanguage it will not be used in this study due to the potential confusion that may arise with prosody as a literary term denoting "the study or science of versification," which is concerned with "meter, rhythm, rhyme and stanza [...] forms" (Cuddon 751).

sound qualities. Consequently, "pitch, volume, voice quality, and timing can be manipulated to achieve an infinite variety of emotional, attitudinal, and stylistic effects," Ann Wennerstrom (200) notes.

For the same reason, Theo Van Leeuwen refrains from attempting to draw up a "code book" in his semiotics of sound, proposing instead that sound production can be classified along the lines of "sound resources" (6) which allow for certain basic choices and gradual modifications. While the resources he lists can be objectively classified according to their physiological origins, there is no definite code to determine the exact extent of their semantic impact. Rather, the choices these sound resources afford specify a "meaning potential" which "will be narrowed down and coloured in the given context" (Van Leeuwen 10). In contrast to verbal language, which operates mostly on the basis of conventionalised codes, Van Leeuwen identifies two principles of meaning-making – "experiential meaning potential" and "provenance" – which account for the 'readability' of non-verbal sound resources, and thus for their communicative use.

Experiential Meaning Potential

Kress and Van Leeuwen define the principle of "experiential meaning potential" as

> the idea that signifiers have a meaning potential deriving from what it is we *do* when we produce them, and from our ability to turn action into knowledge, to extend our practical experience metaphorically, and to grasp similar extensions made by others. (10)

Van Leeuwen cites the physical activity involved in pitch movement as an example. An ascending melody (increasing in pitch) requires "an increase in vocal effort" (103) tantamount to an increase in physical energy, as is commonly experienced in states of anger, for instance. A person's private knowledge of the physical experience that is anger will then permit him or her to interpret someone else's speech melody as 'angry':

> A melody of anger […] might use repeated brief outbursts of energy: to be brief yet energetic is exactly what characterizes any kind of 'outburst'. A harsh and tense voice quality can then make the outburst angry, and repetition will turn the angry phrase into something like a furious cascading of punches rather than a single blow. (Van Leeuwen 105)

Thus, the accumulated physical energy that anger produces is vented through speech, where it is manifest in a higher pitch, increased volume etc. and, in turn, 'readable' for the addressee in accordance with the principle of experiential meaning potential. Van Leeuwen's example is also revealing as to the interdependence of articulatory parameters. One single aspect of sound by itself rarely carries enough information to allow for a well-founded interpretation of a speaker's meaning: vocalic outbursts of energy may equally be taken to express extreme joy, for instance. Only in connection with the "harsh and tense voice" is it possible to ascertain the emotional quality and aim of an utterance, whose meaning potential is further narrowed down by the body's communication through gesture, posture and facial expression, and, of course, by its verbal content.

The principle of experiential meaning potential is related to the concept of empathy, which has recently gained fresh impetus through the discovery of so-called 'mirror neurones.' Tests on monkeys first revealed a type of neuron that discharged "both when the monkey performs a specific hand action and when it observes an individual making a similar action," as Stein Bråten (7) explains. Mirror neurons are activated in the presence of other people and induce the other person's perceived bodily state in the perceiver's neural network, meaning that it is possible for human beings (and animals) to experience each other's pain, for instance. For Bråten, the discovery of mirror neurons is nothing short of a "paradigmatic revolution" in our conception of human beings: "no longer can be upheld as valid Cartesian and Leibnizian assumptions about monadic subjects and disembodied and self-centred minds without windows to each other except as mediated by constructed or symbolic representations" (2). Thus, symbolic representation, such as verbal language, is not the only way in which experiences can be communicated: the body has its very own system of transmitting sensations intersubjectively.

For the perception of articulatory parameters and 'body communication' this means that it is possible to recognise feelings such as anger or sadness because they are transmitted by acoustic or visual perception from body to body (as a certain type of energy, or lack thereof)[4] – they do not have to be

---

[4] Cf. Maurice Merleau-Ponty's concept of embodiment, which points to a kind of non-explicit knowledge which the body has internalised: "To know how to type is not, then, to know the place of each letter among the keys, nor even to have acquired a conditioned reflex for each one, which is set in motion by the letter as it comes before our eye. If habit is neither a form of knowledge nor an involuntary action, what then is it? It is knowledge in the hands, which is forthcoming only when bodily effort is made, and cannot be formulated in detachment from that effort" (*Phenomenology of Perception* 166).

'encoded' in words. Experiential meaning potential thus constitutes a crucial difference between the ways in which a printed poem and a live performance signify.

Provenance

The principle of provenance can be summarised as "where signs come from" (Kress and Van Leeuwen 10). Within a 'semiotics of sound' it refers to the fact that

> we constantly 'import' signs from other contexts (another era, social group, culture) into the context in which we are now making a new sign, in order to signify ideas and values which are associated with that other context by those who import the sign. (Kress and Van Leeuwen 10)

Provenance comes into play, for instance, when people "adopt a fashionable accent or imitate the voice of a movie star or other celebrity," Kress and Van Leeuwen (82) explain.

Van Leeuwen's 'semiotics of sound' and the author's rejection of the idea of a "code book" (Van Leeuwen 6) in favour of the notion of a 'meaning potential' specified by 'sound resources' bear considerable advantages for an analysis of live poetry. He provides a comprehensible classification of sound resources and the choices they afford, based on their physical production, and thus directs the ear towards certain objectifiable levels or qualities of speech to help the listener order his/her acoustic impressions. At the same time he does not claim to hold the key to their deciphering as though there were a definite grammar or dictionary of paralanguage. Instead, his notion of 'meaning potential' pays heed to the fact that while a sound resource such as pitch movement may channel the listener's perception in a certain direction – listeners may disagree as to whether an utterance conveys 'joy' or 'excitement,' for instance, but the same utterance will hardly evoke 'boredom' –, precise evaluations can only be made with reference to the context of the utterance and to the other systems of communication (verbal, physical) involved. Van Leeuwen's notions of provenance and experience as meaning-making principles, as well as his concept of meaning potential, shall therefore underlie the following discussion of articulatory parameters.

Another preliminary point to be made is that while some voice characteristics can be ascribed to the particular way in which a speaker brings forth an utterance in a certain situation, other, more basic, voice qualities are conditioned by a person's physique: by such factors as age or sex, for instance. This distinction is already present in George L. Trager's 1958 article "Paralanguage: A First Approximation," where the author distinguishes between 'voice set' and 'voice quality.' *Voice set* refers to the idiosyncratic background of speech, "the physiological and physical peculiarities resulting in the patterned identification of individuals as members of a societal group and as persons of a certain sex, age, state of health, body build [...]" (Trager 276). I propose the term *voice action* for those qualities of speech resulting from the particular use of voice in a given situation, which are, of course, based on, and influenced by, the physical and physiological factors specified by the voice set. Thus, women's voice set is generally characterised by a higher pitch than men's as the female voice does not undergo the same kind of mutation in puberty that is brought about by a significant lengthening of the male vocal chords. However, a male speaker can choose, as part of his voice action, to speak in a pitch that is comparatively high for him and may thus imitate a woman's speech, according to the principle of provenance. Similarly, hearing the late Harold Pinter recite his poetry one was impressed by the rough, weather-beaten quality of his voice (Pinter suffered from cancer of the oesophagus, which may have impacted on his characteristic timbre). A younger, healthier speaker may choose to modify his voice action so as to imitate just such a voice and evoke the quality of 'toughness.'

The following discussion of paralinguistic features will distinguish between non-verbal sounds (such as whistling and laughter) on the one hand and 'articulatory parameters' (Van Leeuwen 9), such as rhythm and timbre for instance, on the other. Rather than devising a complete paralinguistic theory or 'grammar,' which lies beyond the scope of a study on live poetry, I aim to present a range of 'instruments' or articulatory 'choices' at the disposal of a poet-performer and to trace the ways in which these may shape a poem's audiotext.

4.2 Non-Verbal Sounds

The concept of audiotext, Charles Bernstein argues, should also include "the body's rhythms" – meaning "gasps, stutters, hiccups, burps, coughs, slurs, [...]" which he takes to be "semantic features of the performed poem" rather than "extraneous interruption" (14). While most of the acoustic occurrences whose meaningfulness Bernstein advocates seem to be of an involuntary nature, one example will demonstrate how non-verbal sounds are, in fact, often consciously employed by poet-performers.

On 28 February 2008, Abraham Gibson performed his poem "Nancy and Reeva" at London's Soho Theatre for an "Apples & Snakes" event. The piece revolves around the close friendship between two elderly women in a London council estate – one white, one black – who constitute the two speakers of the poem. In the voice of Reeva, Nancy's "coloured friend," Abraham Gibson talks of a recent hip replacement: "In the hospital I can only say I was frightened, to have teeth replaced gives discomfort but hips? – pfffffff!" ("Nancy and Reeva"). Reeva's account is delivered rapidly and followed by a loud sucking noise Gibson produces with his teeth and whose pitch falls in a great curve, which can be roughly represented in the following way:

"[...] but $^{hips? \: - \: p^{ffff}f_{ff}}$!"

When he performed "Nancy and Reeva" at the Poetry Café in June 2005, the noise occurred in the same place, so it can be taken as a set element of Gibson's piece. After Reeva's speedy comment on the difference between replacing teeth and hips, the sucking produces a comparatively long break in the verbal flow, which heightens the contrast between the verbal and non-verbal elements, producing a comic effect (the audience responds with laughter accordingly). At the same time Gibson's deliberate drawling of the noise suggests an idea which cannot be properly put into words: the very idea of speechlessness in the face of a surgical intervention the scale of which is simply inconceivable for the old woman.

Fernando Poyatos points out that many independent non-verbal utterances are "perfectly integrated in the acoustic body-communication system with language and other nonverbal systems" (380). He calls them "alternants" or "the vocabulary beyond the dictionary" (379), due to their "high degree of semantic lexicality" (380), citing the disgusted "Ugh!" and the reproachful "Tz-tz" (383) as examples as well as clicks, moans, sighs, snorts, or groans. In an early attempt to systematise paralinguistic features, George L. Trager coined the term "vocal segregates" for the same phenomenon, which he defined as segmental, extra-phonemic sounds such as "uh-huh," "sh," clicks, etc. (Trager 277). In the present study the term "non-verbal sounds" will be used for clarity's sake to denote distinct (segmental) non-verbal utterances, which will be distinguished from supra-segmental articulatory parameters that modify verbal utterances. The latter will be discussed in Chapter 4.3. Two further examples from live poetry performances shall demonstrate the potential of non-verbal sounds to be integrated meaningfully into the audiotext.

Shortman's piece "Beautifully Hectic" has already been discussed with respect to the poet's use of audible intakes of breath, which stand in a complementary relation to the written word to underline the poem's theme of haste and breathlessness (see Chapter 3). Rhythmic breathing is clearly part of Shortman's non-verbal acoustic repertoire, as is his scat singing, of which "Beautifully Hectic" contains an impressive example. At the beginning of the piece, Shortman improvises for about half a minute on random syllables at a speed of more than 200 syllables per minute. Below is a transcription of a short excerpt from his scat song, represented in musical notation,[5] with the emphasised syllables in bold print:

daga **do**go da **bo**dogo **da**ga **bo**dogo **gaa** naa do **ba**da **di**gi da

His rhythm is fast and highly regular, his sounds oscillate between two pitch levels, which gives them a playful sing-song quality, though they are spoken more than sung. This illustrates the segmental quality of such non-verbal sounds: like verbal audiotext, they can be modified by articulatory parameters such as pitch or volume, which will be further discussed in the following subchapter.

Although his scat singing is not represented in the print publication, it is a set part of the poem's audiotext, occurring in Shortman's live performances as well as on the video recording of "Beautifully Hectic." While the syllables are delivered at regular intervals, the stresses are distributed in an irregular manner, some delaying the beat, some anticipating it, resulting in a syncopated percussive pattern that suggests haste and chaos and thus anticipates the poem's theme. The idea of chaos is underlined by the fact that Shortman's fast-paced sing-song produces random, seemingly uncontrolled syllables rather than intelligible words. When the verbal text finally sets in, the tempo of the scat song is taken over precisely, giving the impression of unity between the non-verbal and verbal parts of the poem, one merging seamlessly into the other. At the end of his live performance of "Beautifully Hectic," Shortman once more moves from speech into scat song, with the effect that his piece is framed by these fast non-verbal patternings, suggesting that the speaker's life is firmly in the grip of a feverish hurry, which, however, also has its 'beautiful' qualities.

---

[5] This and similar examples of musical notation were created with Octava, a free music composing/ notation software by Obtiv.

The final example is Anthony Joseph's poem "Aranguez," performed by Joseph at the Vienna Lit Festival in 2006. It is an autobiographical poem[6] recounting a visit from his mother, who was despised by his grandparents, with whom Joseph grew up in Trinidad at the time of political unrest. The poem skilfully juxtaposes political uprisings and turbulences within little Anthony's family. In the following transcribed passage Joseph describes his mother's sufferings, evoking a microcosm of different sounds that he pits against each other:

> You see in those days
> the jamette, as they called my mum,
> she wasn't even allowed in the yard.
> It was for what they called her jezebel ways.
> 'a a!'
> And that same strong ghetto jamette mouth
> which held no water to scream and shout
> She would ... ssshake the wire fence
> She would ... rrrattle on the gate
> And it was all that suffer she take for all them years
> which gave she breast cancer.
> From twilight under the orange tree
> she would plead and moan
> until even the dogs stopped barking.
> And the old woman would just peep through her curtains
> while fireflies lit the savannah
> and she remained silent and safe.
> Only a radio possessed sound in the kitchen
> and the radio said
> "Yeah, this is radio 610, the time is now seven forty-nine,
> And this is the Jackson 5."
> And leaving the jamette to the stars would find her
> grinding salt from her eyeballs
> [*sings and flicks his fingers to the beat:*]
> "Oh, baby, I was blind to let you go, let you go baby, baby, [...]"
>
> ("Aranguez")

The verbal text of the above passage contains numerous references to sound: the rattling of gates, screaming, shouting and moaning, dogs barking, the "silence" of the grandmother, and the sound of a radio. Anthony Joseph's performance of the passage in Vienna also contains three signifi-

---

[6] Joseph mentioned in an e-mail interview with the author that "Aranguez" is "a very autobiographical poem about my grandmother's relationship to my mother."

cant uses of non-verbal sounds in the audiotext. Interestingly, Joseph departs from the written version, as published in his chapbook (Joseph, *Excerpts* 19) in several places: the initial "You see" is added, as is "even" (third line) and the "Yeah" of the radio announcer's introduction, which would suggest that "a a!" may have been spontaneously inserted as an improvised vocal comment. It is, however, present in the printed version. On uttering "a a" in a high-pitched voice right after referring to the mother's "jezebel ways" Joseph quickly moves back from the microphone and pulls his arms towards himself. This could easily be 'read' as an expression of disgust, illustrating the public view of a Jezebel – a shameless, immoral woman – as something to withdraw from: a condemnable character needing no further comment than a reproachful "a a."

When Joseph continues to describe the mother's reaction to the exile from her family he again trusts to the communicative force of non-verbal sounds to convey her violent despair:

She would … *sssshake* the wire fence	[*Drumming on mic*
She would … *rrrrattle* on the gate	*simultaneously*]

Joseph prolongs the onset of the words "shake" and "rattle," thus foregrounding their acoustic qualities as a reminder that the activities of shaking and rattling involve a great deal of noise. While he pronounces these words, he quickly drums on the microphone with two fingers of his left hand and on the microphone stand with his right hand. Both noises are amplified by the mic, of course, reminding one faintly of thunder. Although they are neither vocal, nor even oral, they certainly form part of the poem's audiotext in the sense of "the poet's acoustic performance" (Bernstein 13). They are purposefully integrated with the verbal text to illustrate the sounds young Anthony is surrounded by and what they mean to him and the people around him.

A third occurrence of a non-verbal sound in "Aranguez" can be found in the quotation from a song by the 'Jackson 5' that the grandmother is listening to from her safe position inside the house as the mother is begging at the gate to be let in. Joseph sings in a high pitch, "Oh, baby, I was blind to let you go, let you go baby, baby […]," swinging his arms to the rhythm and audibly flicking his fingers to the beat in imitation of the percussion that goes with the song. While the lyrics have a person pleading for love, which comes across as a strange echo of the mother's situation in the poem, Joseph delivers the passage in the carefree tone of 1970s pop music. The noise of his rhythmic finger-flicking together with his dance-like movements turns the analogy into an ironic comment on the dramatic occurrences, pointing towards the absurdity of the grandmother's sitting around listening to radio tunes while Anthony's mother is "rattling on the gates," as well as to the tension this creates.

The examples above demonstrate how consciously artists like Anthony Joseph and Shortman work with the possibilities that live poetry affords as a medium and how they incorporate non-verbal sounds into their audiotexts to achieve specific effects. They also demonstrate the broad variety of non-verbal sounds at the poet-performer's disposal and point towards the close connection between paralanguage and body communication – a point that shall be further investigated in Chapter 5. Non-verbal sounds can be described in terms of their *area of origin*: they may be produced orally – in which case they can be further classified as "voiced or unvoiced" (Poyatos 382), depending on whether the vocal chords are active during their production – or through the nose (snorts), for instance, or even by the hands (as in Joseph's finger-snipping). They can also be defined with regard to their (culturally specific) *degree of conventionality*. Some non-verbal sounds, such as "uh-huh," are almost lexical: they have a set meaning and can easily be 'translated.' Others are identified as meaningful only with reference to the context of their occurrence, such as Shortman's audible intakes of breath in a poem dealing with stress. Finally, as in the case of verbal audiotext, non-verbal sounds can be modified by the articulatory parameters introduced in the following chapter.

To sum up, non-verbal sounds may be applied in live poetry for a variety of effects. They can create a definite mood or atmosphere for a poem, as in the case of Shortman's scat-singing at the beginning and the end of "Beautifully Hectic," which communicates chaos and restlessness. They can illustrate actions, attitudes and feelings, or comment on them. Frequently, they convey ideas that cannot be better expressed in words, such as the idea of amazement resulting in speechlessness. They thus offer the poet-performer a large repertoire of potentially meaningful acoustic elements to be integrated effectively in an audiotext.

4.3 Articulatory Parameters

Paralanguage does not only consist of distinct non-verbal sounds but also provides a range of 'choices,' or "articulatory parameters" (Van Leeuwen 9), for the enunciation of verbal utterances, which serve to support speech communication. The articulatory parameters introduced in this chapter are rhythm, pitch, volume, articulation, and timbre. In contrast to the non-verbal sounds discussed in the previous chapter these are supra-segmental features, meaning that the modifications of speech they effect go beyond the single word, or even beyond a single phrase or sentence. Articulatory parameters are thus paralinguistic features that operate on a different level from non-verbal sounds, never occurring independently of segmental verbal or non-verbal utterances, but rather, qualifying them.

The following presentation of individual articulatory parameters amounts, of course, to an artificial separation of features which normally do not occur in isolation. While it is quite possible to focus one's ear on the parameters of rhythm or pitch only, for the purpose of a close analysis, it should not be forgotten that the ultimate effect of an utterance depends on the interaction of various parameters occurring simultaneously, as will become clear from the examples presented.

4.3.1 Rhythm

Rhythm is a way of structuring spoken language so as to facilitate its production and reception and, by extension, the meaning-making process. In literary studies, the rhythmic analysis of poetry traditionally starts out with one very basic distinction: that between metrical verse and free verse. Metre, according to Derek Attridge, "is a way of organizing rhythm that gives it special regularity and strength" (48), while free verse can be understood as "nonmetrical" (Attridge 219). This opposition of metrical/nonmetrical, which denotes a certain form of (ir)regularity, will emerge as an inadequate analytical tool for live poetry in the following discussion and will consequently be substituted by a more suitable criterion.

In *The Poetry Handbook*, John Lennard explains the practice of 'scansion,' the rhythmic analysis of metrical poetry, as follows:

> In accentual-syllabic prosody the basic unit of poetry is the line, clearly visible on the page, which may be defined as 'a single sequence of characters read from left to right'. [...]
> Once you know the basic foot and line-length, you confront three aspects of metre. The first is the prescribed pattern of stress, as '⌣ x | ⌣ x | ⌣ x | ⌣ x | ⌣ x' for iambic pentameter: the template (or default-setting). The second is the way you would speak the words of the line in every-day conversation, the normal pronunciation of the words (settings you superimpose on some or all of the default-settings). The third is created by the interaction of the first two, the rhythm of that particular line described prosodically; working it out is called *scanning* the line, and the final pattern on which you decide is your *scansion*. (2, 9)

Lennard draws a distinction between "metre," (the "default setting") and "rhythm" (the pattern of "a particular line"), which is frequently found in the literature on poetic rhythm.[7] With 'line' being identified as "the basic [prosodic] unit of poetry," which is "clearly visible on the page" it becomes obvious that the concept of metre is not practicable for live poetry. Iambic pentameter, for instance, is defined as a pattern that consists of five stressed syllables *per line*. Yet if a poet-performer performs a text that is written in unrhymed iambic pentameter in a conversational (irregular) rhythm, the fact that the written poem theoretically contains five stresses per line may easily escape the audience or at least be rendered meaningless. A line is not usually something we can hear.

However, the 'rhythm' of a poem, as specified by the above quotations, is equally tied to the page: it is the rhythm a reader works out in concurrence with the rules of the English language on confronting a written poem, and as such, a product of "evoked aurality" (Stewart 1). Geoffrey Leech, whose essay "Metre" also distinguishes metre from rhythm (he terms it "prose rhythm"), makes this clear: "'Prose rhythm' is not any one particular way of saying a piece of poetry, but rather the *potentiality* of performance according to the rules of English rhythm" (61, my emphasis) – as specified by the written text, we might add. Performance, then, denotes "a particular choice from the aggregate of possible pronunciations" (62), meaning that a poet-performer makes a specific choice from the various possible patternings contained in the 'prose rhythm' of a written poem.

The mere fact that free verse is defined as the opposite of metrical verse, i.e. without a regular number of stresses per line, indicates that the concept of free verse, too, is firmly linked to poetry in its written form. Thus, Attridge observes that "the units into which metrical verse is divided are determined by its own internal structure, whereas the units of free verse are determined by the layout on the page" (7). Accordingly, 'free verse' denotes rhythmically irregular poetry, whose basic unit is defined by a certain layout "on the page," which distinguishes it from prose. Its lines are of irregular length, the stresses distributed unevenly. Charles Bernstein points out, however, that the 'inherent rhythm' of a poem on the page is not necessarily enacted in a performance, which allows, after all, "FOR stressING ("promotING") unstressED syllaBLES, INcluding prepOsitions, artiCLES, aNd conjunctIONS – creatING synCoPAtEd rHyThms […]" (15). Even leaving aside exotic pronunciations such as Bernstein's, one example from rap po-

---

[7] Thus, Derek Attridge declares, "the meter of the poem is something it shares with other poems," whereas "rhythm involves many factors besides meter, and is unique to a particular poem" (8), and for Philip Hobsbaum, "metre is a blueprint; rhythm is the inhabited building. Metre is a skeleton; rhythm is the functioning body. Metre is a map; rhythm is land" (7).

etry suffices to demonstrate how the above definition of free verse can easily be called into question in performance.

Denizen Kane performed his poem "Patriot Act" at Russell Simmons' "Def Poetry" show, which was broadcast on the US TV-channel HBO in 2005. The following lines are a passage from the text published on the channel's website:

> still living in the woods alone
> turn the lights down low, girl, bend down low
> lemme catch a fire, tell you what i know
> when i plant my seed, babydoll, let it grow
> pop a cop but i don't cop a plea
> shoot down sheriffs, not a deputy

An attempt to scan these lines reveals their inherent rhythm to be irregular. The following pattern suggests itself, with stressed syllables marked in bold print:

> **still living** in the **woods** a**lone**
> **turn** the **lights** down **low**, girl, **bend** down **low**
> **lemme catch** a **fire**, **tell** you **what** i **know**
> **when** i **plant** my **seed**, **babydoll**, **let** it **grow**
> **pop** a **cop** but **i** don't **cop** a **plea**
> **shoot** down **sheriffs**, not a **deputy**

The first line would thus be allocated four stressed syllables, the second five, the third and fourth lines six, the fifth line five and the sixth only three stresses. In performance, however, the piece is delivered by Denizen Kane in a highly regular four-beat rhythm, at a fast pace of about 84 beats (crotchets) per minute. Where the syllable count would suggest an excess of beats several syllables are simply drawn together at a higher speed so they can still be 'squeezed' in between beats. In musical notation[8] this can be represented as follows:

still   living in the woods alone   turn the

---

[8]   For a brief explanation of how to work with, and read, musical notation, see Chapter 4.4.

lights down low, girl, bend down low

lemme catch a fire, tell you what i know when i

plant my seed, babydoll, let it grow

pop a cop but i don't cop a plea

shoot down sheriffs, not a deputy

Assigning four beats to each line, the first line break must now be located elsewhere, which is only one of several surprises the performance holds in store. There is no way of predicting from the written text that Kane would deliver "lemme catch a" at double speed so it could still fit in between two beats, for instance, and little evidence to suggest that he would begin the first line on an off-beat.

Thus, rap poetry may sometimes be read as non-metrical verse on the page in the sense that the stresses inherent in the written text result in an irregular rhythmic pattern. Its audible realisation, however, is characterised by a striking regularity to which ordinary every-day speech rhythms are subjected and which is therefore far from 'free.'[9] Consequently, the usefulness of page-bound concepts such as metre and free verse for an analysis of live poetry is very limited.

This study is concerned with the audible rhythmic patterns of performance rather than evoked rhythms inherent in written text. The rhythm of spoken English is created by a succession of stressed and unstressed syllables, 'stress'[10] being defined as relatively greater prominence, which is

---

[9] See also Dana Gioia, "The New Oral Poetry," where the author notes, "Rap's complex syncopation frequently pushes the meter to a breaking point. A reader would not always know exactly where the strong stresses fell" (245).

[10] Note that 'stress' denotes word stress in this study, i.e. "the configuration of strong and weak syllables within a word" (Wennerstrom 47). For 'rhetorical stress,' which

often realised through loudness but may also relate to pitch or duration (see Quirk et. al. 1589). A basic distinction can now be drawn between regular and irregular rhythms to replace that of metrical/non-metrical. If a poem is performed with *regular rhythm*, its stresses – or beats, in analogy to music – occur at equal temporal intervals. 'Equal' in this case means perceptibly equal rather than metronomically precise: i.e. on hearing a poem it is possible to predict when the next beat falls: you can clap your hands to the rhythm. *Irregular rhythm*, by contrast, can be observed in ordinary everyday speech, for instance, where stresses are not spaced out evenly.

Rap poetry or dub poetry, for example, are often performed in regular rhythms, due to the proximity of these genres to musical traditions (hiphop, reggae). The musical character of regular rhythms also suggests the use of musicological terms for their analysis. The term *beat*, which has already been introduced to replace 'stressed syllable,' denotes an audible regular pulse. It can be complemented by '*offbeat*' for syllables in unstressed positions, i.e. syllables that fall between the 'pulses' of the beat. In Kane's performance of "Patriot Act," the word "down" is realised as an off-beat in "bend down low," where it is located between two prominent beats on "bend" and "low." Derek Attridge further distinguishes between "*actual* beat, actual offbeat" – which are "realised in language" – and "*virtual* beat, virtual offbeat," which are not (216). An example for a virtual beat can be found in the above rhythmic transcription, where the initial "still," which is in offbeat position, is preceded by a quaver break on the first beat. This silent beat does not fall on a syllable, but in the regular rhythmic context of the performed poem it can nevertheless be felt clearly. Virtual offbeats are represented by the final breaks in lines 4, 5, and 6. A beat can also be *anticipated*, i.e. delivered earlier than expected, as is the case with "cop" and "plea" in line 5 of Kane's "Patriot Act," which both start just before we expect the next beat and are sustained through it (as represented by the slur in the transcription above). The result is a sense of urgency, of an inability to wait for the point in time that is expected to mark the next beat.

Regular rhythms allow for a division of utterances into '*measures*'[11] of equal duration – in analogy to musical measures (bars) – which begin with a beat. Note the difference between the concept of measure and the traditional prosodic unit of the 'foot,' which may begin with a stress (e.g. trochee) or with an unstressed syllable (e.g. iamb). "Patriot Act" is an example of a piece performed in 4/4 time: in a rhythm with four beats per measure.

has a semantic purpose, the term 'emphasis' will be used (see Attridge 218; see also Chapter 4.3.3).

[11] See also Leech (62) and Van Leeuwen (39) for their use of 'measure' as a rhythmic term.

An example of a different regular rhythm is Brian Patten's "Hair Today, No Her Tomorrow," which the British poet performed at the Vienna Lit Festival in April 2008. It is a humorous piece presenting a man and a woman in a conversation revolving around the man's supposed affair with someone else, which provokes the following exchange (excerpt):

> 'Time for truth,' she said.
> 'For confessions?' I said.
> 'Me too,' she said.
> 'You what?' I said.
> 'Someone else,' she said.
> 'Oh dear,' I said.
> 'So there!' she said.
> 'Ah well,' I said.
> 'Guess who?' she said.
> 'Don't say,' I said.
> 'I will,' she said.
> 'You would,' I said.
> 'Your friend,' she said.
> 'Oh damn,' I said.
> 'And his friend,' she said.
> 'Him too?' I said.
> 'And the rest,' she said.
> 'Good God!' I said.
>
> ("Hair Today, No Her Tomorrow")

In performance, Patten begins the poem in what can roughly be identified as 4/4 time but then moves into a regular rhythm in 6/8 time, with two audible beats per measure (in bold):

The result is a kind of furious waltz rhythm that expresses acoustically what the verbal text reveals on the content level: the fast, inescapable downward spiral of an argument that is going all wrong. The man reveals the long black hair, which has caused the woman's suspicion and her subsequent angry confession, to stem from the new cat. Now Patten almost sings the next passage, comically emphasising the regular rhythm by an equally regular melodic pattern, which drives home to the audience once more the hilarity of this disastrous conversation:

'Oh **no**,' she **said**. 'Oh **yes**,' I **said**. 'Oh **shit!**' she **said**. 'Good**bye**,' I **said**.

The rhythmic pattern of this poem is further reinforced by the regular epistrophic occurrence of "he said" / "she said." Patten's deliberate rhythmic choices for the performance of "Hair Today, No Her Tomorrow" could not have been guessed from a silent reading of the poem on the page. This example demonstrates that the real, actual rhythms of a live poem may add to the meaning of its words and that different articulatory parameters are closely connected and interdependent in live poetry.

A similar kind of regularity can also be observed in John Hegley's short poem "Not Waving," where it has a different effect. The following is a transcription from a CD recording by 57productions:

> I was on a TV magazine show.
> We just discussed blowing the dust off poetry
> And the life of poetry beyond the grave.
> And I could see a monitor with us silhouetted on it a
> Backcloth to the credits
> And craving a bit of fun
> And feeling I'd been un-
> necessarily grave myself
> I waved to camera 2.
> And the floor manager said:
> "We'll do that once more but without the waving, thank you."
>
> ("Not Waving")

In the second line Hegley establishes a slow, regular rhythm that is reinforced by the concurring pitch movement as well as by the rhyme, adding some extra weight to "just" and "-cussed" by an increase in volume and by means of the pauses following these syllables:

We   just   dis-   cussed

The result is a tone that could be described as lethargic (or 'unnecessarily grave' – with reference to the verbal text), and which bears the marks of typically Hegleyan understatement. The next phrase "blowing the dust" is not delivered exactly in the same rhythm as it takes slightly longer but it carries the same pitch movement, with "dust" being uttered in a higher pitch and followed by a pause. It is therefore perceived as belonging to the same regular pattern. In the transcription below, the syllables in higher pitch are represented by raised letters:

We ^just^ ... dis ^cussed^ ... blowing the ^dust^ ... off poe_try_

As in Brian Patten's poem, in which the rhythmic regularity is reinforced by the melody, several factors are working together here, but unlike the Patten poem Hegley's much slower performance communicates boredom and lifelessness, underlining the absurdity of a TV show that professes to "blow the dust off poetry" while refusing the poet even the slightest "bit of fun." The contrast between the two performances points towards the importance of *tempo* as a factor in the rhythmic analysis of live poetry. Poyatos (183) lists a range of attitudinal functions that tempo can fulfil as an expressive device: depending on the evidence provided by other articulatory parameters, the choice of tempo may communicate attitudes such as self-assurance, dominance, or uncertainty (for slow tempo), or gaiety, anger, impatience or haste (for fast tempo). In Hegley's performance, the ironic tension between "the life of poetry" and the "grave"-ness of the conversation is played out nicely by the poet's slow, regular voicing, producing a highly comic over-all effect, which is also a biting comment on the hypocrisy of the TV show producers.

How consciously poet-performers can work not only with the establishing but also with the breaking of regular rhythmic patterns shall be demonstrated by the next example: a famous poem by the late US Pulitzer Prize winner Gwendolyn Brooks. The piece is called "The Pool Players: Seven at the Golden Shovel" and was recorded at the Guggenheim Museum in 1983:

We real cool. We
Left school. We

Lurk late. We
Strike straight. We

Sing sin. We
Thin gin. We

Jazz June. We
Die soon.

("The Pool Players")

In the Guggenheim recording Brooks introduces the poem as her response to seeing "a bunch of boys" in a pool hall one afternoon during school time and wondering "how they feel about themselves" ("The Pool Players"). She performs it in a regular syncopated rhythm in 4/4 time:

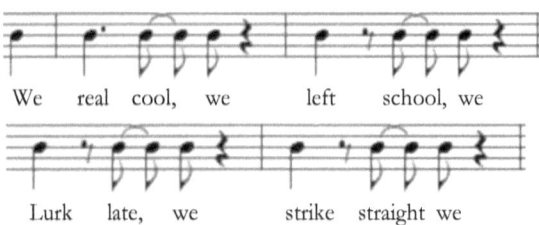

The second syllable of each measure always anticipates the beat of the third crotchet, and the recurring "we" is regularly pronounced just before the final beat, producing a 'jazzy' rhythm that fits in well with the "coolness" of the pool players and the references to "sing" and "jazz." The boys would rather "thin gin" and listen to jazz music than attend school. That the poem is intended as social commentary – a warning to young drop-outs prone to criminal actions and an early death – is strongly emphasised by the striking change in the rhythmic pattern at the very end of the poem:

While so far each measure contained a "we" just before the final beat, the "we" in the last measure is left out. This omission is already conspicuous in the written text but becomes all the more obvious when Brooks shortens "soon" in performance and places it on an offbeat (in "die soon"), giving it lower pitch to express finality. With "die soon" the poem terminates just before the third beat of the last measure, after which another "we" would be expected, in concurrence with the established rhythmic pattern. The "we" is cancelled out by death, expressed by the heavy silence of a virtual beat.

Brooks' performance of "The Pool Players" is a fine example of what Geoffrey Leech calls *"defeated expectancy,"* an effect produced by "a disturbance of the pattern which the reader or listener has been conditioned to expect" (64). The impact of this effect depends, of course, on the rigidity of the pattern previously established: a high degree of regularity will render any deviation strongly noticeable (Leech 65). The examples above have shown that rhythmic regularity can be reinforced by rhyme as well as by concurring patterns of loudness or melody, for instance, again pointing towards the interdependence of various articulatory parameters.

Many poetry performances are not marked by such rhythmic regularity as in the examples discussed above. Often, live poems enact the irregular rhythms of ordinary speech, which are characterized by the principle of isochrony but not structured so as to produce a regularly recurring beat that enables listeners to tap their feet to the rhythm. *Isochrony* specifies the condition that "on some level of analysis, an utterance […] can be split into segments which are *in some sense* of equal duration" (Leech 62). "In some sense" is an important qualification for isochronous utterances, as in stress-timed languages like English "two rhythmic tendencies come into collision," as Derek Attridge (223) explains: while there is a tendency for stresses to be spaced out at intervals of equal duration, several unstressed syllables may occur between two stresses and thus lengthen the time span between them. This is simply due to the fact that although a speaker will strive to accelerate these unstressed syllables so as to squeeze them in between stresses they will still tend to "take up their own time in pronunciation" (Attridge 36). In the context of isochrony critics still speak of the "measure" (Leech 62) as a basic unit, and of an audible "beat" (Bernstein 14), but in contrast to regular rhythms these are not integrated in a predictable, regular pattern and thus cannot be adequately represented by musical notation.[12]

Analysing rhythmically irregular live poetry on the basis of traditional verse prosody would make even less sense, as Charles Bernstein points out: "Regularizing systems of prosodic analysis break down before the sonic profusion of a reading: it's as if 'chaotic' sound patterns are being measured by grid-oriented coordinates whose reliance on context-independent ratios is inadequate" (13). The irregular speech rhythms contributing to what Bernstein calls the "sonic profusion" of a poetry performance can be highly expressive, as the following example will demonstrate. Roger McGough

---

[12] For a discussion of isochrony as a perceptual phenomenon see Rodríguez-Vázquez 46-49.

recited his poem "Bees Cannot Fly" for an audio CD published by 57productions in 2003. The first half is transcribed below, with bold letters indicating greater loudness (and thus stressed syllables) and raised or lowered letters representing a higher or lower pitch. If a word or syllable takes longer to pronounce, the distance between individual letters is increased, and spaces between words are lengthened if a noticeable pause occurs[13]:

Bees can't **fly**.

Scientists have **proved** it.

It's **all** to **do** with **wing span** and **bo**dyweight.

Aerodynamically incapable of sus**tained flight**

bees simply cannot **fly**.

And yet they **do**.   [*faster*]

There's one there,

una**ware** of its **do**dgy **ratios**.

(McGough, "Bees Cannot Fly")

McGough opens the poem with a slow statement pronounced over three heavy beats, as though hammering in an incontestable fact, which is emphasised by the falling pitch movement indicating closure: the fact that bees cannot fly is not open to question. When he explains that "It's all to do with wing span and body weight" and that bees are "Aerodynamically incapable of sustained flight," he falls into a more regular rhythm, which, together with a subdued, up-and-down pitch movement, suggests that he is now quoting the authorities, perhaps even reading from a written document, rather than arguing his own case. "Bees simply cannot fly" is continued in roughly the same rhythm, again marked by the same controlled up-and-down pitch movement and completed by the falling pitch at the end. After a longer pause, McGough suddenly delivers the next phrase at a markedly faster pace:

---

[13] The transcription method proposed here is based on Dennis Tedlock's suggestions for "reperformance" in *The Spoken Word and the Work of Interpretation* (20).

^{And} **yet** ^{they} **do**.

The previously established near-regular beat is broken, a new rhythm sets in, carrying a new point in the argument: the common-sense observation that bees can definitely fly and can even be seen flying.

^{There's} **one** ^{the}**re**

is performed in a far more expressive, irregular rhythm than the allegedly scientific statement about the aerodynamic incapability of bees, indicating that we now hear a more personal utterance, closer to the speaker's heart, which is corroborated by a greater, more expressive pitch range. Thus, McGough's critique of the schematising abstractions of scientific theory and its ultimate inadequacy in the face of nature's profusion is born out in this poem also by the poet's rhythmic choices.

The analysis above was conducted by means of what Elizabeth Fine terms "natural language" (41) and supported by a transcription in ordinary typeset with modifications to indicate paralinguistic features, which can be effected by a standard word processing programme. In *The Folklore Text*, Fine recommends the use of "natural language" as a flexible, easily accessible method and also praises Dennis Tedlock's transcription system (which underlies the transcription above[14]) for its effective fusion of letters with parameters such as pitch. Tedlock's method does not divide pitch notation off from the verbal component: it is a holistic notation of features of speech which occur simultaneously and thus "represents perceptual experience more accurately," as Fine (145) notes. Its information value is much higher than that of a mere rendering of the words alone, as becomes clear from the above transcription of McGough's piece, whose tone can be described as conversational. Its advantages emerge even more distinctly in transcriptions of performances that do not strive to imitate everyday speech but produce a different kind of musicality, as much of Anthony Joseph's live poetry does.

Below is a transcription of the beginning of "Kneedeepnditchdiggerniggersweat," which Joseph performed at the Vienna Lit Festival in 2006. It was first published in a chapbook called *Excerpts from the African Origins of UFOs* and later became part of Joseph's novel of that name. He also published an audio version on a CD and performed the piece live on various occasions, investing it with a life of its own:

---

[14] For a discussion of the functioning and merits of the various transcription methods applied, see Chapter 4.4.

98 *Live Poetry*

His ^(vo)c_e ⋯ had the deep ᵇ ᵘ ʳ ʳ of a m ᵃ n who ¨ kept ¨ **fish** hₒₒₖₛ ¨ in his ᵇ ᵉ ᵃ ʳ ᵈ

This short extract suffices to demonstrate how Anthony Joseph manipulates his speech so as to produce an audiotext whose rhythmic irregularity and expressiveness transcends that of ordinary speech. After shouting out "voice" with an excessive pitch span and high volume he pauses briefly, then to continue at a much faster pace, suddenly taking his time again to pronounce "burr." He speeds up on "of a," stretches "man" and pauses noticeably before racing through "in his," though "beard" is once again delivered slowly, taking up about twice as long as the "in his" leading up to it. There is no regular beat pulsing through these phrases, on the contrary: with their stops and starts and drawn-out syllables they surpass the irregularity of everyday speech by far, just as they exceed the pitch fluctuations one would expect at a poetry 'reading.' The result is a style of speaking that sounds artificial as well as artistic, with a musical playfulness that adds to the poeticity of the verbal text and is also a spectacle in its own right.

To sum up, the rhythm of spoken English is created by a succession of stressed and unstressed syllables. The basic distinction to be made in a rhythmic analysis of live poetry is that between regular and irregular rhythms. The former are characterised by equal temporal intervals occurring between stressed syllables, while in the latter case stresses are not spaced out evenly.

Regular rhythms, which are frequently found in rap poetry for instance, produce an audible regular beat, as in music. The rhythmic regularity can be reinforced by corresponding patterns of rhyme and pitch movement, for instance. The more marked the regularity, the more noticeable a deviance from previously established patterns becomes, according to the principle of 'defeated expectancy.' A beat can be anticipated, for instance, resulting in a sense of urgency. Unstressed syllables between beats are called 'offbeats.' Both beat and offbeat can be realised in language or silence, when they are perceived as 'virtual (off)beats.' Regular rhythms allow for a division of utterances into 'measures' of equal duration which begin with a beat – in analogy to musical measures (bars).

Irregular rhythms, as to be observed in everyday speech, are often marked by isochrony, a tendency to space out stresses at equal intervals which is counteracted by the longer time it takes to pronounce several unstressed syllables in between two beats. Where isochrony is eclipsed by highly irregular rhythms, as in Anthony Joseph's performance, the result may be an audiotext that is more markedly self-reflexive and artistic in effect.

Another expressive factor to be taken into consideration in a rhythmic analysis of live poetry is tempo, which pertains to both regular and irregular rhythms. The tempo of regular rhythms is easily measurable and best expressed in absolute terms, i.e. in beats per minute, while the tempo of irregular rhythms is usually best assessed in relative terms: in relation to the utterances preceding or following the one under scrutiny.

The examples introduced have revealed the uselessness of traditional page-based concepts of rhythmic analysis with regard to live poetry. The written poem is no reliable indicator of the actual rhythms realised in performance. A poet-performer's choices of regular or irregular rhythmic patterns and tempo variations are frequently surprising and often semantically relevant: they may suggest particular moods, for instance, express attitudes or add a sense of humour to a poem.

4.3.2 Pitch

The rhythmic analyses above have already shown how the workings of rhythm and pitch are interconnected in live poetry. Pitch can be defined as the frequency of a sound, ranging from low to high. In speech it is related to the slower or faster vibrations of the vocal cords. Theo Van Leeuwen distinguishes three features of vocal pitch in his semiotics of sound – pitch level, pitch range, and pitch movement – which will be introduced in the following.

Pitch Level

Pitch level can be defined as the "dominant tone in which a portion of speech of whatever length is conducted" (Poyatos 184), "tone" here referring to frequency. The pitch level of a portion of speech will be determined by the speaker's physiological background, i.e. by his/her voice set, as well as by his/her voice action in various situational contexts, which is a matter of choice (conscious or unconscious). Poyatos notes that a *low* pitch level is often "associated with affection, boredom, fear, incredulity or disappointment [...] and *high* level with cheerfulness, joy, alarm, surprise, annoyance, anger, etc." (186). Similarly, Martina Pfeiler claims that a lower pitch may express "emotions such as sadness, seriousness, or sincerity," while a higher pitch can express emotional states or attitudes such as "hysteria, insecurity, or angst, to name just a few" (*Sounds of Poetry* 66). These quotations serve to give an impression of the range of associations pitch level may evoke rather than a complete list of identifiable meanings. As with other articulatory parameters, no definite form-function mapping exists. Furthermore, the value of pitch level is relative: one speaker's high pitch may be low for another. The meaning potential of pitch level will be narrowed down when pitch is regarded in its relation to the complete audiotext and the respective situational context. Van Leeuwen suggests that listeners interpret the meaning potential of pitch level with reference to their own physical experiences of producing utterances of a higher or lower pitch:

> pitch level relates to vocal effort. The higher the pitch level, the greater the effort needed, the more the voice is, literally and figuratively, 'keyed up'. The lower the voice, the more relaxed, and literally and figuratively, 'low key', it will sound. (Van Leeuwen 107)

An interesting example is John Siddique's poem "Yes," which the poet recited twice during the Vienna Lit Festival 2006, first as part of his set, and once again on the day after, to open the Vienna Lit School Slam, a poetry competition for secondary school students. "Yes" is a list poem, citing things that the speaker says 'yes' to, as in "Yes to stardust, I am fleshed by you. [...] Yes I am the same dust as you. Yes to my soul. Yes to my death" ("Yes"). In Siddique's first performance in Vienna, the first two thirds of the piece remained at a rather constant pitch level, oscillating slightly between B♭ and C (approximately)[15]:

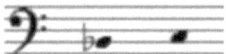

The final third begins with "Yes to falling on the floor crying my heart out. Yes to having a heart to cry," at a slightly higher pitch level, creating an audible climax...

---

[15] Musical notation is used here as a concise way of representing pitch visually that will be familiar to many readers. It is meant to supplement verbal interpretation rather than to function as an analytical tool in its own right. Those unfamiliar with musical notation will still be able to grasp the relative difference in pitch, indicated by the higher or lower position of the notes on the staves. For an explanation of musical notation and its merits for an analysis of live poetry see Chapter 4.4.

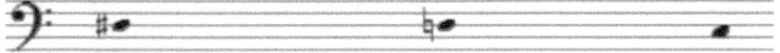

Yes to falling on the floor crying my heart out, Yes to having a heart to cry.

...before the concluding phrases of "Yes to the hand that can write yes. Yes to yes," which are delivered at a lower pitch level to mark the poem's ending. Siddique's second performance on the occasion of the Vienna Lit School Slam sounded quite different, however. While the pitch level of the first two thirds of "Yes" can similarly be located between B♭ and D♯,

Siddique raises the pitch considerably for the climactic phrases towards the end and invests them with a greater loudness:

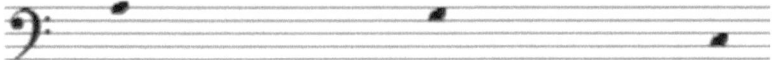

Yes to falling on the floor crying my heart out, Yes to having a heart to cry.

Delivered at a pitch level almost a fifth higher than in his previous performance, these phrases communicate a much higher energy and increased excitement. Van Leeuwen claims that high-pitched, loud voices often come across as "assertive and 'public'" (108), which is certainly true in this case. Siddique is standing in front of a room packed with young people and their parents and friends who have come to support the contestants. Before reciting his poem, Siddique talks about the audience's role in helping the young performers succeed and wishes everyone the best of luck. The atmosphere is crackling with excitement. In this context, the loud, high-pitched phrases towards the end of his piece are heard as a celebratory invocation of a positive attitude towards life and the self and thus constitute a very fitting start for the poetry slam.

High-pitched voices can also be soft, however, which brings another experiential factor into play, as Van Leeuwen observes:

> Our experience also tells us that high-pitched sounds tend to be produced by small people, small animals, [...] and low-pitched sounds by large people, large animals, [...] large engines and so on. Hence low voices are often seen as threatening and dangerous. [...] High voices on the other hand can be used to make ourselves small. (108)

Thus, we are used to soft, high-pitched sounds issuing from small animals or children, for instance, which would not be associated with danger. Van Leeuwen's statement also points towards the gendered nature of pitch level choice, of course. Women's voice set is generally characterised by a higher pitch than men's due to the lengthening of the male vocal cords during puberty. Consequently, high-pitched female voices will be perceived as 'less dangerous,' an impression which some women may actively reinforce by deliberately speaking in a very high, soft pitch reminiscent of a child's speech. The effect is one of 'making themselves small,' as Van Leeuwen calls it, i.e. evoking the innocence and vulnerability of a child, very much in line with traditional gender roles. By contrast, some women – Van Leeuwen cites Lauren Bacall as an example here – are stereotyped as "dark and dangerous temptresses" who "seduce us with a sensuous, low voice" (Van Leeuwen 109). This association of size and pitch level can be observed in Lucy English's poem "Family Prayers" when the speaker's prayer is interrupted by her child sister:

> Hail Mary Full of grace, The lord is with thee, blessed art thou among woman, and blessed is the fruit of thy womb, Jesus – What's a womb? – Shush Mary, we'll tell you later.
>
> ("Family Prayers")

Young Mary is identified as a small child not only by the ignorance that her question reveals but also by the conspicuously higher pitch level English applies. It exceeds the pitch level of "Jesus" by more than an octave and thus marks Mary's question as issuing from a comparatively small person.

Pitch Range

"Besides a characteristic pitch level," Poyatos notes, "each individual possesses a lowest and a highest pitch register, the distance between which is called pitch range, which varies very widely among persons" (187). Again one needs to distinguish between a person's physically predetermined pitch range, i.e. the highest and lowest frequency their vocal cords are capable of producing (as part of their voice set), and the pitch range of a particular utterance (as part of that person's voice action). Van Leeuwen observes that the expression of certain strong feelings, such as surprise for instance, is effected via a comparatively wide pitch range. For a typical pitch curve of an utterance communicating surprise he suggests the following outline, represented on the basis of musical staves (96):

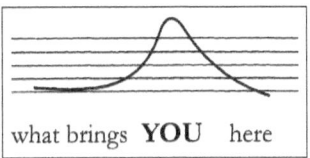

Fig. 2: Surprise pitch curve.

Similarly, Brazil et al. claim that a *wide* pitch range expresses mental states such as excitement, anger, or surprise, while a *narrow* pitch range conveys feelings such as misery or boredom (23). As with pitch level, the perceived meaning potential of pitch range is contingent on experience, on "what it is we *do* when we increase or decrease the pitch range," Van Leeuwen states. "When we increase it we are 'letting more energy out', when we decrease it we are 'holding more energy in', either because we do not have any left, or because we restrain and repress it" (106). A striking example of the repressed energy noticeable behind a narrow pitch range is Adrian Mitchell's famous performance of his poem "To Whom It May Concern" at the 'International Poetry Incarnation' at the Royal Albert Hall in 1965, which was documented in Peter Whitehead's film *Wholly Communion (Peter Whitehead And the Sixties)*. "To Whom It May Concern" has a chorus to which a new phrase is added after each stanza:

Mitchell's pitch range remains rather narrow throughout most of the poem, fluctuating only very slightly around G♭. The result is not the subdued, monotonous sound of boredom, however, as the strong feeling of the poem is conveyed via other parameters: Mitchell makes effective use of pauses, for example before "daisy chains," turning the biting sarcasm of that phrase into an expression of exasperation, as though the thought were absurd and infuriating enough to cause him difficulty even to utter it:

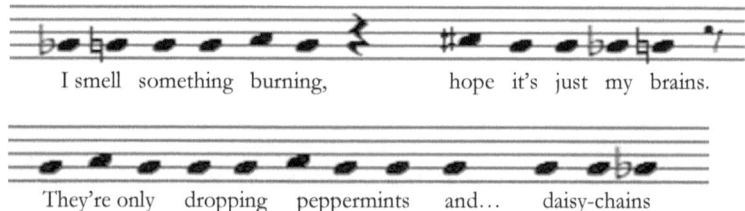

I smell something burning, hope it's just my brains.

They're only dropping peppermints and... daisy-chains

The narrow pitch range then adds a note of despair – a lack of energy for more expansive pitch movements pointing to the powerlessness felt in the face of the crimes against humanity which the poem attacks.

The same narrow pitch range comes across as repressed fury in the last stanza, when Mitchell articulates the chorus as "ssssstick my legs in plaster," making the prolonged initial consonant seem the acoustic equivalent of raising an arm to strike a blow, an impression which is reinforced when he pronounces "lies" in the last "Tell me **lies**" with extra force and a slight downward pitch movement. There is only one passage where the speaker's suppressed rage is vented directly, when he suddenly increases volume and raises his pitch by a fifth before returning quickly to the monotonous, narrow pitch around the G in the following phrase:

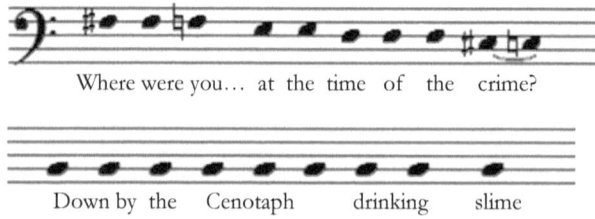

Where were you... at the time of the crime?

Down by the Cenotaph drinking slime

This sudden outburst is all the more noticeable in comparison with the narrow pitch range of the previous phrases and the following utterance "Down by the Cenotaph drinking slime," which is delivered with near-zero pitch range.

In his reflections on the meaning potential of pitch range, Van Leeuwen concludes,

> All we can say is that the wide pitch range allows us to give vent to strong feelings, whether of excitement or shock, of grief or joy, and that the narrow pitch range constrains the expression of strong feelings, whether as the result of a 'stiff upperlip' attitude, or because of modesty or tiredness, or because we are paralysed with fear, to mention just some of the possibilities. (106)

Accordingly, pitch range realises the *"emotional extension"* (111) of a sound act, either in the form of *"emotive expansion"* (in the case of increased pitch range) or *"emotive confinement"* (for decreased pitch range; Van Leeuwen 119), both of which have been illustrated with the help of Adrian Mitchell's poem above.

Pitch Movement

In spoken language, pitch can *rise* or *fall* or remain *level.* The particular patterns of these movements in phrases or whole utterances are generally referred to as 'intonation' or speech 'melody.'[16] Ann Wennerstrom points to the close connection in English between intonation and stress patterns, as pitch accents usually coincide with stresses (46), noting, however, that the rhythmic pattern of speech as such is no predictor of pitch movement: "instead, a speaker decides to associate particular intonation patterns with particular constituents, depending on the discourse context" (17). The relevance of this observation for an analysis of live poetry is twofold: it confirms one of the underlying assumptions of this study, i.e. that paralinguistic features of a performance cannot automatically be deduced from the written text (which presumably contains word stress patterns), and it refers to the ability of speech melody to convey different kinds of information in different contexts.

Considering the experiential meaning potential of pitch movement, Van Leeuwen observes that "vocal effort must be increased to raise the voice and decreased to lower the voice" (111). Consequently, he speaks of *"activation"* (rising pitch), *"stasis"* (level pitch), and *"deactivation"* (falling pitch). In this context the typical "gradual lowering or 'declination' of pitch throughout the duration of an intonational phrase," which Ann Wennerstrom (29) observes and which may be heard at many live poetry performances, can be understood as a standard case of 'deactivation.' A phrase from Roger McGough's poem "Bees Cannot Fly" serves as an example:

---

[16] Quirk et al. draw a distinction between intonation and musical melody based on the observation that in contrast to music, "there is, in speech, no absolute pitch and there are no fixed intervals to be observed in intonation. All pitch distinctions are acoustically relative, however absolute they may be linguistically" (1589). While this is certainly true, 'melody' will be understood in the present study to refer specifically to 'speech melody,' i.e. the particular pattern of ascending and descending pitch movements, rather than musical melody with its implications of fixed pitch intervals. The relative extent of these movements is then captured by the parameter of pitch range.

Aero_{dy}namically _{in}capable _{of sus}tained flight

On a first listening the pitch movement seems to form a fairly regular up-and-down pattern ending on a raised pitch level, but a closer analysis of the stressed syllables surprisingly shows that McGough starts out on an F ("Aero…"), quickly sinks to a D (on "dynamically"), and finally to a B ("flight"). This overall downward movement is hardly noticeable, especially since the last pitch movement from "-tained" to "flight" is a clear rise. Its cause is the natural decrease of the air pressure, and thus of energy, in the speaker's lungs (although it could be heard as a subtle and humorous reinforcement of bees' "incapability of sustained flight" (i.e. descent) in this particular case).

An extreme example of 'stasis' is the level pitch of a phrase in Adrian Mitchell's 1965 performance of "To Whom It May Concern," analysed above. After the aggressively accusatory "Where were you … at the time of the crime" with its falling pitch and wide pitch range the answer Mitchell provides to his own question, "Down by the Cenotaph drinking slime" ("To Whom It May Concern"), sounds remarkably monotonous and disillusioned.

Beyond their ability to indicate physical and emotional conditions, rising and falling pitch movements have an interesting discursive function, which is outlined by Van Leeuwen as follows:

> the end of a melodic phrase either sounds open-ended ('as if there is more to come'), or final ('as if there is no more to come'). In the case of *finality* the end of the melody falls to a low pitch […]. *Continuity* can be realized in a number of ways: by what is sometimes called a 'non-terminal fall', that is a falling pitch which does not fall deep enough to suggest finality; by a level pitch; by a rising pitch. (98)

McGough's poem can again be taken as an example here:

Aero_{dy}namically _{in}capable _{of sus}tained flight
bees _{simply} cannot f_{ly}.

("Bees Cannot Fly")

The poet uses a rising pitch at the end of the phrase, which indicates that 'there is more to come' – in the form of the quasi-authoritative statement "bees simply cannot fly," which ends, appropriately, on a falling pitch.

Van Leeuwen also notes that in conversation, "almost every phrase ends with a continuity intonation" (99), either when speakers indicate that there is 'more to come' or to open the conversation up to the dialogue partner, in a vocal gesture signalling that s/he may "take over and complete what they were saying" (Van Leeuwen 99). He identifies certain speech genres that do not allow for interruptions as characterised by a habitual falling pitch:

> Radio and television newsreaders, for instance, often use finality intonations in the middle of sentences, which not only makes the phrases on which it occurs into self-sufficient morsels of information, unconnected to the rest of the sentence, but also lends a sense of overall authority to the news: the falling pitch is assertive, the tone of definite statements and commands, [...] a deliberate foregrounding of the fact that the speaker has the final word. (100)

The phenomenon Van Leeuwen describes can also be observed at many poetry readings, since 'reading' something out aloud usually implies an absence of dialogue. Wendy Cope's poem "Spared," which was published on Oxfam's *Life Lines* CD in 2006, can be taken as one of many examples here, as the poet continuously produces falling pitch movements at the end of each phrase. The resulting sense of disconnectedness, arising from the fact that each phrase is uttered as though it were complete in itself, clearly marks the poem off from everyday speech. In a live performance, the poem becomes a kind of spoken language that leaves no room for dialogue (although an audience may be invited to comment on the poem via a paratextual cue after the performance). Rather, its individual phrases are 'put on display' like a work of art, a different order of cultural production, whose exceptional status is communicated by pitch movement.

A final point to be made about the communicative potential of pitch movement is the possibility that "intonationally and verbally expressed attitudes can contrast with each other," as Van Leeuwen (101) notes: "What is verbally formulated as a definite statement can sound like a tentative query. What is verbally formulated as a question can sound like a curt command" (101). This is exemplified by Gabriele Pötscher's performance of her poem "Okay" at the Vienna Lit Festival in 2008. The piece is a dialogue poem with two speakers in a relationship about to break up, whose effect relies heavily on the meaning potential of pitch movement:

It's $^{ti}m_e$.

$O_{ka}y$.

I've ^{got} to g_o.

O_{kay}.

I'll ca‍ll, it's not forever.

... Okay.

Be happy, smile. I like it when you smile.

[*smiles*] Okay.

It doesn't pay to be sad. Life goes on. You'll see.

...Okay.

I-It's been really nice. I wish you all the best.

Okay.

I REAlly got to go. I'll call.

Okay.

It's time ...to go. Okay?

Okay. Okay. Ohh.

("Okay")

While the repeated answer "okay" might be read as an expression of consent in print, the way Pötscher raises the pitch at the end of the word in performance gives it the air of a question, as though speaker 2 were waiting for 'more to come.' This latent expectation is apparently sensed by speaker 1, who continues to provide 'more' in the form of reassuring banalities that sound apologetic to begin with, but which soon come across as impatient in the face of speaker 2's persistent incomprehension. While the phrases "It's been really nice. I wish you all the best" sound official and studied with their controlled falling pitch, "I REAlly got to go" is pronounced with extra emphasis, which gives it a sense of greater emotional involvement. Interestingly, "I'll call" is delivered with a rising pitch, as though it were not quite a fact and speaker 1 were not as sure of his/her own promise as the words alone would suggest, leaving them open to challenge. Speaker 2's pseudo-confirmations ("Okay") are occasionally delivered after some hesitation, which reinforces the impression of confusion and helplessness. Finally, speaker 1 aggressively demands speaker 2's consent to leave, asking "okay?" in a sharp tone, after a definite pitch fall on "go" which can leave speaker 2 in no doubt about his/her intentions.

To sum up, pitch refers to the frequency of the vocal cord vibrations during speech, ranging from high to low. Pitch level can be defined as the dominant frequency of a particular portion of speech. It is dependent on the speaker's voice set and on his/her vocal effort, with higher pitches demanding more effort and thus sounding more energised. Pitch range is similarly determined in part by the speaker's basic physical capabilities (voice set) and communicates the emotional extension of an utterance. Pitch movement, finally, can be rising, falling, or level, resulting in 'activation,' 'deactivation,' or 'stasis,' in line with the physical effort involved. It also has a discursive function of marking an utterance as complete (finality) or incomplete (continuity). A poet's use of pitch may thus considerably add to, or modify, the meaning of the verbal text. As with other articulatory parameters, the effect of pitch in live poetry depends on the overall configuration of the respective audiotext and is best studied in conjunction with other acoustic features and the performer's body communication.

4.3.3 Volume

Volume is the articulatory parameter that specifies the loudness of an utterance, or, in physical terms, the intensity of sound, which is manifest in the amplitude of a sound wave. Again we must distinguish between a person's voice set – which predetermines the maximum speech volume s/he is capable of producing – and the volume chosen for particular syllables or phrases as part of his/her voice action.

"Loudness of voice volume, due to respiratory and articulatory muscular effort, is, along with pitch, one of the most obvious ways of lending words [...] special meaningful effects," Poyatos (179) claims. Previous examples have demonstrated how the parameter of volume may interact with rhythm and pitch to produce certain regular patterns or marked irregularities. In John Hegley's poem "Not Waving," for instance, the greater volume of "just," "-cussed" and "dust" – together with rhyme and regular pitch movement – results in a heavy, lethargic tone:

We ^{just} ... dis^{cussed} ... blowing the ^{dust} ... off poe$_{\text{try}}$

("Not Waving")

By contrast, Anthony Joseph's poem "Kneedeepnditchdiggerniggersweat" is characterised by fluctuations in volume, pitch and rhythm which surpass the irregularity of everyday speech by far:

His ᵛᵒⁱcₑ ... had the deep ᵇ ᵘ ʳ ʳ ʳ of a m ᵃ n who ¨ kept ¨ fish hooₖₛ ¨ in his bᵉᵃʳᵈ

The word "voice," for example, is delivered with such force as would not normally occur in day-to-day conversation, which adds to the surrealism of Joseph's self-reflexive tone that is well in line with the poem's science-fictional setting on the planet Kunu Supia in the year 3005.

Previous reflections on rhythm have already pointed towards a crucial function of volume variation in relation to stress patterns, with stress being defined as the relatively greater prominence of certain syllables in speech. This greater prominence is most often associated with an increase in volume but may also relate to other factors such as pitch or duration (see Quirk et. al. 1589). Volume variation within a single word produces lexical stress, which helps speakers of English to distinguish, for instance, between '**re**bel' – a noun – and its corresponding verb to 're**bel**,' in which the second syllable is stressed.

A special kind of stress is emphatic stress, also called "rhetorical stress" (Attridge 218) or '*emphasis*,' which adds extra force to selected stressed syllables. Its function can be to "indicate which word in a sentence provides the new or important information, can give emotional force to one element in an utterance, or can bring out a contrast" (Attridge 33). Thus, an emphasis on "promoted" and "rebuked" in the utterance, "I was not pro**mo**ted, I was re**bu**ked," contrasts 'promote' and 'rebuke,' identifying 'rebuke' as the new or important information. An emphasis on 'I' in the first phrase would ask for a different contrastive emphasis, as in "**I** was not promoted, **Tony** was," indicating that 'Tony' is the focus of the utterance.

Of particular interest to live poetry is the function of emphasis to "give emotional force to one element in an utterance," as Attridge (33) states. In Jeneece Bernard's performance of her poem "Underground" at the Vienna Lit Festival 2006 this was effectively put into practice. The following is a verbal rendering of the poem's beginning:

> Every time I go down that hole
> my thoughts claustrophobe round my skull
> and my spit solidifies until I'm swallowing slabs of indifference and repeating,
> Excuse me! Excuse me!
> all the way down the escalator.

> Sometimes I have to raise my voice and the noise reverbs,
> bouncing around the grey circular tunnel

("Underground")

The poem is delivered in Bernard's usual, insistent tone at a relatively stable volume, except for the double exclamation of "Excuse me!" – which should be transcribed as

> Ex^**CUSE** me! … Ex^**CUSE** me! …

Bernard belts out "Excuse me" in such a manner as though she were actually walking down the stairs of an overcrowded underground station, trying to shout people out of her way. Not only does she increase the volume significantly, but she also raises the pitch to a level that suggests the hysteria of a claustrophobic person in a space that does not seem to be designed for this enormous mass of people to rush through. She continues to explain the discomfort experienced during the dive down into the 'hole' that is the underground station, in the "stilted London space":

> The expectant faces on the other side know
> we've been holding our breaths
> because our bodies are so fragile in this society
> that we can't brush skin or touch hair
> or take a breath of someone else's air

("Underground")

The sudden drastic increase in volume at "Excuse me" communicates exactly that: the panicking reaction at a physical closeness we are not conditioned for, only in a much more startling way than if we read the poem on paper.

Both stress and emphasis are variations in loudness which are observable in one syllable and its immediate context – in the above example it is "-cuse" which is given extra force to indicate emotional extremity. Volume variation may also occur over longer segments of speech, of course, in which case they are most usefully referred to as the '*dynamics*' of an utterance or a passage – in accordance with musical terminology. A striking example of the workings of dynamics has already been pointed out in Adrian Mitchell's performance of "To Whom It May Concern": after a series of near-monotonous utterances Mitchell suddenly delivers the following accusatory question with a marked increase in volume as well as in pitch:

Where were you... at the time of the crime?

Similar to the corresponding pitch variation, this comparatively loud 'outburst' can be understood with recourse to the principle of experiential meaning potential: the energy of suppressed anger at the atrocities of war that could be felt throughout Mitchell's monotonous performance is now vented directly.

Another interesting example is Jackie Kay's poem "My Grandmother," which was recorded on the audio CD *Poetry in Performance Vol. 1* by 57productions. It begins with Kay's calm description of a Scottish grandmother who is "like a Scottish pine, / tall, straight-backed, proud and plentiful" and wears a "plaid shawl." Her face is described as "ploughed land" and she "speaks Gaelic mostly." The image conjured up, apparently in admiration, is that of the stereotypical sturdy highland woman whose eyes "shine rough as amethysts" and who will be "burnt in her croft rather than moved off the land." The poem's middle part provides a sudden twist, however: "My grandmother sits by the fire and swears / *There'll be no darkie baby in this house!*" after which the third part of the poem sets in, which is almost an echo of the first but has very different undertones:

> My grandmother is a Scottish pine,
> tall, straight-backed proud and plentiful,
> her hair tied with pins in a ball of steel wool.
> Her face is tight as ice
> and her eyes are amethysts.
>
> ("My Grandmother")

The toughness and stubbornness are now coupled with a racist bias that makes the old woman's eyes appear as hard and cold as amethysts. The two-part structure of the poem and its striking change in the appreciation of the grandmother is not only communicated through the parallel imagery but is conveyed by a change in volume in the middle part of Kay's audio performance, as can be seen in the diagram below:[17]

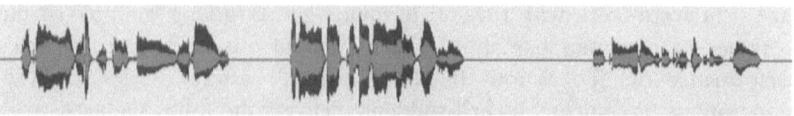

My grandmother sits by the fire... *There'll be no darkie baby...*   My grandmother is...

While "My grandmother sits by the fire and swears" is still uttered in the calm tone of the first part, the grandmother's racist announcement *"There'll be no darkie baby in my house"* is all of a sudden delivered at a greater, more aggressive volume. The startling effect is reinforced by a long pause, giving it more room, before the third part of the poem, "My grandmother is a Scottish pine" sets in at a significantly lower volume, as indicated by the amplitude graph. This quiet passage has an eerie ring to it as the previous violent outburst still reverberates through it, which helps to give the imagery a new meaning, though it may at first sound a mere echo of the poem's beginning.

The function of dynamics to convey emotional states and attitudes in live poetry emerges most distinctly in sound poetry, i.e. poetry in which "sound for its own sake becomes the principal expressive medium, sometimes even at the expense of lexical sense" (Higgins 1182). An example is Peter Finch's poem "Damage," which was conceived as a tribute to Bob Cobbing and begins in the following manner:

> antimacassar cryptography corporate Cirencester
> corpuscular christigineous igneous conflation
> creel cruel scrim cylindrical cricoid
> crankshaft creosote crimson coronet
> cormorant carboniferous cynical cystitis
>
> ("Damage"[18])

In the audio recording on his personal website, Peter Finch introduces the poem with the following words: "Language can be unstable. 'Damage' for Bob Cobbing" ("Damage"). This paratextual announcement is delivered slowly, "Bob Cobbing" is uttered very quietly at the end, with a falling pitch. Consequently, the listener is all the more startled as the poem proper sets in: with his fast-paced performance in a higher pitch and far greater volume Finch provides a striking contrast to the calm words of the introduction:

---

[18] "Damage" was published in Finch's 2006 collection *The Welsh Poems* (61) and is interesting also on a visual level, with certain words rendered in bold print and some being much larger than others. As there is no recognisable correlation between the variations in typeface and paralanguage, however, and since this study is not concerned with visual effects of poetry on the page, I have included only a 'flat' verbal transcription of the poem.

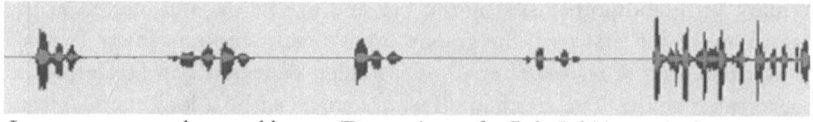

Language   can be unstable.   'Damage'   for Bob Cobbing.   Antimacassar…

"Damage" is a nonsense poem, or "nearsense," as Finch likes to call this type of work, which "loosen[s] the connection between word and meaning" ("Sound Poetry in the UK") so as to put the focus firmly on the sound quality of the words rather than on their representational value. While the verbal text of "Damage" is semantically incoherent, the poem retains the paralinguistic features of 'ordinary' comprehensible speech, which are thus given more weight in the listener's attempt to 'make sense' of what s/he hears. In this respect, sound poetry can be compared to overheard conversations in a foreign language, where paralanguage may be our only clue to the import of the exchange.

The beginning of "Damage" sounds breathless, excited, and almost aggressively loud, as though the speaker were annoyed at someone and railing against them. The dynamics of an audiotext may be described with the help of musical terminology. A "steady increase in dynamic level" can thus be called "*crescendo*," a decrease "*decrescendo*" (Stein and Spillmann 325). In "Damage," a decrescendo occurs further on in the poem and is followed by a crescendo, in a passage that can be transcribed as follows:

> damaged cantonment kings road rusted
> deal dominion antique meal voucher
> real attack rich mangled aromament rings
> sandwiched busted dole liloleum linoleum
> lilomeum lilome lilublbliloneum
> frantic mile pouch racked itch strings minion
> advantaged canton crapper pie-eyed
> kingdom doodle

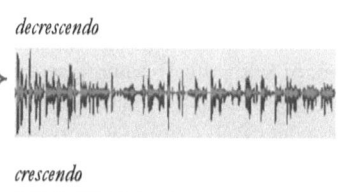

decrescendo

crescendo

("Damage")

The first section, during which volume is gradually diminished, sounds increasingly introvert, as though the speaker were preoccupied with his own tongue action and articulatory efforts, and not so much with getting a message across to a listening public. This impression is reinforced by the prolongation of the 'v' in "voucher," the 'r' in "real," or the 'm' in "mangled" – where the speaker is apparently stuck – and finally by his inability to pronounce the word "linoleum," which results in an incomprehensible babble.

Finally, he finds himself on 'safe ground' again, so to speak: the word "frantic" marks the beginning of a new section which, through a steady crescendo, returns him to his earlier excited tone.

To sum up, volume is the articulatory parameter that specifies the loudness of an utterance, manifest in the amplitude of a sound wave. Volume variations – together with other parameters such as pitch – create stress patterns and thus have a crucial function for the production of regular and irregular rhythms. Emphasis or 'rhetorical stress' adds extra force to selected stressed syllables and relates to the informational focus or emotional force of an utterance. Volume variations that occur over longer segments of speech are referred to as the 'dynamics' of an utterance or a passage. They take the form of a 'crescendo' (increasing loudness) or 'decrescendo' (decreasing loudness) and may convey emotional states and attitudes in live poetry.

4.3.4 Articulation

Articulation refers to the manner in which sounds are connected to, or disconnected from, each other during speech. Just like musical notes, syllables can be uttered in such a way as to join them smoothly together or to articulate them in a disjunctive manner, with pauses in between. In musical terms, the articulation of notes "without any perceptible interruption" is called "*legato*" (Stein and Spillmann 328), the separate articulation of each note "*staccato*" (333).[19] Articulation is linked to syllable duration: if an utterance is first produced with legato articulation and then repeated in staccato at the same tempo, syllable duration will be much shorter in the second instance, due to the pauses between them. Van Leeuwen explains the effects of articulation in relation to the principle of experiential meaning potential:

> Clearly it costs more energy to perform a series of separate attacks than to perform one long, connected motion, and so disjunctive sound production can come to stand for anything that includes the idea of a lively and energetic approach, or a bold and forceful attack [...] Connective sound production, by contrast, can come to stand for anything that includes the idea of a smoother, more relaxed or sensual approach (unless of course most other features point in a different direction). (109-10)

---

[19] Van Leeuwen suggests the terms "connective" and "disjunctive" (109) to specify these contrastive manners of speech articulation. The advantage of "legato" and "staccato" are their wide-reaching familiarity, however, which is why they will be used in this study.

Again, the actual effect of articulation in a given performance must of course be judged in the light of all other features of speech. John Siddique's poem "Yes" is an example of a legato performance that sounds highly energised. Certain lines, such as "Yes to the frozen lakes beneath my fields" are articulated so smoothly and sonorously they are almost reminiscent of incantations. Peter Finch's poem "Damage" provides an extreme example of a staccato performance in its middle passage:

> Cadogan canton capper cyncoed
> Piepowder criddle cree
> crip crip ip oop ip ip oop   } *staccato*
> idle idle ip ip cron crap crap

The amplitude graph displays individual syllables (from "crip" to "crap") as brief outbursts of sound, with breaks in between:

During the staccato section, Finch also plays with pitch variation, represented below:

> crip crip ^{ip} oop ^{ip} ip oop
> idle idle ip ip _{cron} crap crap

This gives the whole passage something bird-like, as though he were imitating bird song or trying to attract chickens (as in 'cluck cluck cluck'). "Damage" is a fine example of how paralanguage can be meaningful: in the absence of comprehensible word denotations the listener is still able to 'make meaning' out of the passage with recourse to paralinguistic features such as articulation, though the meaning generated may be of a different kind.

Syllables are not the only units of sound that can be audibly drawn together or separated in speech. A speaker may bind several words together and articulate them as larger units: phrases. In musical terms, the *phrase* is defined as a "short section of a composition into which the music, whether vocal or instrumental, seems naturally to fall" and which "may be contained within one breath" ("phrase"). With regard to the spoken word Van Leeuwen defines phrases as "moves in the ongoing speech act" and phrasing – i.e. "put[ting] words together as one phrase" – as the act of making these words "belong together as one unit of meaning" (Van Leeuwen 42).

Thus, drawing words together in phrases requires decisions that impact on the meaning-making process: they "add the reader's [performer's] interprettation to the meaning of the written word, just as a musical performance adds the musician's interpretation to the music written by the composer," Van Leeuwen (45) notes.

The lining of a written poem is often understood to indicate speech pauses, i.e. which words belong together as a phrase and where the boundaries between phrases fall. However, as Middleton observes in his analysis of Jackie Kay's poem "Brendan Gallacher" ("How to Read a Reading" 12), this need not be the case: in live poetry words may be grouped together independently of what lineation may suggest. A telling example is Patience Agbabi's 2004 performance of "Ufo Woman" at a college in Cambridge. In her book *Transformatrix* the beginning of the poem is printed off with the following line breaks:

> Mother Earth. Heath Row. Terminal 5. Yo!
> Do I look hip in my space-hopper-green
> Slingbacks, iridescent sky-blue-pink skin
> Pants and hologram hair cut?
>
> ("Ufo Woman")

Agbabi's clever use of richly associative imagery in "Ufo Woman" marks her heroine out as an alien, turning the rather ordinary external appearance of a black woman (slingbacks, skin pants, rasta plaits…) into an ensemble of colourful features that seem to describe some strange creature from a science-fiction movie. When she speaks the poem the phrasing sounds quite different from what the page seems to suggest:

> Mother Earth.
> Heath Row.
> Terminal 5.
> Yo!
> Do I look hip in my
> space-hopper-green slingbacks,
> iridescent sky-blue-pink skin pants and
> hologram hair cut?

The pauses dividing these phrases off from each other also give the beginning of each phrase more weight – in this case the words "space," "iridescent" and "hologram," which are exactly the words that mark the speaker as an alien presence. Conversely, words can also be 'swallowed up' – de-emphasised – by a particular phrasing, as is the case with "pants":

> **ir**idescent sky-blue-pink **skin** pants and
> **ho**logram **hair** cut?

In its position towards the end of the above phrase, "pants" is delivered at a lower volume and lower pitch and quickly followed by "and" before the break marking the end of the phrase. It is thus given far less prominence than the initial "iridescent" and also less than "skin," with the effect that "iridescent" and "skin" remain the most prominent words in the phrase. The strangeness of the speaker's appearance is underlined by de-emphasising the very word that relates "iridescent sky-blue-pink" to her clothes rather than her skin.

Having touched upon the crucial role of pauses for staccato articulation and phrasing, the *pause* deserves special mention here as a stylistic device. Preceding an utterance, pauses may "create suspense" (Pfeiler, *Sounds of Poetry* 69) or express hesitancy, as in Adrian Mitchell's performance of his anti-war poem "To Whom It May Concern," where the poet ironically states "They're only dropping peppermints and … daisy chains," pausing before "daisy chains" as though he had difficulty uttering such an absurd notion. Occurring after an utterance, pauses may function as "carriers of the preceding sound" (Poyatos 137), meaning that they are intensifying the preceding sound by giving it more room. In the middle of her poem "My Grandmother," Jackie Kay pauses effectively after rendering the grandmother's startling, racist announcement *"There'll be no darkie baby in my house"* in an aggressive tone that rings through the pause.

A pause may also "introduce a new theme, or a change of thought" (Pfeiler, *Sounds of Poetry* 69), and it can even acquire significance in its own right, as anyone who has seen Nancy Meyers' film *What Women Want* (2000) will know. Being all of a sudden endowed with the gift of hearing the thoughts of every single woman he passes by, Nick Marshall (Mel Gibson) is exhausted by the profusion of noise and emotional confusion this causes. He finally learns to appreciate the emotional and intellectual capacity of the women around him. Only when he comes face to face with the two ever-smiling, overly made-up secretaries he employed, he is amazed to hear – nothing. With this pause in the constant flow of audible thought-speech, Nancy Meyers must have created one of the funniest silences in the history of film. Similarly, a poet-performer's pause may acquire meaning. In Abraham Gibson's poem with two speakers "Nancy and Reeva," Reeva talks about her time in hospital after a hip replacement operation:

> I was in hospital for three months,
> one of the first operations for that I am told,

and Nancy climbed the stairs to see me every day.
Every day.
I never expected that I'd make it but Nancy made me make it:
sometimes with flowers – flowers she said she had 'borrowed' from the park –
[*A. G. (as Reeva) purses his lips at an imaginary Nancy, A. G. (as Nancy, after a shift of posture) purses his lips back at an imaginary Reeva*]
and cooked food.

("Nancy and Reeva")

Abraham Gibson pauses as Reeva to purse his lips at Nancy in amused disbelief, followed by another pause which can clearly be attributed to Nancy and in which she purses her lips back at Reeva. The impression 'Nancy' gives is one of cheerful defiance at Reeva's mention of the flower theft, as though she were proud of having committed this small crime to support her ailing friend. Gibson indicates the change of speakers by turning his head so that he faces the microphone from a different angle. Normally, this change of posture is accompanied by a change in pitch level – with Reeva talking at a higher pitch and with a slight accent – but in this case there is no audiotext to indicate that Nancy is given a turn in between: the cue is Gibson's body action during the speech pause. Instances such as this strengthen Poyatos' claim that speech ought to be studied in its totality as "a verbal-paralinguistic-kinesic continuum" (122): a pause in the audiotext may be meaningful in conjunction with the poet-performer's body communication.

Furthermore, Abraham Gibson's performance of "Nancy and Reeva" at London's Soho Theatre exemplifies Pfeiler's observation that pauses in poetry performances frequently occur unplanned, in response to audience reactions such as "laughter, supportive or non-supportive comments, cheering, and applause" (*Sounds of Poetry* 69). After the very first utterance in the piece – "Well, I lived on this estate for 55 years now I'd like to be able to say nothing really surprises me but surprise surprise it still does" – which Gibson delivers as Nancy at an extraordinarily fast pace, he is forced to pause so as to give the audience's laughter some room and to make sure his next utterance will be heard. Pauses such as this occur frequently in "Nancy and Reeva." They testify to the fact that a live audience may have a direct impact on the poet-performer's audiotext and even contribute to it: for the individual audience member the laughter of the crowd becomes part of the total audio experience.

To sum up, articulation refers to the manner in which sounds are connected to, or disconnected from, each other during speech. Syllables can be uttered in 'legato' (smoothly connected) or 'staccato' (disconnected) articulation. Several words may be bound together into 'phrases': larger units of meaning usually uttered in one breath. Phrasing may emphasise or deemphasise certain words, thus contributing to the overall meaning of a live poem. For the production of staccato utterances, and to separate phrases from each other, the pause is an important stylistic device. Preceding an utterance, a pause may create expectation and suspense; following an utterance, it gives more room to the preceding sound. Pauses may also introduce new thoughts or themes or signify by themselves, sometimes in connection with body communication. Finally, pauses are often inserted by poet-performers in response to audience reactions.

4.3.5 Timbre

Timbre can be described as "tone-colour: that which distinguishes the quality of tone or voice of one instrument or singer from another" ("timbre"). When a flute and a clarinet produce the same tone they will nevertheless sound different as they have a different timbre. Similarly, different people's voices have different timbres and can thus be distinguished from each other. Timbre is a complex variable relating to factors such as the "frequency spectrum of a sound [i.e. its overtones], and in particular the ways in which different partials grow in amplitude during the starting transient" (Campbell). Unlike pitch or volume, it cannot be measured or represented on a simple one-dimensional scale. Frances Berry therefore proposes 'imaginative description' as a way of capturing the timbre of a person's voice: "a sound's timbre cannot be scientifically measured or objectively described. The timbre of a sound must be imaginatively or subjectively described, e.g. if someone says a voice is metallic, it sounds like metal to a hearer" (11).

Van Leeuwen argues that the trouble with relying exclusively on adjectives such as "metallic" is their impressionistic information value, pointing to the "social semiotics of sound quality" (130). The same component of sound may theoretically be described by very different adjectives, many of which can be evaluative in certain contexts. A tense voice may be described as 'metallic' in a man whereas the same quality may be perceived as 'piercing' in a woman, for instance, as women are expected to sound "soft and sweet" (130). Consequently, Van Leeuwen argues that "we need to go beyond the adjectives, and consider what the sounds actually are, or rather, how they are actually materially produced" and "with what range of meanings and values they can therefore potentially become associated" (130). The following pairs of sound qualities are conceived of as "graded phenomena" rather than "binary opposites" (Van Leeuwen 130):

Tense/Lax

> What happens when you tense the muscles of your throat is an experience we all have in common. The voice becomes higher (lower overtones are reduced, higher overtones increased), sharper, brighter, and, above all, more tense, because in their tensed state the walls of the throat cavity dampen the sound less than they would in relaxed state. When you open your throat and relax your voice, the opposite happens. The voice becomes more relaxed and mellow. (Van Leeuwen 130-1).

An example for a remarkably tense voice is provided by Aoife Mannix in her performance of "Marked" for the Welcome Collection in March 2008. Mannix wrote the poem in response to visiting the Website of Changing Faces – a UK charity supporting "people who have disfigurements to the face, hand or body from any cause," as she explains in the introduction ("Marked"). She was impressed with the courage particularly of young people whose stories told of the ignorance and prejudice they had to cope with daily. "Marked" is an attempt to capture the strength it takes to face hostile gazes, beginning

> Oh give me a face to meet the faces that I meet,
> the cold winter eyes glazed with hostility,
> the mouths with their scalpel tongues,
> the lips bruised harsh purple,
> the judgement stuck in their teeth.
> Give me a mask
> so that I too can be one of the numbing crowd,
> the silent torturers that avert their gazes
> the shuffling of embarrassed feet
> the casual mindless sniggers.
>
> ("Marked")

Aoife Mannix's vocal timbre might be described as 'metallic' or 'sharp,' going straight to the bone. It is certainly 'tense' and can thus convey "a host of [...] meanings which can be said to include the idea of 'tension'" (Van Leeuwen 131). In the case of "Marked" Mannix's tense voice adds a sharpness and concentration to the social commentary of the text that is very fitting for this poem.

Rough/Smooth

> A rough voice is one in which we can hear other things besides the tone of the voice itself – friction sounds, hoarseness, harshness, rasp. The opposite of the rough sound is the clean, smooth, 'well-oiled' sound in which all noisiness is eliminated. (Van Leeuwen 131-2)

The late Harold Pinter's voice, for instance, had a rough, weather-beaten quality: there was a lot of noise in it besides the regular sinus vibrations that the vocal chords produce in the case of a 'smooth' timbre. In terms of its meaning potential, the rough voice is, according to Van Leeuwen, "the vocal equivalent of the weatherbeaten face, the roughly plastered wall, the faded jeans, the battered leather jacket," whereas a smooth timbre is "the vocal equivalent of unblemished young skin, polished surfaces, designer plastic, immaculate tuxedos. How this is valued depends on the context" (132). Van Leeuwen also notes that roughness is often associated with masculinity as it is more audible on lower pitch levels (132). In Pinter's poetry recitals, his characteristic timbre seemed indeed to express a kind of 'tough' masculinity.

Breathiness

> In the breathy voice too, an extraneous sound mixes in with the tone of the voice itself – breath. But the effect is quite different. [...] There is the breathy voice, always also soft, and frequently associated with intimacy. Advertisers use it to give their message a sensual, even erotic appeal, and singers and instrumentalists use it for the same reason. (Van Leeuwen 133)

A case in point is Kat Francois's erotic poem "Anything," which Francois recorded on a self-published CD in 2005 and performed frequently. It is a relishing description of a sexual encounter, with the speaker's voice becoming increasingly breathy:

> Greedily I sniff the air around him.
> I am mesmerized.
> Lips locked hip flipped,
> heart beat skipped,
> clothes discarded and ripped [...].
>
> ("Anything")

The breathiness is coupled with an imprecise articulation, as though the speaker were lacking the energy to pronounce words clearly and to produce a clear (non-breathy) vocal sound. This impression is well in line with her stereotypically feminine willingness to surrender control over herself and be guided by her hyper-masculine lover, as indicated by the previous utterances:

> tall, muscular, I imagine him lifting me effortlessly,
> dominating and controlling,
> a voice so deep and resonating,
> he could say anything and I would do
> whatever he's commanding [...].
>
> ("Anything")

Through her breathy timbre Francois thus audibly enacts the lascivious self-abandonment the text suggests.

Vibrato/Plain

> Sounds are either plain and unwavering, or have some kind of 'grain', some kind of regular or irregular wavering, warbling, vibrating, pulsating, throbbing, rumbling and so on [...]. The vibrating sound literally and figuratively trembles. What makes us tremble? Emotions. Love, for instance. (Van Leeuwen 134)

Brian Patten recorded his famous love poem "Angel Wings" for the *Poetry in Performance* Vol. 1 audio CD, published by 57productions. From the start, there is a slight tremble in Patten's voice:

> In the morning I opened the cupboard
> And found inside it a pair of wings,
> a pair of angel's wings.
> I was not naïve enough to believe them real.
> I wondered who had left them there.
>
> ("Angel Wings")

The poem tells of a love that is "ruined" by "ignorance" and "slaughtered" by "disbelief." Its tone is elegiac, which is partly due to the trembling in Patten's voice, as an expression of the speaker's emotional involvement.

Resonance

> More has been written about nasality than about almost any other aspect of voice quality, partly because it has been difficult to define, and partly because nasality

> judgments have usually been value judgments: the languages, dialects and singing styles and so on which people call 'nasal' are the languages […] they do not like. (Van Leeuwen 134)

The aspect of timbre Van Leeuwen calls 'nasality' – referring to its social perception – is, in fact, part of a broader vocal feature that Poyatos has termed 'resonance.' He distinguishes between "pharyngeal, oral or nasal" resonance, depending on "where the vibrations from the vocal bands find their greatest resonator according to the size and shape of the pharyngeal cavity, oral cavity or nasal cavity" (178). Oral or nasal dominant resonance is most common, Poyatos notes, but sometimes a speaker may enlarge his/her pharyngeal cavity, giving his/her voice a "throaty" timbre (178).

An interesting instance of oral resonance can be found in Lucy English's recording of her poem "Family Prayers," where it is used to indicate a change of speaker:

> Our father who art in heaven
> Hallowed be thy name
> Thy kingdom come
> thy will be done on earth as it is in heaven.
> My father,
> Sitting on the bed
> not kneeling on the floor like the rest of us because he has a bad knee
> his voice beaming straight up to God
> 'Forgive us all our trespasses'   [*increased oral resonance*]
> 'What's a trespasses?'
> 'Shush Mary, we'll tell you later.'
>
> ("Family Prayers")

Poyatos notes that "very oral resonance produces what we call resounding or *orotund* voice (from Lat. 'round mouth'), called by many *resonant, strong* and *rich*," which is often associated with "rather large body size" and positive masculine qualities such as "energy, good health, resourcefulness" (178). The above extract contains some direct speech by the speaker's father, marked by a slightly lower pitch level, which would, however, most certainly go unnoticed if it were not for the sudden increase in oral resonance of English's voice. This different timbre suggests a person larger, more powerful and more determined than the child speaker. The oral resonance is taken back and pitch is raised for the next utterance, which is attributed to the girl Mary, accordingly.

To sum up, timbre is the voice quality that distinguishes individual voices from each other even if they produce sounds of the same pitch and volume. It is also called 'tone colour' and is a complex variable shaped by factors such as overtones. In relation to experiential meaning potential, timbre can be described by graded sound qualities such as tense/lax, rough/smooth, breathy, vibrato/plain, or nasal/oral resonance, bearing in mind that a voice is never characterised by just one of these aspects of timbre. The examples above have demonstrated how timbre can help to characterise a speaker, reveal particular attitudes or emotions in an utterance and thus contribute to the meaning of a live poem.

4.4 Notation

Literary studies has long taken for granted the peculiar fact that verbal language is both its object of investigation and its means of analysing, interpreting and discussing it. Thus, it has always seemed entirely unproblematic to quote a line from a novel in a scholarly essay by simply typing it down with the rest of one's reflections and attaching quotation marks to either side. The materiality of the actual line in the book at hand seems unaffected by this act of transposition, the details of its qualities and texture beside the point. By general consent, the *re*presentation of the original line is treated as a presentation, or at least as an exact copy. Scientists or musicologists, by contrast, have had to face the challenge of representing non-verbal objects and processes by verbal and graphic means for centuries and to devise ways of integrating these representations with the rest of their (verbal) discussions and publications.

The previous chapters have revealed a poem's audiotext to differ so widely from print in its aesthetic, its materiality and means of signification that attempts to quote an utterance from a live poem as though it were a line of printed text will seem quite futile by now. Several techniques of transcription have been employed above to provide appropriate representations of different audiotextual features. In this chapter they shall be reviewed in more depth as to their particular benefits and drawbacks for a discussion of live poetry.[20] Richard Bauman identifies the goal of transcription as "render[ing] the printed texts in such a way as to reveal the essential formal features of the texts presented, a kind of graphological laying bare of the

---

[20] For comprehensive discussions of transcription methods in the verbal arts, folklore and poetry, see Finnegan *Oral Traditions and the Verbal Arts* 199-207, Fine 133-148, and Sherwood 136-137.

features of the device" (*Story, Performance, and Event* ix). Similarly, Elizabeth Fine insists that a live performance must be recorded "as an aesthetic mode of communication" (8). Paralanguage and non-verbal sounds most obviously distinguish a poem's audiotext aesthetically from its written counterpart. While it is always recommendable in live poetry to work with audio or video recordings, which capture a far greater range of the qualities of the original performance, a "graphic transcription helps the critic to draw out relevant paralinguistic features," as Sherwood (137) points out. In order to discuss a particular paralinguistic feature such as pitch movement that is used by a poet in a conspicuous manner it helps to employ ways of representing utterances that highlight the relevant feature in a comprehensible form.

Transcription by definition implies a change from one form into another, which can be problematic. The transformation of live poetry into some form of graphic representation necessitates, like any other kind of transcription, certain choices. Some formal features will be accentuated, some will be left out altogether, meaning that no transcription "can ever capture the whole reality" of a live poem: "in the final analysis, the experience and its representation are never the same thing," as Foley (100-1) notes. The resulting distortion ought to be acknowledged. While "some problems have no satisfactory solution," Ruth Finnegan concedes, "it is at least a mark of intellectual honesty to convey some idea of what is missing, what the points at issue might be, and the rationale for your decisions" (199).

Integrated Verbal Notation

In the following example of a verbal transcription, paralinguistic features are indicated by the visual properties and arrangement of the letters:

His $^{vo^i c}{}_e$ ⋯ had the deep $^b{}^u{}^r{}_r{}_r$ of a $_m{}^a{}_n$ who¨ kept¨ **fish** $h_{oo_{k_s}}$¨

(Anthony Joseph, "Kneedeepnditchdiggerniggersweat")

Paralinguistic features are thus integrated with the typeset, which is why I have chosen to term this form of transcription 'integrated verbal notation.' It is based on Dennis Tedlock's "Guide to Reading Aloud" (20), where Tedlock applies raised and lowered letters and capitals for the representation of pitch and increased volume, respectively. An anthropologist, Tedlock studied verbal art such as Zuni oral narratives and Mayan verse, devising his notation system as a guide to 'reperformance' – i.e. to enable other scholars to read passages of verbal art aloud in a way that resembles the original performance. His system has been refined in this study and serves a different purpose here. In itself, it may still give the reader a rough impression of the acoustic nature of the performance it represents. However, video technology is now widely available to enable a 'reperformance' that conveys a far more accurate impression of the original live performance than any tentative loud reading based on a mere written transcript would. The transcript is intended rather as a supplement to video or audio recordings, visualising certain conspicuous acoustic features that the analyst considers noteworthy. It thus functions as a means of guiding the reader's attention in a discussion of live poetry that will be primarily based on a video or audio recording.

Integrated verbal notation constitutes a flexible means of representing relative pitch (by raising or lowering letters), relative volume (by bold-printing stressed syllables and/or increasing type size), and relative tempo (by increasing or decreasing the spaces between letters) – all of which is easily feasible with a standard word processing programme such as Microsoft Word. As a technique, it is intuitive and easily comprehensible. One of its greatest advantages lies in the fusion of letters and paralinguistic features, which corresponds to our perceptual experience of parameters such as pitch, since "one does not normally hear pitch as a separate element superimposed on words, but rather as a phenomenon occurring simultaneously with words," as Fine (145) notes. Thus, in "voice" in the above transcript we easily recognise a falling pitch, represented by the falling letters. It is also characterised by a comparatively greater volume, indicated by the greater type size and bold print. The letters of "had the deep" are then squeezed together, meaning that these words are pronounced at a relatively faster pace, with the pause before them registering as three dots. To indicate emphasis and/or extreme volume capital letters can be used:

Ex **CUSE** me! ... Ex **CUSE** me!

(Jeneece Bernard, "Underground")

The beginning and end of phrases may be marked by line breaks, as in

iridescent sky-blue-pink **skin** pants and
hologram **hair** cut.

(Patience Agbabi, "Ufo Woman")

128   Live Poetry

Prolonged pronunciations of certain sounds are indicated by the multiplication of letters,

> She would ... ssshake the wire fence
> She would ... rrrattle on the gate

(Anthony Joseph, "Aranguez")

and non-verbal sounds can be represented by letters whose sound values resemble them, accompanied by a verbal description. An example is the "sucking noise" Abraham Gibson "produces with his teeth" in "Nancy and Reeva":

> "[...] but hips? – pffff_fff!"

A weakness of integrated verbal notation is its imprecision. Variables such as pitch or volume are indicated in relative terms, and rhythm can hardly be represented at all, or only very vaguely. This leads us to another method of transcription that is more suitable for a precise notation of rhythm and pitch values.

Musical Notation

Musical notation is a highly accurate method for transcribing regular rhythms. The attributes of individual notes specify their duration in relation to each other as well as their absolute duration – in combination with a tempo indication such as "80 beats per minute."

We   jazz   june we   die   soon.

(Gwendolyn Brooks, "The Pool Players")

The above example is a four-beat rhythm, meaning that one measure lasts for the duration of four crotchets (♩). The 𝄽 sign marks a crotchet break, the 𝄾 sign a quaver break. Quaver notes (♪) and quaver breaks last half as long as crotchets. The ➖ sign marks a break that lasts for half a measure, i.e. two beats. A dot after a note lengthens the note by half its value. There are also half-notes (𝅗𝅥), which last for the duration of two beats, and semi-quavers (𝅘𝅥𝅯), lasting half as long as quavers. The position of a note's head on the staves indicates its pitch, with higher frequencies being positioned higher up on the staves[21]:

'Oh   no,' she said. 'Oh yes,'   I said.   'Oh **shit!**' she said. 'Good**bye**,' I said.

(Brian Patten, "Hair Today, No Her Tomorrow")

If pitch movement is the focus of interest, it may suffice to draw curves over the staves:

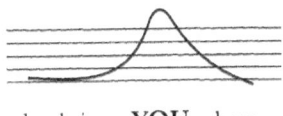

what brings **YOU**   here

The above example of a pitch curve expressing 'surprise' is taken from Van Leeuwen, who explains that in this case the musical staves are used to "give a sense of the scale of the pitch steps, rather than to indicate precise pitches" (96). While the advantage of curves over integrated verbal notation lies in the fact that the shape of the curve does not depend on the graphic length of individual words – which often does not correspond to their duration after all – the use of individual notes gives a more precise indication of the pitch of individual syllables:

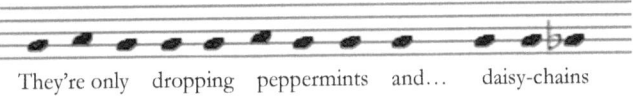

They're only   dropping   peppermints   and…   daisy-chains

(Adrian Mitchell, "To Whom It May Concern")

---

21   Musical notation can be integrated with the verbal text by means of special fonts such as Bach, which was used for several examples above, e.g. ♩♪. The advantage of the Bach characters is that they take up no more space than regular font types, but the font as such is rather difficult to handle. Staves can easily be created with free music composing / notation software such as Obtiv's Octava, in conjunction with image editing software such as the freeware graphics programme Gimp.

The rhythm of the quoted poem is irregular, which is why the stems of the notes and the lines separating measures have been eliminated as they would otherwise be taken to indicate precise durational relations. The duration of individual syllables can still be represented approximately by varying the distance between the respective note heads, as illustrated by the greater space before "daisy chains."

The advantage of musical notation is, of course, its wide-ranging familiarity as a concise means of representing pitch and rhythm visually. However, like any other technique of transcription, it is of little value on its own. It is meant to supplement verbal interpretation rather than to function as an analytical tool in its own right. Those unfamiliar with the precise workings of musical notation may have difficulty reconstructing the rhythm though they will still be able to grasp the relative difference in pitch. They will also find the particularities of the respective utterance described and the potential meaning of the represented paralinguistic features discussed verbally.

Amplitude Graphs

Amplitude graphs are an effective and precise means of registering volume and sound duration:

My grandmother sits by the fire... *There'll be no darkie baby...*   My grandmother is...

This graph represents the dynamics of an excerpt from Jackie Kay's poem "My Grandmother." It demonstrates clearly how the poet increases volume in the middle section, inserts a long pause and finally resumes speaking in a far lower volume than before. The advantage of amplitude graphs is their scientific precision and the relative facility with which they can be produced: all it takes is some simple software for recording and/or editing sounds.[22] They are very useful for visualising patterns of articulation, as in the following example:

---

[22] The two examples are screenshots of graphs created with Audacity, an open source freeware programme, on the basis of an audio recording.

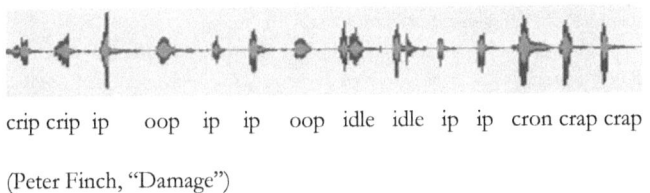

crip crip ip   oop ip ip   oop idle idle ip ip cron crap crap

(Peter Finch, "Damage")

This amplitude graph displays a typical staccato pattern, individual syllables registering as brief outbursts of sound, with breaks in between. As with musical notation, the value of amplitude graphs lies in their ability to represent features of sound visually in a concise manner: they are an auxiliary means for analysis and interpretation, rather than a substitute.

Verbal Description

Elizabeth Fine recommends the use of "natural language" for the analysis of aesthetic speech communication, arguing that "in addition to recording pronunciation, paralinguistic, and kinesic features," it can "describe artifactual and proxemic features as well as details about the aesthetic field. Its strength as a descriptive tool lies in its accessibility and flexibility" (141). In the following examples, a brief description is inserted next to the verbal transcription and clearly set apart from it by italic print and brackets:

My father,
Sitting on the bed
not kneeling on the floor like the rest of us because he has a bad knee
his voice beaming straight up to God
'Forgive us all our trespasses'   [*increased oral resonance*]
'What's a trespasses?'
'Shush Mary, we'll tell you later.'

(Lucy English, "Family Prayers")

Cadogan canton capper cyncoed
Piepowder criddle cree
crip crip ip oop ip ip oop   } *staccato*
idle idle ip ip cron crap crap

(Peter Finch, "Damage")

Longer comments may be inserted in between lines, again being clearly marked off from the verbal transcription:

> I never expected that I'd make it but Nancy made me make it:
> sometimes with flowers – flowers she said she had 'borrowed' from the park –
> [*A. G. (as Reeva) purses his lips at an imaginary Nancy, A. G. (as Nancy, after a shift of posture) purses his lips back at an imaginary Reeva*]
> and cooked food.
>
> (Abraham Gibson, "Nancy and Reeva")

These examples illustrate Fine's observation on the flexibility of "natural language" as a means of recording acoustic as well as kinesic features of an oral performance. Verbal description will generally accompany specialist transcription systems such as musical notation and make possible a smooth transition to interpretive writing. It is often better understood in conjunction with graphic illustrations (staves, amplitude graphs) but also constitutes a valuable analytical tool in itself.

What emerges from this review of notation practices is the need for flexibility: particular features of audiotext lend themselves to different modes of representation. As Kenneth Sherwood correctly observes, "the use of a variety of methods also underscores the necessary insufficiency of any transcription," and he goes so far as to claim that "it may be advisable to develop particularized transcription methods adequate to each genre, performance tradition, even customized to each individual performer" (137). However, the transcription techniques employed in this study are the result of a deliberate selection from available methods according to their suitability for capturing the acoustic particularities of live poetry performances.

4.5 Composite Parameters: Tone of Voice, Accent

Certain qualities of an audiotext can be identified and labelled with relative ease but often cannot be defined with reference to one articulatory parameter only, as they are a conglomerate of features contributing towards a perceptible overall effect. Consequently, these composite parameters – tone of voice and accent – cannot be measured or easily transcribed. They should still be accounted for in an analysis of live poetry, however, since they describe a poem on a different level from parameters such as pitch and rhythm, and thus reveal additional aspects of its audiotext.

Tone of Voice

For Brooks and Warren, "the tone of a poem indicates the speaker's attitude toward his subject and toward his audience, and sometimes toward himself," the term being, in fact, "a metaphor drawn from the tone of voice" (181). According to this view, tone is not an acoustic feature of a poem's audiotext, as the word would suggest: it is only metaphorically related to sound. Other critics have held similar views of the tone in poetry as a configuration of stylistic features expressing the speaker's attitude, such as "word choice, syntax, imagery, metaphors, or other figurative devices" (Brogan and Gudas 1293), rather than an acoustic aspect of orally performed poetry.

In this study, 'tone' is used in its more specific meaning of 'tone of voice,' i.e. "the inflections given to words by speakers [...] and heard by auditors" (Brogan and Gudas 1293) as an expression of the speaker's attitudes or moods. In previous chapters, occasional reference has been made to the tone of an utterance or a whole poem as "excited," "calm," or "aggressive," for instance. In Lucy English's poem "Temple Cloud" the speaker reminisces about a past lover when she happens to drive through his home town: "I didn't think about you much but the bus stopped in Temple Cloud." She remembers his drug problems, the rejection he had to suffer from his family, his unconventional life style and his kindness, before English concludes the poem with a passage whose tone is remarkably tender:

> Do you still sing John Martyn songs?
> May you never lay your head down without a hand to hold.
> May you never make your bed out in the cold.
>
> ("Temple Cloud")

In English's voice there is a tenderness that could also be described as affectionate, well-wishing, and perhaps a little nostalgic. It is brought about by a mixture of low volume and high pitch level, as well as a lax timbre, which suggests that the speaker is letting herself be swept away by her memories rather than communicating actively with her (absent) ex-lover. A series of pauses between phrases seem to point to the speaker's sincerity and genuine feeling by giving her utterances more room.

While descriptive adjectives such as "tender" and "nostalgic" may carry more hermeneutic interpretive significance than a precise description of the dynamics of the above passage, it should be remembered that "the semiotics of tone in ordinary and even in highly structured formal speech is notoriously uncertain," as Peter Quartermain notes: "the fearful voice can be heard as resentful; the shy but friendly as aloof and ironic [...]" (225). For the purpose of analysis it is therefore helpful to indicate what acoustic features have prompted a judgement like "tender," as realised above.

Another example of a distinctive tone of voice in live poetry is provided by Benjamin Zephaniah's poem "Rong Radio Station," which is a long diatribe against the ever-present mass media and their power of manipulation. The poem offers ironic comments on racial stereotyping ("I waz beginning to not trust me, in fact I wanted to arrest me") and the artificial needs created by capitalism ("I've been reciting commercials to my girlfriends, I've been trying to convince myself dat what I really need is a sun bed").

Irony is defined by Claire Colebrook as "saying what is contrary to what is meant" (1). It "draws attention to the gap between saying and said, between speaking position and posited truth" (Colebrook 112). The ironic tone of "Rong Radio Station" is produced not only by the verbal text as such but also by its paralinguistic features in performance:

> I've been trying to convince myself dat I could ease my conscience
> if I gave a few pence or a few cents
> to a starving baby in Africa.
> Because African babies need my favours.
> Because Africa is full of dictators and – oh yeah,
> globalization will bring salvation.
>
> ("Rong Radio Station")

The excessive pitch range and the near-regular rhythm with which Zephaniah delivers his critique of globalization makes it sound like an advertising jingle:

and o$^{h\ ye}$a$_{h,}$

globali^{za}tion... will b r i n g sal^{va}ti$_o$
$\quad\quad\quad\quad\quad\quad\quad\quad\quad\quad\quad\quad\quad\quad\quad\quad$n.

The pitch movement is too exaggerated for the phrase to be taken for a straight-forward statement, marking it out as clearly ironic and thus suggesting that the belief in the benefits of globalization is yet another result of media manipulation that is implanted in people's minds with the suggestive force of advertising tunes.

Finally, Choman Hardi's poem "Journey through the Dead Villages" contains an interesting example of a joyful tone in a poem that tells, in fact, of the poet's painful experience of having to flee from Iraq to Iran as a child after the Iraqi government had used chemical weapons in the Kurdish region during the Anfal campaign:

> Sometimes one journey is the beginning of a hundred journeys,
> each journey undoable, leading to other little journeys,
> each journey entailing … a hundred possibilities,   [*joyful tone*]
> a hundred departures.
>
> ("Journey through the Dead Villages")

The beginning of the poem, where the speaker reflects on the possibilities that journeys open and the new beginnings they afford, sounds cheerful and full of hope. Especially the utterance

> each _{journey en}tailing … a ^{hun}dred possi^{bili}_{ties}
>
> ("Journey through the Dead Villages")

is marked by a joyfully expectant tone, which is due to the wide range of Hardi's pitch rise on "hundred" but also to the particular resonance of "a hundred possibilities." Although audio recordings generally preclude an analysis of facial expressions, this phrase was uttered with an audible smile on the poet's face, which affects its resonance in the oral cavity. The smile is manifest in Hardi's tone, as though the thought of "a hundred possibilities" filled her with pleasure despite the fear and grief which marked the particular journey she relates. The rest of the poem is delivered in a more sober tone as the poet remembers "tears," a "forbidden border" and empty villages where "the scattered sheep without their shepherd were circling in sadness and fear" ("Journey through the Dead Villages"). The poem's account of the family's escape to Iran thus provides an interesting contrast to its joyful beginning.

However, listening closely to the recording there is a possibility that the 'smiling tone' of the poem's beginning stems, at least in part, from a source that has little to do with the poet's attitude or mood. As a Kurdish poet, Hardi speaks English with a slight accent that is manifest, for instance, in her pronunciation of /ɪ/ in 'journey' and 'possibilities,' which are characterised by a much tenser 'i' vowel (as in 'journiiii', 'possibiiliitiiies') than would be expected in standard English. This may entail a tensing of the facial muscles, as when a photographer asks clients to say 'Cheeeese!' in order to provoke a smile. The example demonstrates how tone of voice may be linked to another composite parameter – accent – which shall be briefly discussed in the following section.

Accent

'Accent' can be defined as "the way someone pronounces the words of a language, showing which country or which part of a country they come from" ("Accent"). In its specific sense of regional pronunciation habits, accent is realised as an acoustic phenomenon only. It does not imply, for instance, a particular lexical choice, as 'dialect' does. As such, it affects a poem's audiotext in various ways, one of which is thematised in John Lennard's comment on a dramatic monologue by Tony Harrison titled "V." Harrison's poem contains two lines that end on "book" and "fuck" respectively, and Lennard points out that "in a Leeds accent, especially a thick working-class one, 'book' and 'fuck' are closer to full-rhyme than in most British accents" (209). Thus, what looks like a near rhyme on paper may be manifest as a full rhyme in the audiotext, depending on the performer's accent.

Choman Hardi's poem has shown how the formation of vowels may affect the tone of a poem. Vowel and consonant formation are not the only culturally specific pronunciation habits, however: accents may directly affect stress patterns or intonation, which is why they are discussed under the heading of 'composite parameters.' Christian Habekost notes, for instance, that in contrast to British English, Jamaican Patois "is very lightly stressed" and that the rhythm of Patois lyrics therefore has "a different organising basis" (92).

Apart from their particular sound qualities, accents may be consciously employed in live poetry for speaker characterisation and as a marker of social identity vis à vis the audience. Regarding the latter, Samera Owusu Tutu points out that

> the infusion of dialect [by black performance poets in the UK] initially acted as an indicator of unity between the performer and the audience. It facilitated a clear undercurrent of association between the audience and the performer – and, thus, an affinity. The message was for the people, as was the delivery. (162)

By speaking in a particular accent, the poet-performer can indicate his/her association with an audience and thus convey a sense of cultural authenticity and affiliation. As for speaker characterisation, Abraham Gibson provides an interesting example in his poem "Margaret Thatcher and her African Lover," which he performed at Soho Theatre in London in 2007. The poem is a monologue, and the speaker is clearly identified as African by the accent Gibson is putting on. In contrast to English Received Pronunciation (RP), which is very much stress-based, the African Lover's accent is not characterised by a rhythmic pattern built on the distinction of stressed and unstressed syllables. Instead, all syllables are pronounced with roughly equal duration and prominence but organised by a relatively regular up-and-down pitch movement. An utterance like "it was love at first glance," in which we would normally expect 'was' to be shortened and barely audible in unstressed position, is thus delivered as

> It $_{wos}$ love $_{at}$ first $_{glance,}$

with 'wos' and the preposition 'at' taking up about as much time as the rest of the words. The 'African Lover's' speech is thus produced as a sort of regular sing-song:

> She ^{said} I am ^{going} to ^{take} de ^{power} $_a$way from de ^{unions} and squeeze $_{their}$ balls $_{un}$til $_{they}$ brea$_k$.
>
> ("Margaret Thatcher and her African Lover")

This conscious employment of a foreign accent becomes most obvious when Gibson at one point speaks as Margaret Thatcher after her lover has left her, in perfect RP English, raising the pitch so as to imitate a female voice:

> You know, to spite me she tightened up on the immigration bill.
> She said,
> If this English rose cannot have your sunshine ⎫ *RP accent,*
> then no African azalea will. ⎭ *higher pitch*

Apart from the original explanation of Thatcher's hard-line immigration policy, the passage is interesting for its contrastive speaker characterisation. As Margaret Thatcher, Gibson distinguishes clearly between stressed (more prominent) and unstressed syllables, opposing the 'iron lady's' speech to the level stress pattern of the lover's sing-song which identifies him as an African immigrant.

4.6 Paratext

The audiotext poets produce during a live appearance usually exceeds the 'poems proper': poet-performers will often introduce their poems, or themselves, at the beginning of a performance and explain the origin of a piece or certain allusions for instance, during or after a performance. Among performers, these introductory remarks or comments are usually referred to as 'ad lib,' pointing to their improvised nature.[23] With reference to books, Gérard Genette has coined the term 'paratext': it accompanies the literary text proper in the form of

> a certain number of verbal or other productions, such as an author's name, a title, a preface, illustrations. And although we do not always know whether these productions are to be regarded as belonging to the text, in any case they surround it and extend it, precisely in order to *present* it. (1)

Genette envisions paratext as an "undefined zone" between "text and off-text," lacking "any hard and fast boundary on either the inward side (turned toward the text) or the outward side (turned toward the world's discourse about the text)" (2). This notion of paratext – as elements accompanying a literary text that form a transitional zone between the inside and outside of a literary work – can also be applied to the audiotext of a live literature performance. It is a useful concept, implying an influence exerted "at the service of a better reception for the text and a more pertinent reading of it (more pertinent, of course, in the eyes of the author and his allies)" (Genette 2). That poet-performers are often very conscious of the effects of paratext is made clear by Nathan Penlington:

> Last year I took a one-man spoken-word show to the Edinburgh Festival, an hour's show, but the poems I had written were just written as poems, separate from each other, so then the difficulty was to combine them to make sense as an hour's worth of show. So, the bits in between became as important as the poems themselves, just to carry the audience through. (Penlington interview)

Genette further distinguishes between 'peritext' – a "spatial category" of elements to be found "within the same volume" (4), such as titles or a preface – and 'epitext,' which is "any paratextual element not materially appended to the text within the same volume but circulating, as it were, freely, in a virtually limitless physical and social space" (344), such as author inter-

---

[23] Quite often, the 'ad lib' is not as improvised as it may seem. Many performers will have set introductory phrases for certain poems which they use repeatedly.

views in newspapers. The different paratextual elements of a live poetry event are not materially separable from each other in the same way as elements inside and outside of a book, however, which confirms the onesidedness of Genette's concept: its predication on print. One could argue that the peritext/epitext distinction may be upheld on a temporal level. Peritext would thus be the paratext produced during the event where the literary work proper is being presented, with epitext referring to those paratextual comments originating in temporal distance to the respective event. As this chapter is devoted to a 'close reading' of live poetry, it will focus on peritextual elements. Yet, in view of the notorious slipperiness of 'event' as a temporally defined category,[24] the hypernym 'paratext' will be used in the following discussion.

For an analysis of paratext in live poetry performances, the elements in question should be studied as to their position in relation to the poem and/or the whole event, their originator, and their perceived function. The most common *position* is before a poem, as in Brian Patten's introduction to "Hair Today, No Her Tomorrow" at the Vienna Lit Festival 2008. Patten announces it as "a conversation poem in homage to e.e. cummings," spelling the title out for the audience so they can appreciate the wordplay of 'hair' and 'her.' He then adds: "anybody sitting here thinking of committing adultery, you know, leaving their partner for somebody else tonight – this is a warning, this poem. It has a purpose in life. Unlike most poems" ("Hair Today, No Her Tomorrow"). He takes a sip from his glass, puts it down, positions himself in front of the microphone and – after a short pause in which his gaze is focused on the manuscript in his hands – he begins to read the poem. Interestingly, he announces the title before delivering these comments and does not repeat it later. Patten's introduction is thus inserted between the poem and its title but marked off from the 'text proper' through his body behaviour.

Kenneth Sherwood discusses a similar constellation in his analysis of Amiri Baraka's performance of a poem called "In the Funk World."[25] He points out that it is by no means clear whether the additional material (which does not appear in the book publication) is to be considered "an intervening 'commentary'" or "part of the poem" (126), echoing Genette's notion of the 'transitional zone.' Sherwood transcribes Baraka's performance as follows:

---

[24] See, for instance, Sauter 7.
[25] Published in Baraka's collection *Funk Lore* (72); the recording Sherwood analyses is published online at http://journal.oraltradition.org/issues/21i/sherwood#audio1 (date of access: 24 April 2009).

> In the **Funk World**
>
> Well you know, we created ah, you know, small band music, in New Orleans, and uh, they said it was Dixie Land, and then we created Big Band, and they said it was Swing but it didn't swing,
>
> [audience laughter]
>
> and then they told us that, uh, Paul White Man, was the King of Swing and   no, he was the king of jazz, that's right, Benny Good Man was the king of swing **What I want to kno___w**
>
> **In the Funk World**
> **If El_vis   Presley**
> **is King**
>
> **Who is Ja__mes   Brown?**
> **God?**

Fig. 3: Transcription of "In the Funk World".

Paratext may also be delivered after a poem or a set of poems, for instance in a 'question & answer' session, or as an afterthought to a poem. An example is Mark Gwynne Jones' performance of an (unfinished) series of poems called "Nine Types of Poet" at the Seconds Out Slam at the Contact Theatre in Manchester in February 2007. After "The Clones of Cooper Clarke" Jones plunges straight into the next poem without giving a title. It is revealed to be "The Yorkshire Rapper" – to the delight of the audience – only after he has finished the poem.

Genette refers to paratext as "this fringe, always the conveyor of a commentary that is authorial or more or less legitimated by the author" (2). He draws attention to the fact that the *originator* of a book's paratext must not necessarily be the author. The same is true for live poetry, where MCs, for example, may introduce poets and make comments about their work and thus influence audience expectations and reception of their poetry. A fine example is provided by John Hegley, who introduced the legendary poet and singer-songwriter Fran Landesman at London's Soho Theatre in February 2007 with the following words:

> So our first performer ... what she would suggest is that you shut your eyes, open your ears. So the ... in answer to the question 'where are you from,' the simple answer was 'New York,' and her favourite vegetable is marihuana. Could

you please welcome … with her young son in tow … could you please welcome Fran Landesman, Ladies and Gentlemen. (*A&S in Soho*)

For audience members not familiar with Landesman's work, the announcement of her favourite vegetable must have seemed a somewhat remarkable introduction and raised certain expectations. Hegley's introduction is also exemplary for the fact that it is based on answers to questions he posed to the performer earlier, which certainly renders it 'legitimated by the author,' in Genette's sense. In an instance of 'authorial' paratext, Landesman introduces her second poem that night, a humorous elegy to the freedom smokers used to enjoy, with the words "Loudon Wainwright sings 'in heaven all the angels have ashtrays.' This is called 'The Last Smoker'" (*A&S in Soho*). Landesman's poem contrasts this idea of a heaven where smoking is accepted to the point that angels themselves possess ashtrays to an apocalyptic future when smoking will be severely persecuted in a society that will eventually bury the last smoker "along with the very last joke" ("The Last Smoker") – a horror vision for Landesman.

A definition of paratext as that part of the 'authorised' audiotext that is not the 'poem proper' becomes problematic when we take into account the role of the audience. Audience reactions such as clapping or laughing can be taken as audible commentary that influences other audience members in a way the poet may well have intended. In this sense, they may form an 'authorised' part of the audiotext. However, audience reactions on the whole cannot be entirely controlled. At the 2006 UK Poetry Slam Championships Final (Theatre Stratford East, London, 11 March 2006) one contestant, who was prone to over-emote, was judged rather harshly by the audience but scored well with the professional jury in the first round. When he delivered a similar piece in a hysterical shouting tone for the final round, he received catcalls from the audience and someone even shouted "Judges, be honest!". Such a critical audible comment must be regarded as 'unauthorised,' yet it accompanies the actual poems as part of the overall acoustic event and influences the experience of other audience members. Since an audience has the power to contribute to the shaping of a live event, the concept of paratext becomes difficult to delimit with regard to unexpected audience input. The audience take on the role of co-author, as it were, which makes the entire production process of a live poetry event considerably less predictable than the production of a book.

Paratext can have various *functions* in live poetry. Its function is often *informational*, recounting the motive or manner of composition, explaining certain references, or providing an interpretation. Anthony Joseph's performance of "Aranguez" at the Vienna Lit Festival 2006 contains some phrases that are not included in the print publication *Excerpts from The African Origins of UFOs*:

> You see in those days
> the jammette, as they called my mum,
> she wasn't even allowed in the yard.
> It was for what they called her jezebel ways.
>
> ("Aranguez")

Joseph adds "as they called my mum" to shed light on the identity of the "jammette" for his Viennese audience. This explanatory comment roots the poem in the context of Joseph's life experience and thus leads the audience to 'read' it as an autobiographical piece. Since it is inserted in the middle of "Aranguez" it is not identifiable as a paratextual comment but appears to be an integral part of the poem to anyone not in possession of the written version.

Paratext can also have a *social* function, as British poet Jay Bernard's introduction to her poem "Underground" in Vienna demonstrates:

> So I'm gonna start off by just talking about London, which is where I come from, and it's crazy because here there's a sense of trust… they trust you to buy a ticket for the underground, and for the bus, and for everything else. In London they don't. In London you have a barrier on either end of every single line in the city. […] So it's kind of crazy and I'm gonna begin with this one which is called "Underground." (*VLF 2006*)

This introduction, comparing public transport regulations in two different cities, is Bernard's way of making contact with her audience. By pointing out the "sense of trust" she believes to prevail in Vienna, she expresses her appreciation of the ways of this foreign city, the home of her audience that she is visiting as a guest. At the same time she manages to tie this verbal salutation in with the poem she is going to recite – "Underground" – by pointing out that the experience it describes is one that she shares with her audience despite their different nationalities.

Paratext can further involve the dedication of a poem to a person present in the audience. John Siddique dedicated his performance of "Yes" at the Vienna Lit Festival 2006 to a woman called 'Iga,' whom he had just met in Vienna. These last two examples also highlight the great flexibility of audio-paratext at live events: it is a convenient means of reacting to circumstances quickly and involving an audience by paying attention to one's surroundings or relating poems to current events.

Finally, paratext can also have a *promotional* function. Gabriele Pötscher and Walter Hölbling have co-published a collection of poetry, which Pötscher introduces at the Vienna Lit Festival 2008 after recounting how they teamed up as writers:

> and our first book that we've brought is called 'Love, Lust and Loss,' which we are going to read a little bit from. And we thought we would start with the sad things so that we can get that over with – because it's called 'Love, Lust and Loss,' so we'll start at the back and do the loss first. (*VLF 2008*)

Not only does Pötscher mention the name of the book twice, which the two poets will be reading from, Hölbling – in the background – also picks up a copy of *Love Lust Loss* and holds it up for all to see. After all, the audience will be able to buy it at the festival book stand later. While Pötscher's introduction is certainly informational, it clearly also serves the purpose of increasing book sales.

Paratextual comments should by no means be regarded as a mere add-on to a poem, as they can have considerable effects on the audience's experience of live poetry. An illuminating example is provided by John Siddique, who frequently performs his poetry in public. On the page, many of his poems are serious, contemplative, even melancholy. In performance, however, his framing efforts run counter to the gravitas of the poetry on the page: he talks to his audience in a chatty, approachable voice, makes jokes and relates anecdotes that help understand his poems and turn them into something inter-personal, an attempt to connect with his audience. The paratextual lead-in to his poem "90 Day Theory" at the Vienna Lit Festival 2006 demonstrates this:

> This poem is called "90 Day Theory." I guess if you're sexually active already then you may understand. [*audience laugh*] But, I have this theory that … [*smiles and picks up his drink*] … sorry, I'm just getting very nervous and thirsty. [*audience laugh*]. You know you meet somebody, right, and … for the first three months … you know you've got something that kind of [*swings his arm*] propels you through the relationship, you know what I mean? [*smiles & clenches his fist in a suggestive way*] … and I reckon this period lasts for 90 days where you're completely infatuated and you can't get enough of each other and it's all kind of … you know, bodily fluid and all that sort of thing. And this poem is about what happens on the 91st day. [*audience laugh – JS turns to one of the laughers, points at her and says with a grin:*] Ah, this lady knows the 91st day. [*big high-pitched audience giggle*] Would you like to come and share your experiences … No. … So, if you don't know it then this is it, and if you do know it, well, it's for you. This is for this lady now here [*again points towards her, audience laugh*]. (*VLF 2006*)

"90 Day Theory" is a thoughtful, erotic poem about the transitoriness of love. Siddique recites it in a quiet, serious tone. It can hardly be described as comic, but after his set the audience will probably have remembered his performance as entertaining and amusing, which goes to show how important it is to evaluate live poetry in its context, of which paratext forms a crucial part.

Different poet-performers have different views about paratext, however. Peter Waugh, head of the international writers group "Labyrinth Poets" in Vienna, objects to chatty introductions and lengthy anecdotes, holding the view that a poem should be allowed to speak for itself. This is in line with a view of poetry as a self-sufficient art no way in need of explanation. Accordingly, the group was introduced briefly at the Vienna Lit Festival 2008, with the MC asking the audience not to clap in between poems. The group then went through their set without interruption, their performance being 'undisturbed' by paratextual insertions. Thus, a poet's choice of (not) including paratext in their performance is also revealing as to his/her view of what poetry is and how it is best presented.

5. Body Communication

While the audiotext will undoubtedly be the focus of a 'close reading' of live poetry – an art form that centres on the performed verbal text – the live presentation of poetry involves the physical co-presence of performer and audience, which entails an additional visual level of communication. "If you watch someone speaking, in almost any language and under nearly all circumstances, you will see what appears to be a compulsion to move the hands and arms in conjunction with speech," David McNeill notes (1), pointing towards the body's involvement in speech. The reflections and analytical categories introduced in the previous chapter can technically also be applied to studio-recorded 'audio poetry.' In order to account for the specific aesthetic experience of a live poetry performance, our analytical toolkit must be extended to cover the visual dimension of the performer's body behaviour.

The following chapter is concerned with the body's relation to language, answering the question what body communication is – in order to explore how it can be interpreted. Subsequently, body communication will be discussed in terms of its functions and elements.

5.1 Kinesics: Studying Body Communication

There are as yet no studies that examine body communication in live poetry performances, and even the neighbouring discipline of theatre studies holds little in terms of practicable guidelines. Notably, Erika Fischer-Lichte ("Zeichensprache des Theaters" 238) observes that the 'signs' employed in theatrical communication stem from a range of different cultural systems such as speech, gesture, or music, and that their meaning in theatre can be understood only with recourse to these primary cultural systems. Our ability to 'read' the gestures of a performer speaking on stage thus depends on our knowledge of body communication off stage, rather than on some specific code of live poetry moves. Consequently, it makes sense to consult more general studies on body behaviour, as they have been conducted in the field of kinesics.

"The founding discovery of kinesics" is, according to Keir Elam, "that each culture selects from an immense stock of potential material a strictly limited number of pertinent units of movement" (63). What can be deduced from this statement is that body communication is, to an extent, culturally conditioned, in which it resembles verbal language. The anthropologist Ray L. Birdwhistell, who introduced the term 'kinesics' in his *Introduction* (1952), concluded that our non-verbal body behaviour is not a random by-product of speech but, like language, a systematic form of communication. On the basis of the assumption that "the kinesic system has forms which are astonishingly like words in language" (*Kinesics and Context* 80), Birdwhistell developed his "kinemorphology" as a kind of grammar of body language, whose units – kinemes, kinemorphs, complex kinemorphs, and complex kinemorphic constructions – were organised hierarchically like the units of verbal language, i.e. morphemes, words, and sentences (*Kinesics and Context* 101).

While Birdwhistell's 'grammatical' approach has had its followers (e.g. Fine 120), it has to date often been rejected for its "linguisticism," i.e. for the "simple analogy with language" (Elam 63) that is applied. Language in the narrower sense of a "signification system with recognizable, fairly complex syntactic structures" (Ruthrof 24) implies characteristics such as intentionality, codification (i.e. a close relationship between material sign and signified) and conventionality (Kühn 137). Approaching other forms of communication 'as language' amounts to a "kind of linguistic imperialism that blinds rather than enlightens," Horst Ruthrof notes (22), pointing towards the danger of losing sight of the structural and functional specificities of body communication in an attempt to impose linguistic rules on it. For that reason, the common term 'body language' has been avoided in this study as it falsely implies the possibility of a 'dictionary' or 'grammar' of body communication. Although such dictionaries do exist,[1] Christine Kühn demonstrates how difficult, and indeed futile, it is to try and detect a codified, context-independent meaning of specific gestures. As an example, she points out how the conventional hand-over-heart gesture for swearing may just as well mean 'Me??' – in reaction to an accusation (Kühn 258).

Taking on board many of the challenges body communication poses to the researcher, Fernando Poyatos defines kinesics as the study of

> the conscious or unconscious psychomuscularly-based body movements and intervening or resulting still positions, either learned or somatogenic, of visual, visual-acoustic and tactile or kinaesthetic perception, that, whether isolated or combined with the linguistic and paralinguistic structures and with other somatic

---

[1] See, for example, Schwarz and Schweppe's *Lexikon der Körpersprache*, which defines the expression of 'doubt,' for instance, as a raised eyebrow or a rubbing of the chin. An example in English is Allan Pease's *Body Language: How to Read Others' Thoughts by Their Gestures* (1992). It is only one of many self-help books that promise to enable readers to master the language of the body and thus help them climb up on the career ladder. While Birdwhistell himself rejects the idea of a 'lexicon' of gestures (*Kinesics and Context* 235), his kinemorphology implies a definite syntax of body communication.

and objectual behavioural systems, possess intended or unintended communicative value. (132)

His definition captures some important specificities of body behaviour, such as the fact that it has communicative value though it may not always be conscious: we may unconsciously nod during a conversation and thus encourage our dialogue partner to continue talking (Argyle 11). Furthermore, body communication comprises movements as well as still positions and may occur in isolation or in combination with verbal language. And finally, Poyatos contrasts somatogenic with learned behaviour, suggesting that certain aspects of body communication may originate in the body itself: the mobility of elderly people is often constrained, for instance, so they tend to move slowly and with care. This leads us to a distinction that can be drawn in analogy to the voice set/voice action distinction in audiotext: that between body set and body action. Accordingly, *body set* denotes physical peculiarities such as age, sex, body build, or state of health,[2] while *body action* refers again to the particular body behaviour displayed in a given situation and which is, of course, based on, and relative to, the physical and physiological factors specified by the body set.

In contrast to verbal language (in its sense of an abstract complex communication system) the moving body does not generally bring forth denotative meanings by itself.[3] Seeing a poetry performance on video without the sound will reveal very little about the contents of a poem: body communication is meaningful in live poetry only in its verbal and paralinguistic context. However, body behaviour can modify the meaning suggested by the verbal text, as previous analyses have demonstrated: the body's contribution in a live poetry performance is not simply a redundant add-on to the verbal. Rather, we should conceive of "a triple and inseparable body, language-paralanguage-kinesics" (122), as Poyatos notes. In view of the audience's

---

[2] Note that Ray L. Birdwhistell terms this the 'body base' in his system of 'parakinesics' (*Kinesics and Context* 258-9), which he developed in analogy to paralinguistics. He interpolates a different concept of 'body set,' defining it as an additional level of body communication which includes a range of variable qualities (such as status, health image, age grade) that a person projects in interactions. For example, a sixty-year-old man can "project the image of a forty-year-old," as Fine (122) explains, in which case the body set contradicts the 'body base.' Birdwhistell's concept of body set can easily be subsumed under the function of speaker characterisation (see Chapter 5.2). For clarity's sake, and to avoid having to draw speculative distinctions between the 'real' and the 'projected' body, this study will adhere to the body set/body action distinction outlined above.

[3] An exception are symbolic gestures – a restricted set of 'coded' movements that have denotative meaning, which will be discussed in Chapter 5.3.1.

holistic perception of performance, Alberts similarly claims verbal and non-verbal behaviour to be "total and inseparable elements of the same communication process" (3). An illustrative example of this synthesis is provided by Adam Kendon, who recounts how a student told the story of Little Red Riding Hood, using the verb 'slice' on two different occasions: once when the hunter "sliced the wolf's head off" (51) and a second time when he "sliced the wolf's stomach open" (52). Although the same word was used in both cases, the first instance was accompanied by a quick vertical movement of the hand, the second by a horizontal gesture. The student's body behaviour thus provided information about the directionality and force of the hunter's actions that the word 'slice' by itself did not specify (Kendon 52).

As we are dealing with a highly context-dependent form of communication, the question needs to be considered on what basis body behaviour can be interpreted in live poetry. We cannot extract a lexicon of English body signs and the syntactic rules that govern their combination, as has been done for verbal languages. While cultural norms and conventions provide a rough framework for certain aspects of body communication (for instance how extensively we are expected to move which body parts during speech[4]) and verbal 'translations' for a restricted set of symbolic gestures (such as the V sign for 'victory'), many movements are not easily explicable in terms of a fixed 'code.' Rather, they open up a *meaning potential*, which "will be narrowed down and coloured in the given context" (10), as Theo Van Leeuwen explains in relation to paralinguistic features. Moreover, as with the interpretation of audiotext, this meaning potential may be *experiential*, i.e. it may be rooted in our experience of our own bodies, as "a knowledge of what it is we would physically have to *do*" (Van Leeuwen 94), or feel, to produce a certain facial expression or pattern of gestures.

In Segun Lee-French's performance of his poem "Xmas Kisses" at the "Seconds Out" Slam in Manchester (March 2007), which tells of an office party where "Christmas kisses are falling fast," the speaker notes:

> The walls are dripping,
> Saliva's alive and thick.
> No need to wipe your chin and ask your mate
> Does my breath smell of sick?
> Who cares when the kisses are falling so quick.
> They come in all shapes and sizes,
> some tongueless booby prizes,

---

[4] This point becomes clear when comparing a public speech by Italian premier Silvio Berlusconi with, say, one by Japanese ex Prime Minister Jasuo Fukuda, in terms of their body behaviour.

some wetlipped and mushy, all slobbering and slushy,
some rushed and mistaken identities,
Wait! Wait! [4a]⁵
Ugh! I thought you were your mate! [4b]

Fig. 4a & 4b. Segun Lee-French, "Seconds Out" slam 2007.

When Lee-French exclaims "Wait!" for the first time, he frowns and hastily wipes his mouth with his left hand [4a]. This cleaning gesture – the unwanted kiss and its traces are wiped away by the victim as though the girl could thereby make her mistake undone – is followed up by a facial expression of extreme revulsion [4b]. Our own physical experience tells us that a strong contortion of the face, such as Lee-French displays, is usually provoked by a sense of disgust at a highly disagreeable smell or taste which calls our muscles into action almost involuntarily. In the context of the poem we can therefore understand the girl's displeasure as a familiar physical sensation.

The other principle Van Leeuwen outlines with regard to the meaning of sound – that of *provenance* – can also be transferred to the study of body communication. "[W]hen sound travels," Van Leeuwen notes, "its meaning is associated with the place it comes from and/or the people who originated it, or rather, with the ideas held about that place or those people in the place to which the sound has travelled" (139). Similarly, certain kinds of body behaviour are associated with a particular place or a group of people, meaning that they can evoke an audience's ideas about the place or group. Mark Gwynne Jones's "Nine Types of Poet" series includes a poem called "The Yorkshire Rapper," in which Jones holds the microphone very close to his mouth, producing oral percussion in imitation of a hip hop beat and chanting the following lines in a typical 4-beat rap rhythm:

---

5   The words set in between asterisks and the numbers in brackets refer to the corresponding stills below.

> I move my hands in front of my face
> to distract you from the fact I got nothin' to say
> Yo, I move my hands in front of my face
> to distract you from the fact I got...
> Umm pt ah aUmm pch ah
> Umm pt ah aOoooooooooo
>
> ("The Yorkshire Rapper")

Accordingly, Jones moves his free right hand wildly about, "in front of his face," which together with the biting sarcasm of his audiotext, results in a highly comic effect.

Fig. 5a, 5b, 5c: Mark Gwynne Jones, "Seconds Out" slam 2007.

His gestures and hand position – index finger and little finger outstretched – are familiar from video clips of rappers on TV, as is his aggressive tone and syncopated rhythm. Since his meta-performative mockery centres on the connection between body behaviour and text in rap poetry, his own gestures become crucially important to the meaning of his live performance. Its humour depends entirely on the audience's recognition of the typical rap moves he is acting out.

In view of the lack of lexically decodable body signs in theatre, Peter Boenisch calls for a non-denotative approach to body communication (*körPERformance* 124). Like Van Leeuwen, he conceives of a meaning potential ("Möglichkeitsspielraum" 82) of body behaviour that is intersubjective in the sense that it is grounded in the audience's common experience of a performance. The individual spectator will then interpret elements of the performance s/he has conjointly watched with other audience members as more or less meaningful. What this means to the researcher of live performances, Guido Hiß notes in his introduction to the analysis of theatrical performance, is that we must make our interpretations traceable in order to avoid seemingly arbitrary judgements: we must specify the criteria of our selection of significant elements and their perceived relation to the context (80f). In this respect, the interpretation of body behaviour in live poetry can, in fact, be related to the interpretation of poetry on the page: both cases require researchers to justify their conclusions by pointing out specific elements or aspects in the written text or performance respectively, arguing in what ways these can be understood as meaningful in the given context. No matter whether experienced in performance or in a silent reading: poetry often leaves room for various 'readings.' Being confronted with a non-denotative communicative practice that is closely interlinked with the verbal text, it seems futile to try and posit *the* meaning of body behaviour. What individual researchers can do is to argue their case as one possible and comprehensible 'pathway' through the 'jungle' of potentially meaningful signs – to borrow Peter Boenisch's metaphor (*körPERformance* 78).

Nevertheless, certain general criteria for a differentiated examination of body communication can be discerned that may help direct the researcher's gaze towards different aspects of body behaviour in live poetry. The following sections will explore the workings of body communication in terms of its functions (5.2) and in view of the various elements – postural, gestural, facial, artefactual – it consists of (5.3).

5.2 Functions of Body Communication

In *The Expressive Body* David Alberts cites the following functions of movements and gestures: "(1) to express emotion; (2) to regulate interpersonal interactions; (3) to present one's personality to others; (4) to convey interpersonal attitudes and relationships, and (5) to replace or accompany speech" (15). In one form or another, these are all applicable to live poetry performances. A performer may choose to *express emotions*, for instance, through a 'sad face' or 'angry movements.' In Lucy English's monologue "I want to be a bitch," the speaker has an imaginary conversation with her family, telling them everything she has always wanted to say, as for example in her address to her son, which is clearly marked by anger:

> And you smell.
> I mean really bad, like last month's cheese,
> and can you look at me instead of at your feet
> and take that bloody woolly hat off, please!

("I want to be a bitch")

The phrase "**bloo**dy ... *woo**ll**y .*. **hat** off ... **please**" [6a][6b] is delivered with a deliberate regular rhythm of increased stresses that are accompanied by forward thrusts of the head and a downward movement of the hands [6a]. The words are thus rendered as repeated outbursts of aggression that register in the tone as well as on the body, as though an imaginary push was added to the imaginary dressing-down.

Fig. 6a & 6b: Lucy English, "Apples & Snakes in Soho" 2007.

A performer cannot only express emotions through her/his body communication, however, but also her/his *attitude towards the addressee or topic of speech*, as in the address to the speaker's partner in the same poem:

> And I wanna say to my partner:
> Just do it. Go and buy a Harley and black leathers
> and work out your midlife crisis.
> And I know, I know,
> your *job's a bore   [6c]
> you're *out of shape   [6d]
> you *don't know where it's all* going   [6e]

("I want to be a bitch")

At "job" English sarcastically rolls her eyes [6c], at "out" she touches her stomach [6d] and during "you don't know where it's all going" she waves about with her uplifted arms and shakes her head in an exaggerated manner [6e]. From her body behaviour and her tone it becomes clear that the imaginary addressee is being mocked – not taken seriously at all. The speaker adopts a sarcastic attitude.

Fig. 6c, 6d, 6e: Lucy English, "Apples & Snakes in Soho" 2007.

To *regulate interpersonal interactions* may not appear to be an obvious function of body communication in live poetry, and many poets make little use of this regulating potential of the body's signals, which seems to pertain to everyday conversations and dialogues rather than to the presentation of poetry. However, some poet-performers work very consciously with audiences and their reactions, as the following example demonstrates. Andy Craven-Griffiths' poem "Lottery Mentality" relates a series of scenes from the lives of different people who have all taken chances in some way:

> Four gifts to choose from, one was guaranteed.
> Maureen only had to call to claim her plasma screen TV,
> Caribbean cruise,
> 10,000 pounds in cash
> or a personalised luxury yacht for free.
> What about that...
> But first, the monotone monologue of
> an automated machine had to explain
> in painstaking ways, taking days, it seemed,
> the conditions of her inestimable fortune:
> The scratch card is invalid if it's torn or damaged,
> This includes misuse of nails, indents from being chewed,
> it's even void if *fingerprints can be found   [7a]
> or if it has suffered exposure to noise. *...   [7b]

> ("Lottery Mentality")

Through most of the passage quoted above, Craven-Griffiths holds the microphone close to his mouth with his right hand while gesticulating with his left hand, as can be seen in the first still [7a]. After "exposure to noise" he pauses, drops his arms and makes a doubtful face at the audience [7b].

Fig. 7a & 7b: Andy Craven-Griffiths, "Apples & Snakes in Soho" 2007.

While his facial expression – an uncomprehending frown – is a silent comment on the absurdity of this notion, the fact that he has removed the microphone from his mouth and dropped his hand to keep it still for a moment is a clear signal to the audience that he is leaving room for their reaction – permitting them to laugh, so to speak – and they promptly oblige. Ekman and Friesen have termed movements that govern speech interaction "regulators" (82). Prior to his performance Craven-Griffiths asked the audience to participate in the poem by responding to his refrain question "What are the odds?" with "So Long," as in the following passage:

> But maybe the next time
> the booby prize will be a colon
> that doesn't go wrong.
> But what are the *odds? *...   [7c] [7d]
> AUDIENCE: So long.
>
> ("Lottery Mentality")

At "What are the odds" he moves his left arm forward, its palm extended towards the audience in 'taking' position [7c], inviting them to respond. In the pause that follows he drops his left hand as well as the right hand with the microphone [7d], again to signal that it is now the audience's turn to exclaim "So Long." Thus, Craven-Griffiths employs gesture and face communication effectively to orchestrate his piece in verbal and non-verbal interaction with the audience.

Body Communication 155

Fig. 7c & 7d: Andy Craven-Griffiths, "Apples & Snakes in Soho" 2007.

To 'present one's personality to others' refers to the functions of *performer characterisation* and/or *speaker (persona) characterisation*. Of course everybody has a way of moving and carrying themselves that is peculiar to that particular person. Judgements such as 'an upright person' have a visual as well as a metaphorical dimension: they refer to posture and personality alike, pointing towards the assumed connection between them. A poet-performer is thus also characterised and identified by his/her non-verbal behaviour. While the function of performer characterisation refers to the poet's 'performance self,' which will be discussed in some detail in Chapter 6.2.1, the body may equally be employed to characterise and identify a persona, i.e. a fictive speaker that is clearly distinguished from the poet him- or herself. In Abraham Gibson's poem "Nancy and Reeva," the two characters emerging from the text are visually kept apart by a simple change of posture, as Gibson explains in an interview:

> what I do is I give myself a couple of pointers. So with Nancy and Reeva, all I do is fold my arms to play Nancy and then I hold one of my arms to play Reeva and that's the pointer and I just stick to that and then anything else that happens, they do and it can't be repeated. It looks really shocking when someone is trying too hard. It's poetry; it's not an Academy Award, you know. I keep it as simple as possible. (Gibson interview)

The two 'pointers' Gibson mentions are captured by the stills below:

Fig. 8a & 8b: Abraham Gibson, "Apples & Snakes in Soho" 2007.

The proud posture Gibson adopts to signal to the audience that it is now Nancy who is speaking [8a] does not only characterise Nancy as a haughty elderly woman, it also identifies her as Nancy, in opposition to the more soft-spoken Reeva, who is visually cued by a less defiant posture [8b]. Interestingly, Gibson's comment about the Academy Award reveals the body as still an uneasy participant in live poetry. While Gibson has clearly given some thought to the visual presentation of his piece, he is quick to point out that his body action really plays a minor role in his poetry performances. 'Trying too hard,' i.e. an attempt at 'acting,' would apparently be 'shocking' and entirely inappropriate for poetry, which is, after all, primarily a verbal art.

Fig. 9: Mark Gwynne Jones, "Seconds Out" slam 2007.

Another function of body communication is to convey *interpersonal attitudes and relationships*. In live poetry, this is particularly interesting with regard to the relation a poet-performer establishes with his/her audience. This is effectively thematised by Mark Gwynne Jones in his poem "Mumblemumblewoeisme," which is part of the series "Nine Types of Poet" that he delivered in Manchester in 2007. Jones mumbles the piece barely audibly from behind a book where he is 'hiding,' one could say. All the time he keeps his head low and has no eye contact with his audience whatsoever, thus acting out a particularly self-conscious type of poet-performer. Body behaviour may not only disclose a poet's confidence vis-à-vis an audience, however, it may also be telling as to the poet's willingness to engage with audiences. This ties in with previous reflections on the function of paratext, which may have a social dimension. Poets may employ paratext to engage with their audience or point to a view of poetry as a self-sufficient aesthetic 'object' that should speak for itself, if they do not. Similarly, body communication can indicate whether a poet views live poetry as a form of communication that visibly acknowledges and implicates the audience or as a one-way presentation that takes place more or less independently of an audience.

The last function of movement and gestures Alberts lists is "to *replace or accompany speech*" (15). It does not actually stand in opposition to the previous categories, as the body may well express emotions, for instance, or indicate interpersonal attitudes during speech. Furthermore, it must be extended to include the function of *modifying speech* – rather than just accompanying it. The visible body may convey additional aesthetic and semantic information that is not contained in the audiotext alone. The sarcasm of the speaker's imaginary address to her partner in Lucy English's poem "I want to be a bitch" is primarily communicated through the poet's body action, for instance. Also, in motioning towards her abdomen when referring to the 'partner' as "out of shape" [6d], English makes it clear that the addressee is dissatisfied with his growing belly rather than an undersized biceps, for example. Her use of gesture thus disambiguates her speech.

Lucy English's use of body communication in her live poetry performances may perhaps be regarded as special in the sense that English speaks of herself as a 'performance poet' who puts a lot of effort into the live presentation. She employs her voice very consciously and, by reciting her pieces by heart rather than reading them from a book, frees up her hands and her gaze to make the most of the communicative possibilities her body affords. However, poet-performers will always communicate via their bodies in some way, consciously or unconsciously, and the analyses above have already demonstrated that there are many different kinds of movements that may have very different effects.

To sum up, body communication may fulfil various different functions in live poetry: it is employed to express emotions and attitudes towards an implied addressee or the topic of speech; it can serve to regulate interpersonal interactions between performer and audience; it contributes to performer characterisation or helps to characterise a persona, and it reveals interpersonal attitudes and relationships. On the whole, it does not only replace or accompany speech; it can actually modify its meaning.

5.3 Elements of Body Communication

In the following, body communication will be discussed under the rubrics of gesture and posture, facial communication, and artefactual communication. The division is, of course, artificial to the extent that these elements of body communication must be read in relation to each other, as will be demonstrated in due course. The aim is to give an insight into different forms of body behaviour and to propose ways of 'reading' them in the context of live poetry rather than a comprehensive theory of kinesics, which is beyond the scope of this study. The functions of body communication discussed in the previous chapter apply to all forms introduced in the following.

5.3.1 Gesture and Posture

Fig. 10a: Posture: Anthony Joseph.

A gesture, according to David Alberts, is "any physical action that involves using a limited area of the body – usually the fingers, hands, or head – to express or emphasize an idea, an emotion, or an attitude, or to convey information" (2). Posture, by contrast, is a more static form of body behaviour that involves the whole body (Boenisch, *körPERformance* 97). *Posture* is an important "means of conveying interpersonal attitudes" and "emotional states," as Argyle (276) notes. Following Albert Mehrabian, he identifies two main dimensions of posture: *immediacy* is marked by a forward lean and corresponds to "non-postural variables" such as "proximity, gaze, [and] direct orientation" (Argyle 276). *Relaxation*, its opposite, may consist of "asymmetrical arm positions, sideways lean, asymmetrical leg positions, hand relaxation, [and] backwards lean" (276). Stills 10a, b, and c catch poets Anthony Joseph and John Siddique in postures of immediacy, and Abraham Gibson in relaxation.

Joseph bends forward and looks directly at his audience while relating the conflict between his mother and grandmother in his autobiographical poem "Aranguez":

> You see in those days
> the jamette, as they called my mum,
> she wasn't even *allowed in the yard. [10a]

Body Communication 159

Fig. 10b: Posture: John Siddique.

Fig. 10c: Posture: Abraham Gibson.

He knows this piece by heart and speaks it straight at the audience. At "allowed" he reaches into the auditorium as though he were 'handing over' an explanation to them, in an attempt to establish a direct ('immediate') physical relationship between himself and his audience. Posture and gesture are closely interlinked in the overall impression of immediacy he creates. John Siddique also looks directly at the audience, connecting to them via his gaze. His posture is very straight and upright, pointing towards an overall tension and alertness that holds his body up [10b]. It provides a contrast to that of Abraham Gibson [10c], who has comfortably shifted his weight onto one leg, bending his head to the right and generally giving a more 'laid back' – i.e. 'relaxed' – impression.

It is this greater physical tension that underlies the notion of 'immediacy.' Drawing on the human capacity for empathy, it can be transferred to the audience as a kind of alertness. Thus, it can be no coincidence that most politicians conduct public speeches in standing position: sitting automatically makes for a greater degree of relaxation, which may be out of place if a speaker aims for a direct relationship with the audience and to induce in them a state of alert attention, or even excitement.

In contrast to postures, *gestures* are instances of body behaviour that are of shorter duration and involve only a limited area of the body, such as the hands or the head. Poyatos identifies three basic qualifiers for the description of gestures: intensity, range, and speed (134). *Range* is defined by Alberts as "the amount of space an activity occupies or encompasses in its performance relative to the activity itself" (12). He adds '*direction*' as another spatial qualifier of gesture that relates to "the actual path of the movement in space relative to the body" (12). *Intensity* can be understood as "the apparent expenditure of energy required to perform a particular physical activity or the level of energy purposely imposed on an activity" (12), while the relative *speed* of a movement and its *duration* (12) determine its temporal configuration.

Gestures have been variously categorised by researchers of kinesics. Ray Birdwhistell's 'grammatical' classification distinguishes gestures "according to the classes of lexical items with which they are regularly associated" (*Kinesics and Context* 120). Thus, Birdwhistell identifies such movements as "kinesic pronominal markers" (121) and "pluralization markers" (122).[6] Paul Ekman and Wallace Friesen's (1969) functional classification postulates the basic categories of "emblems," "illustrators," "affect displays," "regulators," and "adaptors." It has influenced a number of more recent studies such as Krauss, Chen, and Gottesman's essay "Lexical Gestures." The authors note that they "espouse a minimalist approach to gesture categories, based on our belief that some of the proposed typologies make distinctions of questionable utility and reliability" (262). They propose four broad categories of gestures which seem to be loosely based on Ekman and Friesen's system, albeit with altered labels: "symbolic gestures," "deictic gestures," "motor gestures," and "lexical gestures." Except for the lexical gestures, their classification is well suited for an analysis of body communication in live poetry and will be taken up in this study. It provides very basic categories combined with a lucid terminology that prevents researchers from overloading their analyses with an excess of kinesic terms.

Krauss, Chen, and Gottesman define "*symbolic gestures*" as "hand configurations and movements with widely recognized conventionalized meanings" (262). In Ekman and Friesen's system these "nonverbal acts which have a direct verbal translation" (63) are termed "emblems." The V sign for 'victory' may again serve as an example here, or the fist as a threatening gesture. Symbolic gestures may occur simultaneously with speech, but they can also signify on their own. They constitute conscious instances of non-verbal communication, which is why they are relatively rare in live poetry as few poets will choreograph their pieces in such a way as to include pre-planned symbolic gestures. An example can be found in Anthony Joseph's "Aranguez," where the poet indicates the age of his child self not only verbally but also by holding up three

Fig. 11: Anthony Joseph, Vienna Lit Festival 2006.

---

6   Fernando Poyatos has chosen a similar approach, specifying "punctuation markers," for instance, as either "syntactical," "quantitative," or "qualitative" (149).

fingers:

> But that morning my mother brought my sister to meet me
> My grandmother let me
> And I ran to the gate, man, I was *three.   [11]

("Aranguez")

Deictic gestures consist "of indicative or pointing movements" and are usually "used to indicate persons, objects, directions, or locations, but they may also be used to 'point to' unseen, abstract, or imaginary things" (Krauss, Chen, and Gottesman 262). An example of a deictic gesture has already been discussed in connection with Lucy English's performance of "I want to be a bitch," where the poet points to her belly when speaking of the addressee as "out of shape" (see *Fig.* 6d). A deictic gesture also occurs in Brian Patten's performance of "Hair Today, No Her Tomorrow" in the following passage:

Fig. 12: Brian Patten, Vienna Lit Festival 2008.

> What's *that, she said.   [12]
> What's what, I said.
> That noise, she said.
> Upstairs? I said.
> Yes, she said.
> The new cat, I said.

("Hair Today, No Her Tomorrow")

At "What's that" Patten points upwards with his index finger, indicating that it is something located above the adulteress ("she") that attracts her attention, even before the verbal text fills the audience in on the "noise" she hears "upstairs."

"*Motor gestures*" consist of "simple, repetitive, rhythmic movements that bear no obvious relation to the semantic content of the accompanying speech" (Krauss, Chen, and Gottesman 263). Ekman and Friesen termed these gestures "batons," defining them as "movements which time out, accent or emphasize a particular word or phrase, 'beat the tempo of mental locomotion'" (68). We have already encountered them for instance in Lucy English's performance of "I want to be a bitch" (see *Fig.* 6a, 6b), where the phrase "and take that bloody... woolly... hat off... please" is delivered with a regular rhythm of increased stresses that are accompanied by a downward movement of the hands. In this case, the aggression of English's tone is emphasised by her vehement motor gestures. When David McNeill observes a universal "compulsion to move the hands and arms in conjunction with speech" (1), motor gestures are most likely what he has in mind: they occur highly frequently in everyday speech as well as in live poetry.

The last category Krauss, Chen, and Gottesman propose is that of "lexical gestures," which "occur only as accompaniments to speech, but unlike motor gestures, they vary considerably in length and are non-repetitive, complex, and changing in form, and many appear to bear a meaningful relation to the semantic content of the speech they accompany" (263). The term "lexical gesture" is potentially misleading as it suggests that the movements it describes have a denotative lexical meaning and can be 'translated,' potentially resulting in confusion with symbolic gestures. Ekman and Friesen have coined the term *'illustrators'* for these "movements which are directly tied to speech, serving to illustrate what is being said verbally" (68). They identify various sub-types,[7] three of which shall be introduced here: *spatial gestures* are gestures "depicting a spatial relationship" (68); *kinetographs* "depict a bodily action" (68), and *pictographs* "draw a picture of their referent" (68). Felix de Mendelssohn's performance of his poem "Kyoto Conversation" relates a conversation between a Japanese shopkeeper and her English-language customer who is trying to buy a game of Go:

> To the lady who owns the shop I say:
> "I want to buy a game of Go!"
> "Oh – a...game?" she looks at me quizzically.
> "A game" I say, making appropriate descriptive gestures.
>
> ("Kyoto Conversation")

When de Mendelssohn mentions the "appropriate descriptive gestures," he provides a pictograph with his right hand, drawing a shape in the air that can be identified as roughly quadrangular and suggesting the approximate size of the board game the speaker is asking for. The following passage from

---

[7] Ekman and Friesen also include 'batons,' 'ideographs' and 'deictic movements' among the group of 'illustrators.' For clarity's sake this study uses 'illustrators' only as a hypernym for spatial gestures, kinetographs, and pictographs, retaining Krauss, Chen, and Gottesman's terms for the categories previously introduced, i.e. symbolic, deictic, and motor gestures. Ekman and Friesen's "spatial movements" are referred to as "spatial gestures" in this study to avoid the confusion potentially entailed in introducing yet another term.

Abraham Gibson's performance of "Margaret Thatcher and her African Lover" contains a spatial gesture as well as a kinetograph:

> She said,
> You were once under the British *Empire.   [13a]
> You remember when Britain was great.
> She said,
> I am going to take the power away from the Unions
> and *squeeze their balls* until they break.   [13b]

("Margaret Thatcher")

Fig. 13a & 13b: Abraham Gibson, "Apples & Snakes in Soho" 2007.

At his mentioning of the British Empire, Gibson stretches out his arm and points to a far distance, in a spatial gesture indicating the 'greatness' and enormous geographical scale of the former British Empire. At "squeeze their balls" shortly after, he reaches down in front of him and closes his fingers, seemingly grabbing at the testicles of an unseen adversary. Thus, his gesture – a kinetograph – depicts the bodily action that his words describe, adding a concrete visual humour to the metaphorical 'ball-breaking.'

To sum up, gesture – a movement of only a limited area of the body – must be distinguished from posture, which is a more static form of body communication involving the whole body. Postures are characterised by the two basic dimensions of immediacy (forward lean, more energised and energising) or relaxation (sideways or backwards lean, asymmetrical). They are not only indicative of the speaker's bodily (and mental) state but may also induce this state in the audience. Gestures can be described in terms of the basic qualifiers of range, direction, intensity, speed, and duration. We distinguish between symbolic gestures (conventionalised movements with a direct verbal translation), deictic gestures (pointing towards persons, objects, directions or locations), motor gestures (rhythmic movements that accent particular words or phrases), and illustrators, i.e. movements that illustrate the verbal text, providing information on spatial relations (spatial gestures), depicting bodily action (kinetographs), or drawing a picture of their referent (pictographs). The examples discussed have demonstrated that gestures can be effectively used to express or emphasise an idea or to render it more precise and thereby add new information to the verbal text. Posture and gesture thus constitute important instruments of communication that can be drawn on by poets in performance.

5.3.2 Facial Communication

The face is often thought to play the most significant part in the communication of the body due to its high expressive potential – 'expression' (of emotions, attitudes, etc.) therefore being a major function (see for example Argyle 211). Facial communication involves dozens of fine muscles that allow for a multiplicity of expressions. The face is also the area of the body that is the visual focus during speech: people will usually look their conversation partners in the face rather than stare at their shoes, for instance. Earlier approaches to studying the face conceived of facial communication in terms of the often-quoted 'seven main facial expressions' – happiness, surprise, fear, sadness, anger, disgust, and interest – and focused on the development of schemata and scoring systems to 'decode' them.[8] More recently, Russell and Fernández-Dols (22) have rightly observed that the relation between emotions and their expression on the face is far too complex to allow for a simple classification into seven basic emotions. While they concede that a link between emotions and facial expression certainly does exist, they point out that even the assumed causality implied in the idea of 'expression' – i.e. the prior existence of an emotion which then finds its expression on the face – "remains untested" (17). This point is crucial for an understanding of live poetry. "Facial displays" can be "expressive *to* another person" rather than just "expressive *of* an underlying state," as Nicole Chovil (333) points out. Her statement stresses the intentionality and control often involved in facial communication. Poet-performers may 'express' sadness or surprise to their audience via the face without actually having to experience

---

[8] See Argyle 214-217. See also Birdwhistell, *Kinesics and Context* 260 for an elaborate transcription code for facial movements.

these emotions during the performance. In this way, the performer's face can communicate a wide variety of emotions and attitudes in live poetry, in accordance with the text. Rather than proposing a typology of facial moves, dividing the face into distinct areas which must ultimately be understood in their total effect anyway, I will point out with the help of an example how the face can be interpreted on the basis of one's own experience and understanding of nonverbal communication.

The possibilities of facial communication are effectively demonstrated in Felix de Mendelssohn's performance of his poem "Kyoto Conversation" (Vienna Lit Festival 2008), part of which is transcribed below. The asterisks and the numbers in brackets again refer to the corresponding stills:

> To the lady who owns the shop I say:
> "I want to buy a game of Go!"
> "Oh – a…game?" she looks at me quizzically.
> "A game" I say, making appropriate descriptive gestures.
> *"Ah – a game!" she says – knowingly. "What game?" [14a]
> "Go" I say. She looks at me disturbingly as if I were disturbed.
> *"Go?" [14b]
> "Yes", I say, "Go, you know, the game."
> "Go?"
> "Go" I answer.
> "Go?" She doesn't get me at all.
> *"Go" I say, somewhat defiantly. [14c]
> She looks up in the air as if I were mad. "Go?"
> *"Go" I say, pleadingly now, "Go. Go." [14d]
> She ponders, worried, unsure of her next move.
>
> ("Kyoto Conversation")

The poem revolves around a strained conversation between a Japanese shopkeeper and her English-speaking customer. When the shopkeeper understands, after some confusion, that it is a game that is being asked for, her sudden comprehension registers on de Mendelssohn's face as a sudden raising of the eyebrows, with eyes and mouth wide open [14a]. When she inquires what game her customer is looking for he responds somewhat impatiently "Go," with a falling pitch curve and increased volume, making it sound like a command. When she asks back "Go?" her confusion is apparent in de Mendelssohn's moving forward of the head and his squinting [14b] – a common expression of incomprehension that suggests a moving closer to the dialogue partner in order to see and hear better.

Fig. 14a & 14b. Felix de Mendelssohn, Vienna Lit Festival 2008.

In the course of this conversation the customer's tone progresses from polite to impatient, aggressive, and desperate, and the poet's facial behaviour follows suit, specifying the speech it accompanies and being interpreted by it in turn. When the shopkeeper repeatedly responds "Go?" the customer repeats the name of the game once more, "somewhat defiantly." This defiance finds its lively expression in de Mendelssohn's frown as he is slightly bending forward and emphasising his loud, angry utterance of "Go" with an accompanying hand gesture [14c].

Fig. 14c & 14d. Felix de Mendelssohn, Vienna Lit Festival 2008.

The speaker's final attempt at making himself understood is uttered "pleadingly," right palm turned upwards in taking (or begging) position. The poet's face indicates how the customer is frustrated with his inability to communicate his wish: he is suffering. His gaze and the position of his eyebrows (the outer ends pulled down) suggest that he may begin to cry any minute: his is a desperate plea. It is reinforced by a change in posture: de Mendelssohn ducks his head, thus shortening his neck, and looks upward as though he were trying to make himself small – a stance that is well in line with the act of 'pleading' [14d]. Much of the poem's effect derives from de Mendelssohn's facial expressions and his lively delivery of audiotext. "Kyoto Conversation" demonstrates very well how different aspects of nonverbal communication – facial expression, gesture, posture, pitch – are interlinked in live poetry and must consequently be interpreted holistically rather than in isolation.[9]

A factor in facial communication that deserves separate mention is the performer's eye behaviour. We have already seen how eye behaviour is deliberately employed in live poetry to express surprise (de Mendelssohn's "Kyoto Conversation") or a sarcastic attitude (English's "I want to be a bitch"), for instance. It also plays a crucial role in audience interaction, as Mark Gwynne Jones' refusal of eye contact in "Mumblemumblewoeisme" has shown. During a conversation, "looking is used to collect feedback, at strategic points," (243) as Michael Argyle notes. The gaze establishes a connection between the performer and the audience and thus not only contributes to 'immediacy' as one of the basic postural dimensions (see Chapter 5.3.1) but also signals to the audience a willingness to engage with them in a reciprocal relationship.

The face is the area of the body that will normally receive the most attention during conversation and allows for a multiplicity of muscular configurations. Due to its high expressive potential and its ability to establish a connection with the audience through the gaze, the face is an important factor in a poet's body communication.

---

[9] Christine Kühn substantiates her plea for an integrative interpretation of body communication with an impressive example: in an experiment, scientists turned the head of Botticelli's "Astronomia" a little downwards, by means of a computer graphics programme. Although only her posture was changed, interviewees would predominantly interpret Astronomia's facial expression as proud, self-confident and arrogant in the original but thought she looked modest, submissive and dreamy in the altered version (Kühn 156).

5.3.3 Artefactual Communication

"'Artifactual' communication refers to the communicative use of objects, including cosmetics and clothing" (131), Elizabeth Fine explains. A poet's external appearance and use of objects forms part of the visual information the audience receive during a performance and is closely connected to other aspects of body communication.

Live poetry is generally performed without props, an exception being the microphone and a book or piece of paper the poet may be reading from. Objects that poets hold in their hands may have a significant effect on audience interaction. For Patience Agbabi, "paper is a barrier, even if you're reading really really well" (Agbabi interview). Agbabi points out how paper may be impeding audience interaction by limiting the performer's ability to establish eye contact and notes that reciting poetry by heart "just frees you up as a performer" (Agbabi interview). However, reading from a newly published book – putting it on display, so to speak – may also be a way of advertising it, enticing the audience to buy a copy after the performance. A microphone may on the one hand limit the performer's hand gestures – and consequently, their natural expressivity – but can, on the other hand, serve as an interactive tool, for example when the poet points the microphone towards the audience to indicate that it is their turn to speak a chorus line or repeat a phrase.

In contrast to costumes in theatre, clothing is generally regarded as deserving of little attention in live literature. A brief anecdote will illustrate this point. In September 2006 the National Live Literature Consortium in the UK organised a live literature conference and showcase titled "LitUp." One writer read out a short story about a young woman afflicted by a magic spell that caused her to live in a permanent drought. During her reading, the author suddenly took off her shirt – apparently to visualise the heat her character was suffering from – and stood before the audience in a black sports bra. In the break after her performance various people remarked on the indecency of her little 'striptease,' stating that it had been 'quite unnecessary.' Although she did not read out poetry but a short story, the implications of these reactions count for both genres: as a writer presenting a work of literature (rather than a dancer or an actress in the theatre) it was inappropriate of her to take off her top and thus draw attention to her (un)clothing.

Thus, the amount of artefactual communication conventionally 'permitted' in live poetry ties in with the definition of live poetry as an artistic medium that is primarily focused on the verbal. However, poets will nevertheless make strategic choices when dressing for a performance in order to achieve a particular visual effect. Patience Agbabi notes that she chooses her clothes very consciously, sometimes adapting her outfit to the size of the performance venue ("if it's a really big stage I tend to wear my sequins, sequins look really nice [...] but you've got to have the lights on them for them to really work," Agbabi interview). Her outfit thus adds a note of grandeur to her performance, framing it as a special celebratory occasion. For Abraham Gibson it is not uncommon to adapt his choice of clothing to his audience, especially if the event organisers suggest a particular type of outfit such as a suit (Gibson interview), and Rommi Smith sometimes selects her stage outfit according to the work she is presenting:

> I'm working with a character at the moment, in this sequence of work, I think it's really – for me – important to look quite glamorous when I go on stage because that's her. You know, like on Saturday I wore a dress with some glitter in it, I wore some heels, I don't always. (Smith interview)

Smith's collection *Mornings and Midnights* contains many monologues, occasioning her to refer to her character Gloria as 'I' in performance. The first person pronoun makes it easy for the audience to identify Smith to some degree with her fictional jazz diva Gloria. Her glamorous stage outfit and make-up are appropriate for a jazz singer and thus help to create a more concrete visual image of Gloria – as a means of persona characterisation. In *The Analysis of Performance Art*, Anthony Howell notes that clothing can take on "a multiplicity of uses: to simulate, camouflage or intimidate, in its mimicry mode; to lure or to protect in its display mode" (16). Rommi Smith's choice of clothing can be regarded as an instance of mimicry, imitating the looks of a jazz diva, while the black sports bra of the author who took off her shirt at the "LitUp" showcase may have identified her body as a "lure," putting it on "display" to "attract others" (Howell 15).

To sum up, artefactual communication in live poetry is effected through objects such as microphones, books, clothes and make-up. Objects that poets hold in their hands (microphones, books) may impede their ability to gesture or establish eye contact, though they may also serve a specific purpose, such as advertising a new publication or regulating audience interaction. A poet's external appearance is determined in part by clothes and make-up, which serve as a means of performer or persona characterisation. The choice of an outfit may reveal a poet's attitude towards the occasion or the audience ('dressed up,' formal, casual) and identify him/her as (not) belonging to a particular group.

170   *Live Poetry*

5.4 Notating Body Communication

As with the study of audiotext, the interpretation of body communication in live poetry is best undertaken with the help of a video recording, which provides a less ephemeral, albeit remediatised, impression of the live performance. The act of interpreting itself requires the performer's body behaviour to be in some way put into writing, i.e. verbalised, notated, described. As can be seen from the examples above, the analyses in this study are conducted without the use of elaborate systems of graphic notation as they are sometimes employed in theatrical performance analyses.[10] In the audiotext chapter I proposed the use of *verbal description* – what Elizabeth Fine terms "natural language" (141) – due to its flexibility and accessibility. The same reasoning can be applied to body communication in live poetry: rather than overloading analyses with a bulk of kinesic terminology and an elaborate system of graphic symbols to represent individual body parts and their various movements, simple descriptions in 'natural language' can be used for paralinguistic, kinesic, and contextual features alike and have the advantage of being generally comprehensible. Furthermore, kinesic and paralinguistic features are best discussed in relation to each other and to the context of the performance rather than in isolation, and verbal description allows for a smooth transition between them.

To illustrate verbal descriptions of body behaviour – which is, after all, a visual component of live poetry – *stills* can be used as a visual cue. They effectively capture postures and provide snapshots of significant movements. A succession of two or three stills can indicate the direction and range of movements and thus visualise and specify the action described verbally.

These reflections on the body's role in live poetry already point towards the significance of the performer's presence. While audiotext still evokes the conventional notion of 'text' and, by implication, of a familiar 'readability,' the idea of live poetry as text becomes more problematic in the case of body behaviour, a form of communication that centres on the physical presence of the performing body. The situation is complicated further by the fact that the performer also happens to be the author of his/her text, and by an audience that is co-present and reacting directly to a performance, in a real physical – rather than a merely evoked – space and time. Like body be-

---

[10]   See, for example, Peter Boenisch (*körPERformance* 91). His study of theatrical body communication is based on 'labanotation,' a complex system of dance notation describing patterns of movement in terms of their duration and direction.

haviour, these factors are foreign to literary studies and its traditional occupation with verbal text. They are, however, immanent to the aesthetic specificity of poetry performances and must be accounted for in an approach to live poetry.

6. Contextualising the Performance

According to our earlier definition, live poetry is characterised by the direct encounter and physical co-presence of poet-performer and audience. This encounter occurs in a specific spatio-temporal situation, and it is this definite 'situatedness' that constitutes the performance's essence as shared experience. The material book may be stored away in a library for decades or centuries after it was printed and may be rediscovered long after the author's death to be perused at leisure on public transport, in bed, or wherever its reader happens to take it. A live poetry performance, by contrast, is marked by the simultaneity and collectivity of its production and reception. It depends on the common effort of poet and audience to make it happen in the here and now, and on the direct influence they have on each other by way of their physical presence. Audience members may be provoked to smile, sigh, or clap enthusiastically, by the poet as well as by each other. They may in turn provoke a poet to alter the tempo of his/her delivery. They may prompt him/her to change the order of his/her pieces, or to skip a line. They may drown out parts of a poem in loud laughter and request that other poems be repeated. A different audience means a different performance, as anyone who has seen the 'same' theatre performance or heard the 'same' poem twice on different occasions might testify.

The unpredictability of live performances, arising from these spatially and temporally defined performer-audience relations, leads Erika Fischer-Lichte to question the usefulness of traditional hermeneutic and semiotic approaches that are founded on the distinction between production, work, and reception:

> If there is no work of art that exists independently of its producer and recipient, if we are instead dealing with an *event*, in which everyone – though to a different degree and in a different function – is involved, if, in that sense, "production" and "reception" occur in the same space and at the same time, it seems highly problematic to continue to operate with parameters, categories, and criteria that were developed in separating aesthetics of production, work, and reception.
>
> ("Denn wenn es nicht mehr ein Kunstwerk gibt, das über eine vom Produzenten und Rezipienten unabhängige Existenz verfügt, wenn wir es statt dessen mit einem *Ereignis* zu tun haben, in das alle – wenn auch in unterschiedlichem Ausmaß und unterschiedlicher Funktion – involviert sind, „Produktion" und „Rezeption" also in diesem Sinne im selben Raum und zur selben Zeit vollzogen werden, erscheint es höchst problematisch, weiter mit Parametern, Kategorien und Kriterien zu operieren, die in separierenden Produktions-, Werk- und Rezeptionsästhetiken entwickelt wurden." 21-22, my translation)

Although Fischer-Lichte is reflecting here on the aesthetics of performance art, her point also holds true for live poetry, as a poetry performance is not a tangible object that can be studied independently of the spatio-temporal frame of its occurrence in any meaningful way. Neither can it be regarded as a product of pure chance brought forth by the spontaneous verbal outbursts of a poet in dialogue with his/her audience. Most poets craft their work carefully, after all, before committing it to print or performing it. In this sense, live poetry must be viewed as what Richard Schechner famously termed "restored" or "twice-behaved behaviour" (28) in his introduction *Performance Studies*: as "actions that people train for and rehearse" (28). These actions are to an extent pre-planned – 'restored' – while being marked at the same time by an 'emergent' quality in relation to their spatio-temporal setting. Schechner therefore regards the "aesthetic reality" of performance as "neither the same nor the opposite of ordinary daily reality. It is its own realm, an intermediary, liminal, transitional, maya-lila time-space" (124). With specific reference to verbal art, Richard Bauman and Charles L. Briggs explain this liminal condition of live performance in terms of a twofold process of decontextualisation and recontextualisation, defining performance as

> a specially marked, artful way of speaking that sets up or represents a special interpretative frame within which the act of speaking is to be understood. Performance puts the act of speaking on display – objectifies it, lifts it to a degree from its interactional setting and opens it to scrutiny by an audience. Performance heightens awareness of the act of speaking and licenses the audience to evaluate the skill and effectiveness of the performer's accomplishment. By its very nature, then, performance potentiates decontextualization. (73)

Bauman and Briggs conclude that "decontextualization from one social context involves recontextualization in another" (74), as part of the same transformational process. They thus locate the essence of live performance in the relation of the performer's speech to different contexts – echoing Schechner's notion of "twice-behaved behaviour" – and consequently call for a genuine 'performance approach' to verbal art: one that marks "a shift from a study of texts to the analysis of the emergence of texts in contexts" (66).

It might be argued, of course, that the scholars quoted above are associated with disciplines that have little to do with the study of live poetry as defined in this study and therefore their theoretical reflections are of limited use for our present purpose. Fischer-Lichte's performative aesthetic, for example, draws on the more radical forms of performance art that depend to a much greater degree on the audience's engagement, or even intervention, with the performer.[1] Schechner's performance theory is rooted in an overly inclusive concept of performance, one that comprises cultural practices as diverse as "ritual, play, sports, popular entertainments, the performing arts (theatre, dance, music), and everyday life performances to the enactment of social, professional, gender, race, and class roles, and on to healing (from shamanism to surgery)" (2). Bauman and Briggs concern themselves with verbal art in a very broad sense from the point of view of linguistic anthropology, often dealing with performances that involve a high degree of variability, improvisation, and audience participation, as well as an element of 'foreignness.'

Regardless of the disparities between their definitions of performance, the general conclusions drawn by these critics as to the context-dependence of live performance are highly applicable to live poetry. Like Fischer-Lichte, Schechner, Bauman and Briggs also reject the conceptual distinction between an objectified 'work proper' in live performance and its production and reception, pointing out the defining role of the social 'time-space' in which the three converge.[2] Live poetry is a verbal art form, and an "analysis of the emergence of texts in contexts" (Bauman and Briggs 66) by no means precludes a close analysis of verbal texts in all their complex materiality, which was, after all, the central concern of the previous chapters. Examples from these chapters have also shown that live poetry cannot be divided off from the physicality of the performer or the presence of an audience, who may participate in, or intrude upon, a performance in various ways in their specific place and time. If an audience can be regarded, to an extent, as co-producers (rather than mere 'recipients') of the performance, then traditional models of literary communication must be reconsidered so that interpretations of live poetry might factor in the social and spatio-temporal conditions of performance.

---

[1] Fischer-Lichte cites examples such as the ritualistic performances of Marina Abramovic, which often involve self-harming and may end with audience members dragging the performer off a block of ice in a decision to terminate her self-inflicted suffering, for example. See *Ästhetik des Performativen* 9-11.

[2] The anthropologists Elizabeth Fine and Clifford Geertz have also stressed the defining role of contextual structures for live performances. Fine's method for the analysis of folklore performances stipulates the need for a "report" of the "aesthetic field" in which a performance occurs, "if it is to be understood by readers unfamiliar with the live performance" (94). More famously, Geertz's ethnographic method of 'thick description' starts out from the recognition that forms of cultural performance only ever make sense in their specific context, which means that the researcher must relate them to that context: to "something within which they can be intelligibly – that is, thickly – described" (14).

6.1 A Communication Model for Live Poetry

In their *Introduction to the Study of English and American Literature,* Vera and Ansgar Nünning note that "the speech situation is one of the fundamental structuring principles of literary texts" (53), proposing the following communication model for poetry (53)[3]

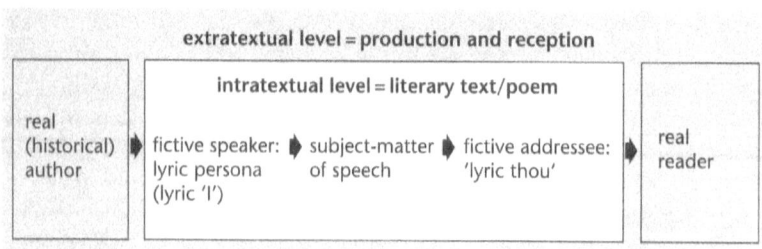

Fig. 15: A communication model for poetry (Nünning & Nünning).

Nünning and Nünning's model identifies, as its "central issues," "firstly, who the textual speaker is, secondly, to whom his or her remarks are addressed, and thirdly, where and when both speaker and addressee are situated" (52-53). These issues concern only the "intratextual level," which includes the "fictive speaker," "subject-matter," and "fictive addressee" of the text, and which the authors contrast with the "extratextual level" of production and reception, to which the "real (historical) author" and the "real reader" belong. The temporal separation between an intratextual level (the 'poem proper'), author, and reader – represented by the left-to-right orientation of the above diagram – traces the workings of print culture: the book has a material existence independent of 'historical author' and 'real reader.'

Live poetry – in which poems are realised anew in each performance in every new space and time, and in collaboration with each new audience – offers no 'poem proper' that can easily be dissociated from its producer and receiver. The following diagram outlines a modified communication model that takes this particularity of live performance into account:

---

[3] Nünning and Nünning's communication model reflects the basic constituents – addresser, message, and addressee – of Roman Jakobson's earlier model (cf. "Closing Statements: Linguistics and Poetics," 1960), which also points to the role of the context within which a message operates. The intratextual level containing a fictive speaker (or narrator) is also identified by Wayne Booth, whose *Rhetoric of Fiction* (1961) postulates a third level of literary communication which constitutes the 'implied author' – a notion on which Wolfgang Iser's concept of the 'implied reader' is predicated.

Contextualising the Performance 177

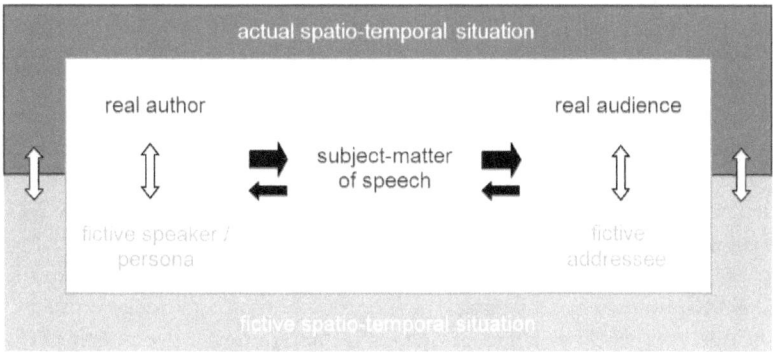

Fig. 16: A communication model for live poetry.

In this model, 'real author' and 'real audience' are located in the same box in order to underscore their direct encounter within a shared space and time. The arrows between author and audience point both ways, visualising the ongoing exchange between them. While their contributions to a performance cannot be said to carry the same weight – the poet is the main shaper and focus of the performance, after all, as indicated by the greater prominence of the upper arrows – the audience's contribution can be substantial and must not be neglected.

'Fictive speaker' and 'fictive addressee' – what Nünning and Nünning would call the "intratextual level" – are marked in light grey, together with the fictive spatio-temporal situation to which they belong.[4] They are represented underneath the 'actual spatio-temporal situaton' that includes 'real author' and 'real audience' to indicate that they are accessible only within, and via, this actual configuration of performance participants and time-space. The fictive speaker of a poem, as a textual function, is experienced by the audience simultaneously with, and through, the physically present poet-performer in a concrete space and time.

Furthermore, previous observations on the nature of performance as "twice-behaved behaviour" (Schechner 28), as a two-fold process of decontextualisation and recontextualisation (Bauman and Briggs 74), point to live poetry's simultaneous relation to different 'contexts': to different social, spatio-temporal settings. When a poem's fictional time-space, addressee, and

---

[4] The terms 'lyric I' and 'lyric thou' have been deliberately avoided in the above communication model for live poetry. They are problematic in so far as they imply the presence of a speaking (and listening) subject in a poem that is explicitly referred to as 'I' and 'you' ('thou'). Nünning and Nünning distinguish between "implicit and explicit subjectivity" (54), conceding that the fictive speaker materialises as a subject to varying degrees in different poems and that an explicit "I" may often be lacking.

speaker are brought together, through performance, with its actual speaker, audience, and setting, these may overlap or jar. In live poetry, the relationship between them is key. It is represented in the diagram by the vertical, bi-directional arrows.

Relating the different contexts of a live poem to each other thus forms part of its interpretation. The difficulty with 'contexts,' however, is that they are neither bounded nor coherent. A theatrical event, according to Willmar Sauter, is "defined by its position in the theatrical, cultural and social world at large" (11). The same is true of live poetry, in which events exist within an almost infinite range of circles of literary, cultural, and social contexts. To include "the world at large" in one's interpretation of a live poetry performance seems a rather vague demand, however. Defining 'context' as "the general situation in which something happens, which helps to explain it" ("Context") makes it clear once more that the decision as to what "helps to explain" a live poetry performance will ultimately depend on the researcher's own judgement as well as on her/his particular research interest. For Peter Middleton, it is crucial, at the very least, to provide information about "poet, venue, audience, reading series, [and] type of poetry" ("How to Read a Reading" 14). In her study of folklore performances, Elizabeth Fine further calls for an examination of the "ends" (i.e. aims) and "act sequence" (159) of a performance.

Starting out from the modified communication model presented above and integrating the contextual factors cited by Middleton and Fine, the following sections aim to direct the researcher's attention towards different aspects of live poetry performances so as to provide him/her with a range of questions from which to begin an analysis of the context of a performance.

6.2 Participants

The participants constitute, of course, an important factor for the contextualisation of live poetry. Elizabeth Fine proposes "participants" as a descriptive category that includes the performer(s) as well as the audience (158). As a hypernym, it has the advantage of indicating the collective nature of live poetry performances. A basic distinction can be made between *overt participants* – i.e. those who are visibly present during a performance in a recognisable role, such as the poet-performer, the M.C. (master of ceremonies), and the audience – and *covert participants*, who play a decisive role in shaping an event, yet may not be as visible in their function during the performance, such as a producer or curator.

The various participants' roles and significance in live poetry will be discussed in the following, as well as the aims and formats of poetry performances determined by the participants. These performance variables – poet-performer, audience, MC, producer, and aims and format – will be examined separately for the sake of clarity. They are, however, strongly interdependent and their significance is relational, since performance "takes place as action, interaction, and relation" (30), as Richard Schechner stresses repeatedly.

6.2.1 The Poet-Performer

Cast in the double role of author and presenter of his/her poetry, the poet-performer is the main shaper and focus of a live poetry performance.[5] Depending on the researcher's interest, s/he will provide such *basic information* as age, gender, ethnicity, physical appearance, and biographical information (e.g. training, vocation, or political background). This can be derived from various sources: from paratextual comments, interviews, critical literature, promotional material, or the researcher's own observations.

An example where the performers' appearance was made to play a decisive role was an event titled "Lip Up Fatty!", staged by "Shortfuse," London's "only weekly fusion of stand-up poetry, performance comedy and spoken word" ("Lip Up Fatty"), on 1 March 2007. It was advertised as "featuring the five best heavyweight poets and performers in London," and the order of performance would be "decided by a live weigh-in" as is common at boxing matches. The audience had a chance to win "a hamper of fat bloke food" if they guessed the collective weight of all five poets plus that of host Nathan Penlington, "the skinniest man in poetry" ("Lip Up Fatty"). Thus, the poets' corpulence functioned as a structuring principle and running gag throughout the night, with one poet – Roddy Lumsden – even adapting his performance to the evening's theme by reciting only poetry that had to do with food.

Frederick C. Stern cites a telling example of a poetry reading that centred on the poet-performer's biography. In 1987, young Russian poet Irina Ratushinskaya was released from labour camp in the Soviet Union and emigrated to the USA. Soon after, Stern attended her reading at the University of Illinois, Chicago, which he remembers as follows:

> The reading takes place on a lovely evening in April. The room where we often have poetry readings is too large for the audience, but that is frequently the case.

---

5   On the conventionalisation of the author/performer constellation in the twentieth century, see Middleton "Performing an Experiment" 33.

> As with many readings which have a political or other special element – readings by African-American or Latino poets, for example, which often bring out people who are there as a show of solidarity or support, rather than out of an intrinsic interest in poetry – there are people here whom we don't see at other poetry readings. Many of them are elderly, some of them, we surmise, Soviet immigrants. (70)

Although I would not subscribe to the view that the audiences attracted by African-American or Latino poets have no "intrinsic interest in poetry," Stern makes the important point that interest for a live poetry event may arise on the grounds of the poet's biography. Information about Ratushinskaya's plight was obviously a crucial factor for her reading, not only as a reason to invite her but also because it drew people who wanted to show their political solidarity with the poet. The event – an encounter of poet and audience – was thus shaped by Ratushinskaya's life history, and her poetry will have been understood in that light.

Another biography-related factor to investigate is the poet-performer's standing in the literary world, i.e. their *position in the literary field*, as Bourdieu terms it (*Rules of Art* 231-234). Bourdieu conceives of the conditions of production and reception of literature as a structured field in which agents take up various relational positions. These reflect the distribution of power in the field, according to the "*capital*" that the agents can command and which "governs success in the field" ("The Field of Cultural Production" 312). This capital is not necessarily of an economic order but can also be "symbolic capital," which comes in the form of honours and prestige, such as a literary prize may confer, for example (*Rules of Art* 142, 168, 221). When Nobel Laureate Seamus Heaney was invited to read at the opening of an Irish Studies conference at the University of Vienna in September 2009, his fame attracted a large audience that included several ambassadors. Heaney was introduced by way of a lengthy laudation and conducted his reading/talk from the richly decorated rostrum of the university's main ceremonial chamber. With a Nobel Prize, several honorary doctorates and a Professorship of poetry from Oxford University to his name, Heaney has a wealth of symbolic capital at his disposal that secures his prominent position in the literary field. Thus, his appearance at the conference opening attracted not only the attention of Irish Literature specialists, but also of major national newspapers and radio stations and brought to the event a mixed audience of academics, dignitaries, people with a particular interest in Heaney's poetry and those with a general interest in culture who wanted to witness a reading by a Nobel Prize laureate. What also emerges clearly here is the relation between the poet-performer's status, the audience, and the place of performance: the rostrum of the magnificent ceremonial chamber seemed a fitting place from which a Nobel laureate might deliver his talk but would have been a less obvious choice for, say, a young poet presenting his first book publication. The choice of the main ceremonial chamber as a location not only confirmed the prestige of Heaney's reading but also resulted in a particular audience composition. Had the event been staged in an Irish pub, for instance (provided that a Nobel laureate would agree to such a thing), it is doubtful whether the audience would have been the same.

According to Bourdieu, there are tensions between the various positions in the literary field which result in part from agents' struggles to see their own artistic practice legitimised, i.e. from conflicts over the definition and delimitation of the field itself ("The Field of Cultural Production" 322-23), which become manifest in questions such as what is literature/poetry and who is a (true) poet. With regard to live poetry, such tensions are noticeable in relation to the poetry slam, for instance, an event format based on open competition between poet-performers, who are judged by the audience. Jeffrey McDaniel, a well-known representative of the US performance poetry scene, remembers that "[w]hen slam first emerged in the national consciousness courtesy of the media in the early '90s, academic poets vilified it, saying, "That's not poetry!" Over the years that stance has been modified to guarded acceptance" (35). In the UK, slam has given rise to ongoing controversies among writers ever since it attained great popularity in the early 1990s, with many publicly voicing their dislike of poetry slams. When British novelist Martin Amis declared poetry dead, he conjured up slam as its "ghoulish afterlife" (qtd. in Hart). Anthony Joseph, a poet who also refers to himself as a "spoken word artist" (Joseph Home page) and frequently performs his work, calls it "the pornography of poetry" (Joseph personal interview). McDaniel, by contrast, insists that "even with its shortcomings, most slams are a lot of fun, which is more than can be said about some poetry readings" (37).[6]

One of the noticeable tensions within literary fields in the US and the UK alike is that between poets who see slam as an opportunity to present their work to a public and who appreciate its capacity for entertainment ("a lot of fun") and those who regard it as a sell-out to the audience. According

---

[6] McDaniel also points out that there are, in fact, striking parallels between the poetry slam and what he calls the "academic" poetry scene: "The academics initially criticized the slam for its competitive nature, which is strange, considering that one of the main ways page-based poets get a first book published is through fierce manuscript competitions that charge up to twenty bucks to enter, and are often plagued with whispers of nepotism. And arts organizations dispensing highly coveted creative writing grants often have a panel of experts score the applicants, not unlike the way one gets scored in a slam" (36).

to the latter view, slam is an event format that brings forth work of minor quality, or "not poetry." Thus, a poet's position in the literary field is indicative of his/her views of poetry and performance in general, as the example of slam demonstrates. Consequently, positioning oneself in the literary field affects other aspects of performance, such as the kind of venue a poet will (not) appear in or the type of literary organisation s/he will (not) collaborate with.

Another interesting aspect with regard to the contextualisation of live poetry is how a poet's performance style – understood as a configuration of audiotextual features and body communication – relates her/him to a particular *performance tradition*. The question of a poet's relations to a specific poetic school and tradition has long been a concern of literary critics. It has usually been studied in terms of factors such as diction, (evoked) rhythm, or subject matter. This approach can certainly shed light on live poetry performances (dub poetry as a genre is often politically motivated, for instance). It should, however, be complemented by an examination of the *performance* aspects of a poet's work (discussed in Chapters 4 and 5) as they relate to *performance* traditions, bearing in mind that a poet's individual performance style is also subject to his/her personal artistic development and may, of course, change over time.[7] While it lies beyond the scope of this chapter to provide a complete overview of stylistic currents and traditions identifiable even in contemporary English-language live poetry – something that Marsh, Middleton, and Sheppard (46) have postulated as one of the great desiderata of literary studies[8] – the following selected examples point to the historical and cultural contingency of performance styles, as well as serving to demonstrate the pertinence of a performance-oriented approach to poetic tradition.

In British poetry recordings from the nineteenth and early twentieth centuries we often encounter what Jed Rasula calls the "liturgical style" (236).

---

[7] For example, a comparison of Rommi Smith's first collection *Moveable Type* (which also came out on CD) with her performance of poems from her forthcoming collection *Mornings & Midnights* reveals a striking change from a fast-paced, witty mode of delivery to a more measured, relaxed style that is well in line with the jazz characters evoked in *Mornings & Midnights*.

[8] In "'Blasts of Language': Changes in Oral Poetics in Britain since 1965" the authors roughly sketch out the development of live poetry practices in the UK over the past 40 years, deploring the fact that since "the proliferation of readings and other more performative, theatrical, and musical forms of poetry events has not attracted historians, much of this work is already lost—neither recorded nor reviewed, despite its evident importance for poetry" (46). Lesley Wheeler strikes a similar note for the USA, locating one of the difficulties for researching historical live poetry practices in their "inherently ephemeral" nature (3).

Rasula cites Lord Tennyson as an example, describing his reading style as "ore rotundo" (236) – with oral resonance. Another representative is Irish poet William Butler Yeats, whose poetry recordings are reminiscent of religious incantations, associating poetry with spirituality and notions of the sublime. In Yeats's BBC recording of "The Lake Isle of Innisfree" (1932), published on *The Poetry Archive* website, the line "And I shall have some peace there, for peace comes dropping slow" is uttered – or rather, sung – almost on a single pitch, "slow" being drawn out with a vibrato that is far from the ordinary speaking voice.[9] According to Rasula,

> the liturgical style stresses (often unwittingly) an alliance between the high sublime and the sound poem, disclosing both as exercises in not understanding. The incantatory mode, then, legislates between the bardic posture of superior wisdom and a less privileged endowment, which is that of the stupefied or narcotically enchanted believer. (236)

Thus, following this performance tradition also meant subscribing to a view of poetry as a kind of elevated speech that has little to do with everyday life. This view can be traced back to earlier writers, for instance to Sir Joshua Reynolds' classicist *Discourses on Art*, where the author states that "the manner in which poetry is offered to the ear, the tone in which it is recited, should be as far removed from the tone of conversation, as the words of which that Poetry is composed" (206).[10]

While Rasula criticises the "bardic posture of superior wisdom" that the liturgical style apparently implied, he also offers some interesting thoughts on what he sees as the dominant style of contemporary American live poetry:

> Recently there has been a flight from or an evasion of sound, particularly the sounds that would awaken an understanding of that not-understanding which is so consistently bound up with poetry's heritage. Contemporary (or post-Vietnam) American poetry has developed a laconic, speech-oriented vocalization, wary of the narcotic blur of panegyric intonation and liturgical recitative. This idiomatic plainness reflects a semantic penury, a "commonsense" appeal encoded thematically to vindicate those who have felt threatened by the archaic claims of a presentient soundworld, the "raw being" of language; those for whom the sound of "plain speech" reassuringly disavows the need to glance below the surface of words. The measured sanity of the pedestrian reading voice certifies the

---

[9] The 'liturgical' style can also be observed in recordings of T. S. Eliot and Ezra Pound, for example.

[10] See also Engler 42-43 for a discussion of various historical poets' attitudes towards oral performance.

semantic stability of words on the page by means of its vocal autoregulation. (255)

For Rasula, this "laconic talk-poetry style" thus veils "a fear of what poetry might become if words wander too far off the page" (255).

However, contemporary live poetry is not restricted to only one performance style but rather comprises a multitude of performance trends. British performance poet John Cooper Clarke provides an example of a performance style that is far from 'plain speech.' Cooper Clarke rose to fame in the late 1970s coming from a punk background. As in punk music, where cover versions of Rock 'n' Roll songs were done at twice the original speed, he adopted a regular, high-speed mode of delivery (Penlington 16f) and made the 'electrified' hairstyle his trademark, signalling his alliance with the punk scene visually as well as acoustically. Similarly, dub poets such as Linton Kwesi Johnson and Benjamin Zephaniah draw on Caribbean reggae traditions in their poetry performances. Like reggae music, dub poetry is often delivered in Patois, over reggae "riddim patterns" (Habekost 2). Johnson's live poetry is especially marked by highly regular rhythms that hint at what Oku Onuora called the "built-in reggae rhythm" of dub poetry (qtd. in Habekost 3). Zephaniah's Rasta dreadlocks and his expressive use of his whole body in performance again associate him visually with reggae traditions.

The above examples illustrate that poetic style is not simply a question of a poet's belonging to a particular school of writing but that in live poetry a poet's individual performance style can also be related to traditions of performance. These have a historical as well as a cultural dimension and may originate in extra-literary fields such as music. Locating poet-performers in a performance tradition may reveal their attitude towards performance and, by extension, their view of poetry, and will thus broaden the researcher's understanding of their art.

The communication model represented in Figure 16 visualises the fact that a poem's 'fictive speaker' – a textual function – is experienced in live poetry simultaneously with, and via, the physically present 'real author.' Performance has been explained as a simultaneous relation to different contexts, i.e. different social, spatio-temporal settings. A central question for the interpretation of live poetry is therefore how these contexts relate to each other: *what relationship is established between poet and fictive speaker in performance; who is being performed?* For this purpose, it pays to reflect once more on the relationship between performer and (fictive) dramatic speaker, or 'character,' in theatre.

"In traditional dramatic performance," Keir Elam notes, "the actor's body acquires its mimetic and representational powers by becoming something other than itself, more and less than individual. This applies equally to his speech" (7). When actor Patrick Stewart plays Claudius in *Hamlet*, the audience is aware that they are expected to identify the real-life person before them with a fictional character: to 'read' Stewart's actions as the actions of Claudius, and his words as the speech of Claudius. The actor is thus turned into "an icon of the character being performed," as Fernando de Toro notes (76). Umberto Eco explains this condition of dramatic performance in terms of two parallel speech acts. The first speech act is the actor's: it is an implicit utterance telling the audience "I am play-acting this" ("Ich spiele das" 273). According to Eco, this utterance is truthful in the sense that the actor is informing the audience that from now on s/he will be telling lies. The second speech act is of a different order: it is the pretended utterance that is attributed to the dramatic character rather than the actor (274). The audience recognises it as such, which is the reason why no one in the theatre jumps up to call the police when Claudius is plotting to murder Hamlet. This differentiation between the levels of speech of actor and character is easily possible in dramatic performance (although the audience are simultaneously asked to conflate the two temporarily in order to partake of the aesthetic illusion that the theatre aims to create). Its conventionalisation is rendered obvious in programme brochures that announce the actor's name next to that of the character s/he represents.

Eco's reflections relate to J. L. Austin's speech act theory as set forth in *How to Do Things With Words*. Austin's concept of 'performatives' stipulates that certain utterances, such as "I name this ship the *Queen Elizabeth*" (Austin 5), are a means of performing an act if they are produced in the right circumstances. Austin notes that "a performative utterance will, for example, be *in a peculiar way* hollow or void if said by an actor on the stage, or if introduced in a poem, or spoken in soliloquy" (22). What he has in mind is again the fact that in the theatre no one will have actor Patrick Stewart arrested when he threatens Hamlet in the guise of Claudius, for example. For Austin, then, both theatre and poetry performances apparently create circumstances that render a speaker's utterances "void." As noted above, Umberto Eco suggests, by contrast, that the speaker performs two speech acts in theatre, one of which is truthful ("I am play-acting this"), while the other one simply operates on a different level – that of the fictional character. Similarly, Richard Bauman and Charles L. Briggs explain verbal performance (in a broad sense) as "a specially marked, artful way of speaking that sets up or represents a special interpretative frame within which the act of speaking is to be understood" (73). Thus, rather than treating it as a 'lie' or a 'void' speech act, they insist that verbal performance functions within a different frame, within which it must be interpreted. This is a condition that dramatic performances share with live poetry. If a poet recites a piece about pain, no one will get up and offer help. Although the poet's words are spoken to an audience in the present, they operate within a different frame.

However, unlike in theatre, live poetry audiences cannot usually draw on a conventionalised distinction between a real-life actor and an easily identifiable character whose name can be listed in the programme. The differences between the two art forms were also sketched out in Chapter 2.2, and two of these differences are of particular interest for an analysis of the relation between real author and fictive speaker. One is the fact that in live poetry the poet-performer presents him- or herself rather than *re*presenting a fictitious character, the other one is the identity of author and performer. What does it mean, though, to 'present oneself,' and what is the significance of the author's self-presentation in relation to a poem's fictive speaker?

Rather than 'standing for' a fictive character as a person, the poet presents his/her own text and thus "*performs* authorship" in live poetry, as Peter Middleton notes (*Distant Reading* 33): "when the speaker is the author [...] the moment of reading acts as a figure of an imaginary moment of composition" ("The Contemporary Poetry Reading" 268). Middleton raises several interesting points. The 'performance of authorship' alludes to the fact that poet-performers are not actually composing their poetry during performance but are 're-inhabiting'[11] words they have composed previously, i.e. they are presenting their poetry in a different context to the one in which it was composed and themselves as originators. This ties in with previous reflections on live poetry functioning within 'a different frame,' of which the audience is aware. Even if a text is autobiographical and expresses an emotion or idea experienced acutely by the poet when s/he composed it, the 're-inhabiting' in performance – though it may seem spontaneous and emotionally coloured – is recognised by the audience as temporally removed from the poem's composition. What matters, however, is that the poems they hear were composed by the person before them, who is now presenting his/her own thoughts and ideas.

The 'performance of authorship' – the author's presence in a live poetry performance – can be said to add value to an event, as Middleton notes:

> Authorship fascinates poets and audiences because the author is the subjective crossroads for the enormously complex transactions of institutional legitimation in the contemporary world. Unremitting efforts go into maintaining the authority of specialized knowledges and the rights of individuals to be its authors, critics, and revisionists. ("The Contemporary Poetry Reading" 269)

---

[11] US poet Jane Hirshfield talks of "re-inhabiting" a poem in performance; see Scott Dillard, "The Art of Performing Poetry" 219.

Thus, authorship is valued highly in our society and as such it makes a difference whether a poem is presented by its author or by a performer who is 'interpreting' someone else's words. The added value created by the author's presence consists, on the one hand, of his/her assumed superior rendering of a poem due to his/her first-hand knowledge of 'what it means,'[12] i.e. his/her performance is endowed with an exclusive kind of authenticity. On the other hand, the valorisation of authorship creates an interest in the poet-performer's personality that often exists independently of a particular rendering of a poem, leading to what Mark Robinson calls the "poet as personality cult" (40), which confers an air of "secular blessing" (40) upon book signings after a performance. This aspect of live poetry performances shifts the focus onto the poet's personality as perceived on stage.

Discounting any notions of a poet-performer's 'true self,' Anthony Howell points out that performers are "projecting a self or a persona through posture, through body language and through their clothing. They are acting being themselves, or, to put it another way, constructing a *performance self*" (16). While Howell is concerned with performance art, he is making a point about the absence of a dramatic character to be represented which also holds true for live poetry. At the same time he points out that the performer 'projects' a 'constructed' personality, which is, perhaps, not so different from enacting a 'character' after all. Just as the staged character in theatre is the only 'personality' an audience can witness, a poet's 'performance self' is, in fact, the only one that the audience has access to, whatever else they believe to be served.[13] Significantly, this 'performance self' is also

---

[12] Peter Quartermain criticises this "pursuit of the authentic," i.e. the belief on the part of the audience to be "in touch with the genuine and originary poetic voice" as the "archaeological fallacy" (226). Especially with regard to recordings, Quartermain sees a real danger of "establish[ing] some readings as normative and suggest[ing] that a 'good' reading is timelessly stable [and] transcendent" (226). Interestingly, in the modernist era it was assumed that the poet would "rarely be the best oral interpreter of her own poetry," as Lesley Wheeler points out, and that "superior recitation required unusual skill and sensitivity in the performer" (4).

[13] The notion of a knowable 'true' self or personality beyond a performance context is also rendered problematic in view of sociological and poststructuralist theories of performance. Ever since the publication of Erving Goffman's influential book *The Presentation of Self in Everyday Life* in 1959, the idea has taken hold that all human behaviour in social interaction can be conceived of in terms of a theatrical performance and captured by theatrical metaphors. Decades later, Judith Butler's equally influential *Gender Trouble* (1990) proposes a view of gender identity as 'performed' rather than essentially given. Gender, in this sense, is not naturally possessed: it is being

present when the text offers little in the way of an 'I' or a clearly-defined speaker/subject. Even in performances of texts that constitute more radical attempts at "decentring the self/subject," as is the case in L=A=N=G=U=A=G=E poetry (Diehl 96), the poet-performer's presence will be perceived to lend the text a subjective colouring through his/her performance self.

The main distinction in this regard between live poetry and theatre, however, lies in the conventional understanding of a theatrical character's personality as 'definitely not the performer's' (and usually not the author's either). Author and performer are rarely the same person in theatre and the performer's own life experience will not be assumed to be biographically inscribed into the dramatic text. Programme brochures citing the actor's name next to that of the character s/he represents render obvious the conventionalised distinction between the two, on which their representational relation is founded, turning the actor into "an icon of the character" (de Toro 76).

By contrast, no such set distinction applies to live poetry performances.[14] Its absence makes it easier, and seemingly more legitimate, to speculate on the extent to which the poet embodies the fictive speaker of the text s/he has composed and which s/he is now performing, i.e. this indeterminacy often invites the audience to enter the "autobiographical pact" (Lejeune). This is not to suggest that poet-performer and fictive speaker can simply be conflated in live poetry: one is a real-life person, after all, the other one a function of the poetic text. However, it is interesting to observe the ways in which poets consciously employ both the 'performance of authorship' and

---

'done,' and Butler goes so far as to claim that there is no "subject who might be said to preexist the deed" but that the subject is "performatively constituted" (34) through it, under social regulation. Although Goffman and Butler stem from widely differing research traditions and have different agendas, they share a view of social interaction, and – by extension – social identity, as a kind of performance. In that sense it could be concluded that any witnessed 'self' in a social context is inevitably a 'performance self.'

[14] The dramatic monologue may be cited as an exception here. As a genre, it is marked by the presence of a clearly-defined fictive character that is by definition not the author's (Meyer 29) and may thus lend itself more easily to the kind of impersonation that the conventional actor-character constellation in the theatre entails. However, even in dramatic monologues the poet-performer will never be 'read' as "an icon of the character" (de Toro 76) to the same degree as the actor performing in the theatre. This also relates to the fact that poetry as a genre rarely generates the powerful aesthetic illusion that theatre performances often create (see Chapter 2.2).

the frequently ambiguous relation between poet-performer and fictive speaker, as the following two examples will demonstrate.

In 2002, Patricia Smith, a famous African American writer and four-time National Poetry Slam champion, was invited to perform her poem "Skinhead" in HBO's "Def Poetry" series. "Skinhead" is a dramatic monologue, i.e. a poem that "implies the presence of a listener and insists on the difference between author and persona," the latter of whom "defines the pronoun 'I'" (Meyer 29). Its fictive speaker is a white supremacist, a skinhead who complains,

> I sit here and watch niggers take over my TV set,
> walking like kings up and down the sidewalks in my head,
> [...] So I move out into the sun
> where my beauty makes them lower their
> heads,
> or into the night
> with a lead pipe up my sleeve,
> a razor tucked in my boot.
> I was born to make things right.
>
> ("Skinhead")

Fig. 17a: Patricia Smith, "Def Poetry" 2002.

Smith's delivery is aggressive, her face is contorted. She spits out her consonants, her voice is tense, her words come out at a fast pace and high volume:

> I get hard listening to their skin burst.
> I was born to make things right.
> [...]
> I'm just a white boy who loves his race,
> fighting for a pure country.
> [...]
> I'm riding the top rung of the perfect race,
> my face scraped pink and brilliant.

That the poem cannot be autobiographical – or rather, that the 'I' of the poem cannot be conflated with its author – is obvious. Smith is visibly part of a "race" that is not "pure" and "perfect" in the skinhead's view. If she encountered someone like him in the street she might well be in great danger.

Fig. 17b: Patricia Smith, "Def Poetry" 2002.

And yet these words emanate from Smith's mouth – they are the speech of a black woman, an instance of visible irony, making for a startling effect. They are also her own thoughts, her own composition, which underscores the sincerity of her performance. The identity of the poet – who is performing authorship here – and its relation to the fictive speaker matter a great deal in this performance: it would not be the same if the words were uttered by a white poet, for instance. When Smith quietly pronounces the final words of the poem, her deictic gesture towards the floor in front of her at "right here" breaks down the boundaries between performance and everyday-life:

> I'm your baby, America, your boy,
> drunk on my own spit, I am goddamned fuckin' beautiful.
> And I was born
> and raised
> right here.
>
> ("Skinhead")

Smith is in America, after all, speaking to a crowd who are aware of the crimes against humanity committed daily by people like her skinhead character, and she speaks out to the audience as a black woman, addressing them as "America" in what can be understood as an implicit reproach. Thus, she makes conscious use of her presence in performance, drawing on the incongruity and tension between her own ethnic identity and that of her poem's self-righteous speaker.

Another example is offered by Patricia Foster's performance of her poem "Lips" at London's Spit Lit Festival 2007. Foster appears as part of the writers' collective "Malika's Kitchen" and recites "Lips" in a section devoted to childhood. She introduces the poem only by saying "let me tell you about Esther" and plunges straight in without announcing the title, thus giving her monologue an air of immediacy: "My lips seem to amuse Esther" ("Lips"). Foster speaks as a child giving an account of the harassment she experiences at school at the hands of a girl called Esther. Esther keeps making fun of the speaker's "dry rubber lips" ("Lips") and

Fig. 18: Patricia Foster, Spit-Lit Festival 2007.

incites the rest of the class to do the same. The poem then switches to a holiday in Jamaica the year before, where the speaker is taken care of by her grandmother:

> She'd just say
> 'come darling!', scoop up a bit of white jelly -
> smooth it over my lips with a protective touch.
> The heavy sun would just melt the Vaseline
> and keep them plump and moist all day.
> Then as I'd run off,
> Granny would tell me
> to 'take time and talk good with your lips'.
> That's why… that's why, perhaps, I can't say anything to Esther now.
>
> ("Lips")

From the passage about the holiday in Jamaica it can be inferred that the poem's speaker is the child of Jamaican parents who immigrated to the UK, just as Foster herself is a Black British poet with Jamaican roots. The poet thus seems to embody the 'I' of her poem, creating the impression that "Lips" is an account of an experience she actually lived through herself. This impression is reinforced by Foster's identificatory mode of delivery: when she utters thoughts such as "maybe my lips are big, as she says" ("Lips") she invests them with all the insecurity and sadness of a young, tormented child, pausing before and after, and speaking in a breathy voice that suggest she may be close to tears. However, the "dry rubber lips" instance is, in fact, made up, as Foster admits.

> Yes, the incident and Esther are both made up. […] I was inspired to write it because I wanted to document my own personal experiences of being teased and bullied by several people during my childhood and decided to create one character who embodied ALL the perpetrators – that character being Esther. (Foster interview)

Foster notes that she consciously chose the first person pronoun as she thought it "would be the most powerful way to convey the impact made by Esther on her 'victim'" (Foster interview). In a similar vein, John Siddique reveals that his first-person poem "Neckgrip" is not about his own experiences, although it may easily be read as autobiographical (the speaker's parents are introduced as "a black marrying a white woman," and Siddique's father came to Europe from Pakistan). He also consciously uses the pronoun 'I,' explaining that

> a closely observed personal poem gives the appearance of the author talking about themselves, which allows the reader to see a narrative happening that is removed from them [...]. That is the device [...], that the reader will empathise and see. By me saying the word "I" it takes the pressure off them. Very much like in the 1960's *Star Trek*: issues that were happening on earth, racism and war, were handed out to alien races so that we could talk about them. (Siddique, "Of You and I" 180-81)

Like John Siddique, Patricia Foster regards the first-person pronoun as a powerful device allowing the reader to empathise. Her performance of "Lips" at the Spit Lit Festival shows that this effect is particularly noticeable in live poetry where the poet is physically present, appearing to 'embody' the 'I' she pronounces and delivering the poem in a way that suggests her emotional involvement with the text.

This double role of 'poet-performer' in live poetry is particularly significant given that the ontological differentiation between artefact and reality counts as one of the axiomatic laws of literary studies – indeed, one of the first concepts students of English literature encounter is that of 'persona,' as they are instructed to refer to what 'the narrator says' or 'the speaker says' rather than what 'the author says' when discussing a text. In live poetry, however, it is indeed the author who is standing in front of an audience uttering the words that must technically be attributed to the 'fictive speaker,' i.e. to an intratextual construct rather than a real-life person. As the 'speaker' emerges in performance through the person of the author, this conceptual split is much harder for the audience to realise in live poetry than when dealing with print. The spoken word still seems to be "entirely tied up with the person," as Sybille Krämer observes ("Das gesprochene Wort scheint in seiner Fluidität noch ein Attribut des Sprechers zu sein, ganz und gar verwoben mit ihm als Person. Erst die Institution der Schrift, also der Text, eröffnet den Raum für eine Epistemologie, die auf der Dissoziierung von Können und Person beruht." 340, my translation). The point of Foster's example is not, however, to annihilate, or even to question, the distinction in literary studies between the author of a text and its speaker, but rather to reveal how poet-performers deliberately play with the fact that they, as a person who is visible and audible in performance, can easily be 'read into' the performed text.

To what extent the audience will feel called upon to make this connection depends on several factors, which can be deduced from the examples above. First of all, how far the poet-performer seems to 'embody' a poem's speaker will depend on the composition of the text: A poem that contains many instances of an 'I' and is marked by a clearly-defined subjectivity will more readily be understood as imparting personal life experience in performance than one that is lacking these attributes. Second, a poet's performance style, especially his/her perceived emotional involvement in the material, gives the audience more or less reason to assume a biographical connection between author and text. And finally, an important factor is the noticeable overlap of character traits and biographical facts, i.e. the extent to which a poem's (fictive) speaker has been assigned experiences or qualities that also characterise the poet. These may sometimes be visible – Patricia Smith is quite obviously not of the same sex and ethnicity as the "Skinhead" of her poem – or the relevant information may be provided in the paratext.

The potential impact of the poet-performer's double role, through the extent to which s/he is perceived to embody the poem's speaker and how the real and fictive relate to each other, becomes clear in the case of US poet Amiri Baraka, who was made to resign from his post of New Jersey's poet laureate in 2003. Certain passages in Baraka's poem "Somebody Blew Up America" had been interpreted as an incitement to anti-Semitism, insinuating that the attacks of 9/11 had been the product of a Jewish conspiracy. The poem can be understood as an extended anaphoric rant against various forms of injustice, oppression, and imperialism, as in

> [...]
> Who killed Malcolm, Kennedy & his Brother
> Who killed Dr King, Who would want such a thing?
>   Are they linked to the murder of Lincoln?
> Who invaded Grenada
> Who made money from apartheid
> Who keep the Irish a colony
> Who overthrow Chile and Nicaragua later
> [...]
>
> ("Somebody Blew Up America")

Dennis Büscher-Ulbrich notes that "Baraka consciously brings into play existing conspiracy theories to underline one of the poem's central issues – the shaping of public opinion on the basis of fabricated 'facts' and the manufacturing of consent in times of political crisis" (94). One of these conspiracy theories concerned the alleged Israeli involvement in 9/11:

> Who knew the World Trade Center was gonna get bombed
> Who told 4000 Israeli workers at the Twin Towers
>   To stay home that day
>
> ("Somebody Blew Up America")

Although Baraka had performed the poem before on several other occasions, the controversy was triggered by his performance at a major poetry festival in New Jersey, in September 2002 (Büscher-Ulbrich 90). Those who accused him of ideological slant explicitly mentioned his performance at the festival, at which he was introduced as Poet Laureate of New Jersey and where he recited the poem to a large audience (Davidson and Goldstein). Apparently, Baraka's "'angry' persona" (90) – his aggressive performance style – was a deciding factor in the accusations against him. In this instance, Baraka's critics did not distinguish between the poem's fictive speaker and its author: they read (heard) the said passage out of context, as a direct public statement by a political activist, "with profound real world implications" (Büscher-Ulbrich 89). Researchers of live poetry ought, of course, to distinguish between real-life author and fictive speaker, the latter of which is a textual function rather than a living subject. However, Amiri Baraka's historical case seems to confirm Sybille Krämer's claim that on a perceptual level the spoken word still appears to listeners as "entirely tied up" with the speaker (340, my translation).

6.2.2 The Audience

Listing the audience as 'participants' in, rather than 'recipients' of, live poetry points towards their definitive role in a poetry performance. For Nicholas Abercrombie, the very notion of performance in general as "a kind of activity in which the person performing accentuates his or her behaviour under the scrutiny of others" (40) implies some kind of audience. In live poetry specifically we are dealing with what he terms the "simple audience," (44), as opposed to the "mass audience" of television, for instance. Simple audiences are marked by "high attention," a certain "ceremonial quality," and "a communication of some kind between a sender and a receiver" that is "fairly direct" and typically takes place in a "public space" (Abercrombie 44).

In theatre, which equally caters to 'simple audiences,' the role of the spectator has been described as a form of "patronage" which "can be said to *initiate* the communicative circuit (his arrival and readiness being, as it were, the preliminary signals which provoke the performers proper into action [...])" (Elam 30). Thus, the mere presence of an audience makes a performance possible by giving it its raison d'être, but 'presence' alone does not exhaust the audience's role in, and power over, a performance, as the following statement by poet Denise Levertov demonstrates: "I am exhilarated by a good response and feel flat when there's a flat one; and a good response for one poem makes one read the next one better, & so on" (qtd. in Ginsberg 91). Similarly, Anthony Joseph notes that a good performance for him means "getting the *acknowledgement* from the audience that you're connected" (Joseph personal interview, my emphasis). Thus, not only is the audience present, it can also respond to a performance in various noticeable ways and thereby impact directly on the quality of the performance. A live poetry performance, in this sense, is the result of the communication between performer and audience: it is a collective experience that is time-bound as well as space-bound. The audience takes on the function of co-creator, which is why Erika Fischer-Lichte calls for an approach to live performances that transcends the traditional distinction between production, work, and reception (*Ästhetik* 21-22).

This raises obvious methodological questions as regards the analysis and interpretation of live poetry. Reader response theory – the branch of literary studies that most obviously deals with the 'reader's' contribution to literary communication – assumes a 'solitary reader' on the receiving end of literature, so much so that the actual response of this isolated individual cannot be accessed by researchers and must thus be theorised, as in Wolfgang Iser's concept of the 'implied reader' (*Der implizite Leser*). With the de-individualised 'implied reader' being studied as a function of the literary text, Iser renders questions about the response of actual readers superfluous while at the same time upholding the conceptual separation of production, reception, and 'work proper' (to which he attributes control over the reading experience).[15]

In live poetry, however, production, text and reception merge in the eventness of a performance that is effected before, and with, an actual audi-

---

[15] That is not to say that reader response theory as a whole has nothing to offer for an interpretation of live poetry: Hans Robert Jauß's concept of the reader's 'horizon of expectations' ("Erwartungshorizont," *Toward an Aesthetic of Reception*) foregrounds the historical situatedness of all literary activity, which is certainly a valid point for the study of an art form as context-dependent as live poetry. Stanley Fish's notion of 'interpretive communities' (*Is There A Text in This Class?*), moreover, insists that a reader's response to a text is culturally shaped as the individual reader is part of a (cultural/social/professional…) community that shares certain strategies of interpretation which are brought to a text. On the whole, reader response theory must be credited with shifting the focus towards the reader as the locus of meaning and raising awareness of the act of reading as a historically and culturally contingent process. It nevertheless posits the reader's experience as an individual, 'solitary' experience, disregarding the possibility of a collective reception in which an audience's visible and audible responses directly impact on each other and on the poet-performer. For a discussion of reader response theory in relation to theatre, see Susan Bennett 34-54.

ence rather than just an implied one. Like the performer, the audience of live poetry is observable and can be described as a group in terms of *basic characteristics* such as age, gender, ethnicity, political orientation or social background, depending again on the researcher's particular interest and the information available. Information that is deemed relevant but which cannot be gained by observation alone may sometimes be obtained from the event organiser, who may be able to provide audience statistics, for instance. A description of the audience should also include the size of the group, particularly in relation to the venue.

A live audience responds, to some degree, visibly and audibly to the activity of the poet-performer. "*Spectator-performer communication*," as Elam (86) terms it, may take on the form of anything from clapping, laughter, tears, yawning, and nodding to appreciative cheers, derisive catcalls, and verbal comments (such as the loud demand "Judges be honest!" uttered by an audience member at the 2006 UK Poetry Slam Championships at Stratford East Theatre, as an expression of his discontent with a performer who was prone to over-emote). Malte Möhrmann distinguishes between "*latent*" and "*manifest*" audience response (166), depending on the degree of its conspicuity. Extreme audience reactions such as catcalls are thus classified as 'manifest' while the behaviour of an audience that is sending few distinct audible and visible signals ranges nearer the pole of 'latent.' The use of the term 'latent' is significant in that it points to the fact that human beings "cannot not react" upon each other when they meet, as Erika Fischer-Lichte (*Ästhetik* 67) states in imitation of Watzlawick's famous dictum.[16] This is not only true for the audience but also, of course, for the poet-performer, who will in turn react to the audience signals s/he perceives. In this context Fischer-Lichte speaks of a self-regulating "*feedback loop*" ("feedback-Schleife," *Ästhetik* 59), whose workings are never entirely predictable.

For some performers the audience's reactions may appear to be of minor importance – though Keir Elam claims in a theatre context that spectator-performer communication "will affect, if nothing else, the degree of the actor's commitment to his work" (86-7).[17] Others deliberately activate the feedback loop and play upon the audience's power to respond and contribute actively to a performance. Dub poets, for instance, often include call-and-response patterns in their live poetry as a tribute to its social significance as a group experience (Habekost 92).

---

[16] "Man kann nicht nicht kommunizieren." Watzlawick et al 1990, 53.
[17] This is corroborated by Rommi Smith's claim, "I feed off the audience's energy" (Smith interview).

However, it must be remembered that the audience does not only react to the poet-performer: audience members also react to each other's presence in what Elam terms "*spectator-spectator communication*" (87). He identifies three main effects audience members may have on each other:

> *stimulation* (laughter in one part of the auditorium provokes a similar reaction elsewhere), *confirmation* (spectators find their own responses reinforced by others) and *integration* (the single audience member is encouraged, in consequence, to surrender his individual function in favour of the larger unit of which he is a part). (Elam 87)

What this means is that groups tend towards homogeneity in their response to a performance: "In almost all cases, laughter, derision, and applause is infectious," as Susan Bennett notes (153).[18] Sometimes, the visible or audible reactions of other audience members are not only infectious; they are potentially eye-opening as well. A personal experience will serve as an example here: Suzanne Andrade's performance of her narrative poem "Goring-by-Sea" at "OneTaste," an event organised as part of the "Shot from the Lip" Season at Bedford's Globe Theatre on 4 March 2007. I had listened to the poem on Andrade's self-published audio CD *Thousands of Men and Women Running* long before the event. The recording features the same eerie background music that was put on during Andrade's performance at "OneTaste": a computer-generated sound reminiscent of slow, painful mewing, which added a surreal, uncanny note to Andrade's remarkably sober recitation. As in the recording, Andrade at The Globe delivered the piece in a serious tone, with few dynamic or pitch variations, and kept a perfectly straight face:

> [...] Their bedsit smells of butter.
> The wallpaper is covered in crayon clouds and birds.
> The carpet is crawling with silverfish.
> Carol feels around under the sofa,
> finds an open tin of tuna and a fork.
> She still collects Natwest pigs.
> They stand porkishly on top of the gas fire.
> She doesn't open the curtains any more.
> With a mouth full of tuna and brine
> and a face full of fear she says

---

[18] The metaphor of 'contagiousness' is also applied by Fischer-Lichte ("Ansteckung," *Ästhetik* 55) and Anne Ubersfeld (128) to denote the fact that a live performance is in part determined by what happens between individual spectators.

Was that the door? [...]

("Goring-by-Sea")

In her Eton crop, dark eye-liner, and frilled collar Andrade looked like a 1920's flapper. When I had listened to the recorded poem and its surreal text, the uncanny sound effects had made such a strong impression on me that all I had sensed was a grotesque air of unease and foreboding. However, I was surprised to find that the audience at the Globe laughed heartily in several places, and it was only on account of their reactions that I suddenly realised how outrageously funny Andrade's poem was, a fact which had somehow escaped me. Thus, the reaction of other audience members was a revelation for me: it radically changed my perception of the fictitious world the poem evoked.

Consequently, the audience's experience of a live poetry event is not only dependent on the poet's performance and the impression s/he makes on her/his audience but also on the audience itself and the dynamic relationship between individual audience responses. Live poetry thus provides an aesthetic experience as well as a social one. The 'contagiousness' of audience response can, of course, also affect the researcher of live poetry as an audience member, who should therefore be aware of the workings of spectator-spectator communication.

Both the development of spectator-performer communication and spectator-spectator communication during an event also depend on the "implicit or explicit *expectations for performance*" (Fine 62) as raised by a range of interrelated factors such as time and location, type of event (e.g. open mic vs. high-profile reading by Nobel prize winner), or the genre(s) presented (e.g. humorous poetry vs. elegy) – in other words, on the different frames of reference activated. Audience expectation – and, by extension, audience behaviour – can be guided by pre-performance elements such as publicity, as well as during performance. An example is the event "Lip Up Fatty!," which, as previously mentioned, was advertised as "Featuring the five best heavyweight poets and performers in London," and the order of performance would be "decided by a live weigh-in" as is common at boxing matches. "Lip Up Fatty!" is the title of a single released by British ska revival band Bad Manners and refers to the obesity of its front man Buster Bloodvessel. Together with the announcement of "heavyweight poets" and the "live weigh-in," this title signalled to prospective attendees that they could expect an evening of poetry that would also be entertaining in an unusual and rather informal way. The venue was a function room above a North London pub and held approximately fifty people. The audience appeared rather young, loud, and cheerful, at the beginning they were chatting away, drink in hand, as the pub location suggested. About half the audience were standing, which added a different kind of energy to the event, as it required a higher degree of wakefulness (being comfortably seated makes it easier to let one's attention wander). The host Nathan Penlington wore blue denims and a white shirt hanging loosely over his trousers, stressing the laid-back atmosphere of the event. The live weigh-in was carried out with the help of bathroom scales and raised the mood of the crowd further. When one of the performers, Phill Jupitus, walked on stage in his casual red T-shirt, denim shirt, hat and earring for the weigh-in he grumbled "Get another scale" when the scales could not accommodate his body weight, prompting more audience laughter. Then one spectator noisily advised Jupitus to "take your hat off" and the poet complied, which finally caused an eruption of laughter from the audience.

All this was happening before the performers presented their poetry, creating a friendly, informal atmosphere in which audience response was obviously welcome and encouraged. It was carried over into the readings, making for plenty of hearty applause and cheers for the poets when they were announced as well as when they had completed their set. And a good audience response functions, in turn, not only as a measure of success for the producer of the event but also impacts back on the poet-performers, encouraging them to "read the next one better," as Denise Levertov (qtd. in Ginsberg 91) notes.

Just as the physical presence of the poet-performer raises questions about the perceived overlap between real-life author and fictive speaker, live poetry may create an interesting *relationship between the physically present audience and a poem's fictive addressee(s)*. While the 'fictive addressee' emerges through the poet's rendering of a poem, the poet is simultaneously confronted with a real-life audience to whom s/he addresses his/her words. Again, some poet-performers deliberately play on the physical co-presence of author and audience in this respect, as, for example, Mirha-Soleil Ross, a transsexual Canadian spoken-word performer, sex workers' rights activist and prostitute. Trish Salah explains that in Ross's monologues,

> Ross's audience is positioned as the audience of the character she is performing. Consequently, audience members find themselves repeatedly addressed by and implicated in overlapping discursive contexts about abolitionist feminism, liberal 'co-existing with prostitutes' programs that aim for the precise opposite and whore hunting. Uncovering the ground shared by feminist discourses that purport to rescue prostitutes, 'shame the johns campaigns,' and serial murderers of prostitutes, Ross [...] provides analysis [...] in which audience members' affective implication in anti-prostitution attitudes is surfaced [...]; her mobilization of audience discomfort, anxiety, irritation, animosity, shame and/or apprehension is

sustained throughout the performance, reconfigured and deployed to keep her audience busy with thinking. (Salah 66)

As with the fictive speaker, a sense of direct audience address will also depend on the poem's deixis. Apostrophe – the use of the pronoun 'you' – has a much greater effect in live poetry, where 'you' finds a real-life target and can be understood as implicating the present audience in the speech act, as in the example of Patricia Smith's "Skinhead." After evoking the views of a white supremacist, Smith's piece ends on the words

> I'm your baby, America, your boy,
> […]
> And I was born
> and raised
> right here.
>
> ("Skinhead")

When Smith performs "Skinhead" to an American audience, the poem's deixis ("your," "here") powerfully roots it in the present of her performance, in which her address of "America" overlaps with her address of the audience before her. Spectators thus find themselves accused as part of a nation that has given rise to the racist views and deeds of the self-righteous skinhead. Rather than having to take this accusation personal, however, the nature of performance as "twice-behaved behaviour" (Schechner 28) at the same time gives the audience license to think of Smith's words as one step removed: as belonging to a different, artistic frame. This gives them the opportunity to take in what they hear – and take Smith's criticism seriously – without, for instance, feeling obliged to defend themselves, which is why Richard Schechner conceives of performance as a "liminal" experience: its "aesthetic reality" being "neither the same nor the opposite of ordinary daily reality" (124).

6.2.3 The MC

A crucial participant in many live poetry events is the MC (master of ceremonies) or host. As the person who guides poet-performer(s) and audience members through the proceedings, s/he can shape an event by introducing the featured poet-performers, providing information about them that guides audience expectation, regulating audience interaction and the structure of an event (e.g. the order of appearance when there are several poet-performers).

A fine example of guiding audience expectation is Jackie Kay's appearance at the Vienna Lit Festival 2008, where the Scottish poet was introduced as "one of Great Britain's leading literary voices" by MC Susanne Reichl. After a brief outline of Kay's university education and early writing career, Reichl mentioned "an impressive collection of publications" – naming and holding up various books for the audience to see –, "an impressive amount of literary prizes," Kay's fellowship of the Royal Society of Literature, as well as Kay's MBE for her services in literature and her current post as professor of Creative Writing at the University of Newcastle. She thus emphasised Jackie Kay's fame and achievements as a writer rather than, for instance, the major themes of her work, which were addressed much later in the Q&A, thus setting her up as a literary celebrity.

Interestingly enough, Kay comments immediately on this awe-inspiring introduction before she begins to read from *The Adoption Papers*:

> Thank you very much, that was a lovely introduction! I was very impressed – not a single note, either – she didn't read from any notes! [...] It was so enjoyable actually. I could have sat there for quite a time. [*audience laughs*] Thank you very much. [...] It's nice to see such a packed room full of people! What – have you not got anything better to do on Saturday night? What is wrong with you? [*audience laughs*]. (*VLF* 2008)

Rather than adopting the pose of the 'grande dame of British Literature,' suggested by the MC's laudation, Kay presents herself as a relaxed, chatty, and approachable performer who likes to have fun with her audience. Her performance self thus gives an interesting twist to the expectations raised by the MC, whose introduction has, however, established Kay's credentials as an author right from the beginning.

A very different approach to the role of MC could be witnessed at the 2006 UK Poetry Slam Championships Final (Theatre Stratford East, London, 11 March 2006), hosted by spoken-word poet and former world slam champion (2005) Kat Francois. As is common at slams, the MC has an active role to play throughout the event: Francois explains the rules at the beginning and introduces the

Fig. 19: Kat Francois, UK Poetry Slam Championships 2006.

judges. She then introduces individual slammers before they mount the stage and maintains a dialogue with the competition judges after each performance, announcing the scores. She also regulates audience response by repeatedly asking for applause after each performance. Boris Preckwitz outlines the challenges of the MC's job at poetry slams as raising the spirit of lethargic audiences and calming down overexcited ('rowdy') audiences, as both tendencies may compromise the success of a slam (Preckwitz 55). Kat Francois skilfully maintains a high level of energy by shouting out phrases such as "put your hands together for…," or "make some noise" (*UK Poetry Slam Championships*) so as to entice the audience to lend their audible support to the contestants. Her appearance is well in line with the celebratory mood she creates: she is wearing a short dress with a low neck and glittery appliqués, and high heels, which altogether comes across as a party or club outfit and provides a contrast to the sober attire of most MCs at the more formal poetry readings. This framing of the poet's performances also paves the way for particular kinds of poems: those which are equally delivered in a high-energy mode (i.e. fast-paced, at high volume and pitch range, stirring excitement or laughter). Poems which employ a more reflective tone – few as they are – do not receive high scores.

Introducing featured poet-performers and regulating the order of appearance as well as audience interaction, the MC may thus enjoy considerable influence on the shape of a live poetry event.

6.2.4 The Producer

Just as publishing houses employ various behind-the-scenes people to enable book publications, and as theatre companies work with backstage figures such as directors, live poetry performances often depend on the initiative and commitment of a producer who for the most part does not have a visible role during the event yet still contributes a great deal to its realisation. As a 'covert' participant, the producer determines the frame of an event, for instance by curating a literature festival or spoken-word tour with regard to specific aims and selecting a suitable space and particular poet-performers to take part. The producer may decide on a format for an event and on the order of appearance (to be carried out by the MC or pre-arranged with the poet-performers), s/he oversees the public relations work and the production of publicity material and often makes an event possible in the first place by raising sufficient funds.[19] The following example will illustrate the breadth of tasks that a producer may have to perform.

Melanie Abrahams is the founder and creative director of "Renaissance One," an agency that curates and organises events which "present the full range of contemporary writing and spoken word" ("About Renaissance One"). In 2001, she produced "Modern Love," a show involving 13 writers presenting poetry and prose texts about love and modern relationships. "Modern Love" toured 20 towns and cities in the UK – among them Luton, London, Sheffield, Leeds, and Manchester – and was subsequently presented in seven European countries. Abrahams chose the theme of modern love for its universal appeal and its topicality: at the turn of the millennium it seemed appropriate to explore how relationships had changed, and "what was in the air" (Abrahams interview). She selected writers for the tour – among them Francesca Beard, Anthony Joseph, Charly Dark, and Malika Booker – with a view to diversity of style, genre, and ethnicity. She was in charge of the budget, three quarters of which came from East Midlands Arts, the rest being earned through fees paid by the tour venues. Abrahams took care of the logistics, pitching the show to appropriate venues, arranging tour dates, compiling critical paths etc. She hired and briefed a PR agent and made sure each venue took care of their own marketing, providing all the relevant information and material. She had professional photos taken of the writers and worked with a graphic designer to create a tour flyer that would appeal to the right target groups. She also coordinated the performances as such, deciding on a suitable format for each venue (reading/performance with or without musical accompaniment, with or without a Q&A, with or without visuals, etc). Abrahams decided on an order of appearance of the individual performers, which resulted in a particular narrative thread running through the show, and she took part in rehearsals with musicians in order to add elements of humour or pathos to particular pieces, thus actively shaping the artistic 'product.' When asked whether she ever mounted the stage herself during the tour, Abrahams said that she arranged for a local writer or for the host at each venue to introduce the show and individual performers, while she would merely provide them with the necessary information. She added, however, that she would sometimes host shows herself when appropriate, for instance in the case of her regular "London Liming" events, which combine spoken word and music and draw on a Trinidadian tradition (as Abrahams has Trinidadian roots herself). Thus, a producer may occa-

---

[19] Occasionally, these various functions may be divided between different people, depending on the size and shape of the organisation backing the individual producer, if there is one.

sionally appear onstage, either to make a general announcement about an event or to act as MC her/himself. As the example of Melanie Abrahams shows, the producer's role is not only administrative, but can also be creative.

6.2.5 Aims and Format

Participants also determine the aims and format of a live poetry event.[20] These two crucial aspects are often closely connected, i.e. a particular format is chosen to serve a certain overall purpose. An event's aims and format are also closely connected to other aspects of performance, such as the choice of poet-performer(s) featured, or the performance space. Poetry events staged by the organisation "Poets Against War," for instance, will feature only poets whose political outlook corresponds to that of the organisers and who take part in order to "read their works as a powerful statement of public and collective resistance to the Bush administration's drive toward war in Iraq" (*Poets Against War* website). Maya Angelou's performance of "On the Pulse of Morning" at Bill Clinton's presidential inauguration ceremony in 1993 was conducted from the Capitol as part of a large celebratory event whose location was entirely tied up with its aims. Furthermore, Angelou had composed the poem especially for Clinton's inauguration, which is an example of how the prospect of performing at a particular event and its purpose can govern literary creation, rather than just the other way round.

The aspects of format and aims also involve the question of whether a particular event forms part of a *series* or larger *scheme*. When Apples & Snakes' London coordinator Russell Thompson programmed "Apples & Snakes in Soho," which took place at London's Soho Theatre on 28 February 2007, his aim was to celebrate the organisation's 25th birthday by featuring "a combination of well-known people, cult figures, people that should be well known that aren't, and people who I think are the future," in order to present a "broad cross-section of what Apples & Snakes does" (Thompson interview 2007). The format of the event was chosen accordingly: as a series of eight ten-minute performances, with spoken-word and comedy star John Hegley as MC. At the same time the event marked the launch of the "Shot from the Lip" Season, a series of "written spoken word events" presented by "a collective of London's spoken word artists and

---

[20] Elizabeth Fine calls for an examination of the "ends" of a verbal performance in *The Folklore Text* (159), by which she means the purpose or aims of a performance.

promoters to bring the thriving underground scene a little closer to the surface" (*Shot from the Lip*). "Apples & Snakes in Soho" thus constituted a profiling event in a double sense, its aims being to present and celebrate the organisation "Apples & Snakes" and to reach out to new audiences for spoken word as part of the larger "Shot from the Lip" project.

An example of an event that forms part of a series and whose format and aims are very closely connected is "Poetry Idol," a series of competitive live poetry events run over several years by "Shortfuse." "Poetry Idol" is, of course, marketed in imitation of the pop knock-out TV show "Pop Idol." "Poetry Idol" nights are cast in a competition format similar to that of a poetry slam: six poet-performers are chosen by the producers to compete against each other and the outcome is determined by audience votes. Host Nathan Penlington outlines the aims of "Poetry Idol" in the following manner:

Fig. 20: Poetry Idol logo.

> we were looking for a format to get people that normally do open mics to sort of progress a little bit, because the thing with only doing open mics is that [...] perhaps ... you can sometimes only see bad poets and bad performers and bad writing because there's no criticism [...]. So that's why we started up Poetry Idol. We get people to send us tapes, and we listen to the tapes and choose. (Penlington interview)

Penlington's explanation also points to a difference between Poetry Idol and the standard *slam* format, which does not normally entail a pre-selection of performers by the organisers. Thus, Poetry Idol introduces an initial stage of 'quality control,' signalling to the audience that the event will most likely be more worth their while than a regular open mic or slam. At the same time, the event draws upon a knock-out competition mode that has obviously been hugely popular in the mass media over the last few years – "Big Brother" and "Britain's Got Talent" being prime examples. "Shortfuse" market their live poetry on the back of this popular culture format, as "a way of getting an audience in that wouldn't necessarily come to a poetry thing but because they might have heard of Pop Idol and so [...] they can understand the format," as Penlington admits (Penlington interview). Consequently, "Poetry Idol" is an event whose format is closely tied to the organisers' audience development aims; and "Shortfuse" indeed have a fantastic record of drawing crowds that would not normally attend literary events, albeit on a small scale.

Another presentation format "Shortfuse" have successfully implemented to achieve similar aims is "Speed Poetry" – in analogy to speed dating – where the audience are divided into small groups which listen to each performer in turn and every poet has seven minutes to impress them:

> Think Speed Dating but with literary chat-up lines, intelligence, wit, and an opportunity to meet some of London's finest poetry and spokenword performers face-to-face [...]. Speed Poetry could be your perfect introduction to a new relationship with literature. Couples, singles, and groups of any number welcome. Who you wake up with in the morning is your own business. (Holland)

Again, the familiarity of a pre-existing format is used to make a live poetry event more appealing to new audiences who "would not normally attend literary events."

A frequent live poetry format mentioned by Nathan Penlington is the *open mic*. Its modus operandi is summarised by Fortner Anderson: "Whether it is gibberish, schmaltz or genius, all of it must be welcomed and heard without judgment. Only the limits of time and the length of the sign-up sheet protect the public from punishment worthy of Dante's *Inferno*" (44). Anderson is referring to the fact that there is no "gatekeeper" at open mics who "exercises a curatorial function" (44). As with poetry slams, there is usually no quality control on the part of the organiser: s/he only determines the time span each poet-performer is allowed, usually about five minutes. For Geraldine Collinge, Director of the live poetry organisation "Apples & Snakes," this accessibility of live poetry as a form of publication is one of its greatest advantages, "because you don't have to go to drama school or to … you know you don't have to borrow money to put on a show, you just go to an open mic and do it. So it's completely democratic" (Collinge interview). Thus, open mics are an especially important forum for beginners, or for poets who want to test how a live audience will receive a work in progress. The poems presented usually have a rough, unpolished quality about them, which is reinforced by the lack of curatorial order: the audience has no way of knowing in advance what kind of poetry will be presented to them and by whom.[21] The open mic format also offers a fluid distinction between poet-performer and audience: performers will mount the stage and thus take up a

---

[21] In order to compensate for the lack of artistic control, some organisers have developed hybrid formats such as the open mic that is interrupted by a featured poet who is assigned a longer slot and whose name will appear in advertising announcements. In Vienna, the international poetry group "Labyrinth Poets" regularly invite a featured poet to perform for 20 minutes at the end of the first half of their monthly open mic.

special position vis-à-vis the audience for five minutes, yet as audience members themselves they are not distinguished from their fellow spectators for the majority of the event. This blurring of the lines between performer and audience adds to the rather informal workshop character of the open mic. Its open accessible format is thus in line with its purpose of providing a forum for all types of live poetry performances, without censorship.

Finally, it should not be forgotten that the various live poetry participants – poet-performer, audience, MC, and producer – may pursue different aims with regard to the same event. A producer may want to stage an event with the general aim of developing an audience for spoken word, for example, while the featured poet may be chiefly interested in marketing her/his new book and collecting her/his fee. With regard to the audience, there are probably as many reasons for attending a live poetry event as there are audience members: from supporting one's poet-friend, spending an interesting evening with colleagues, meeting an admired writer face to face, becoming acquainted with the latest trends in contemporary poetry, to simply wanting to be entertained. The audience can be counted on to appear if the over-all purpose of the event fits their own remit for spending their valuable free time.

The format of an event – whether it forms part of a series or larger project or stands by itself – is thus closely connected to the aesthetic, ideological, and social aims of its participants and to the producer's audience development efforts. While certain standard formats have developed over recent years, such as the open mic or the poetry slam, a great variety of, and experimentation with, event formats is noticeable in live poetry.

6.3 Spatio-Temporal Situation

6.3.1 Localised Audiences in 'Borrowed Spaces'

The physical co-presence of poet and audience in a live poetry performance presupposes its occurrence at a certain time and in a definite space. It constitutes what Nicholas Abercrombie calls a "simple audience performance" (55), simple audience being defined as the people "within earshot or range of vision"[22] who inhabit "localized – and often specialized – spaces which often lie unused for long periods of time when there is no performance" (55). The specialisation of these public spaces, together with the co-presence of performer and audience, enhances the "ceremonial and celebratory as-

---

[22] This may be moderately extended by a microphone, for instance.

pects" of live performances as they "allow, encourage, and demand a *condensed*, intense experience," Abercrombie (55) adds. Among the examples of simple audience spaces that he cites are the football stadium and the theatre building. That space is an important component of each live performance rather than just its 'background' is a point often emphasised in theatre studies. Rick Knowles, for instance, states that "to shift physical and/or social space is to shift meaning" (63). Similarly, Michael Hays notes that

> It is, in fact, the choice of location which first announces the conceptual as well as the spatial structure of the theatre event since position, size, and shape of the place determine the physical and perceptual relationships between the participants as well as their number. (3)

While most of these observations also hold true for live poetry performances, few purpose-built spaces exist that have been created to suit the requirements of live literature – along the lines of theatre buildings. Space is "still an uneasy participant in the poetry reading," as Peter Middleton notes ("The Contemporary Poetry Reading" 271), pointing out that many live poetry events

> take place in borrowed spaces – pubs, bars, lecture rooms, art galleries, halls, and theatres where the readers [i.e. the poet-performers] stumble over stage sets, talk above the noise of drinkers returning from the bar, or try to figure out how best to use a PA system installed for other purposes. (270)

Whether space is strategically integrated in a live poetry performance or merely 'borrowed' without seeming to play a decisive role in the poet's activities, it sets a physical limit to the performance and influences the flow of spectator-performer communication, as well as spectator-spectator communication. Consequently, an analysis of a live poetry performance should also give some thought to the ways in which space impacts on the performance.

Space can shape a performance on various levels. Christopher B. Balme suggests four categories of theatrical space which can be adapted to live poetry performances. "Theatrical space" denotes "the architectural conditions of theatre, usually a building" (Balme 48). "Scenic space" or "stage space" refers to the space "where the actors perform" (48), "place of performance" designates the location of an event in its "wider civic or other environment" (49), and "dramatic space" is the space "evoked by the theatrical text" (49). In the following, these concepts will be examined in relation to live poetry. Instead of 'theatrical space' I propose the term 'performance space' to refer to the building or any other site at which a live poetry event takes place. The performance space can be said to incorporate the "stage space" as well as the "spectator space" (Balme 48) – the auditorium. "Dramatic space," finally, will be renamed "fictive space" to indicate its alliance with the fictive speaker and addressee of a poem.

6.3.2 The Performance Space

Considering the shape of the performance space, i.e. the immediate "architectural conditions" (Balme 48) of a performance, Balme follows Marvin Carlson's typology of theatrical spaces developed in "Histoires des codes," distinguishing between five basic spatial structures that determine "the interactive relationship between performers and spectators" (Balme 49). The spatial arrangement of *"confrontation"* is associated with the proscenium stage, which is based on a clear, linear division of stage space and audience space. It is also associated with naturalistic theatre practices that position the audience behind an invisible "fourth wall,"[23] which allows the actors to act as though no audience were present and which turns the spectator into a passive *voyeur*. Live poetry is, of course, not necessarily staged in a theatre building, but rather can be encountered in all sorts of borrowed spaces. Thus, 'confrontational' structures may also be in place in a university lecture hall, for instance, where the space of the lecturer and his/her rostrum are clearly divided off from the auditorium s/he is facing frontally. The thrust or *apron stage*, common in Elizabethan theatre, is characterised by an extension of the stage space into the spectator space, with audiences positioned on three sides of the 'apron.' The stage space of an *arena* theatre is "entirely surrounded by the audience" (Balme 50). *Environmental* theatre, finally, is marked by a high degree of flexibility: spectators "can surround the stage/playing area(s) or vice versa" (Balme 50).[24] The underlying criterion to distinguish between these various spatial arrangements is the kind of interaction between spectators and performers that they encourage. Additionally, one should ask what relationship a particular spatial arrangement establishes between audience members[25]: when spectators are positioned in such a way that they are facing other audience members, for instance, spectator-spectator communication is facilitated by mutual visibility.

---

23 Cf. *Oeuvres de théâtre de M. Diderot* (339).
24 The fifth category Carlson proposes, the "divided" space, is of no relevance to live poetry: it denotes a spatial separation of performers and audience, as is the case in cinematic productions.
25 See also Elam 50.

A further factor is the presence or absence of a stage, in the sense of a raised platform. Its absence often brings about a sense of "closeness," as Samera Owusu Tutu observes: "being on the same level creates a feeling of equality. There is a heightened sense of community. The performers are not untouchable" (165). Tutu's statement evokes the concept of *social distance*.[26] Performers basically acquire a certain "mystique" which sets them apart from the audience, as Abercrombie notes: "They are a separate order of beings inhabiting an extra-mundane world" (42). The extent to which the poet-performer appears as an 'extra-mundane' being will in part be dependent on his/her physical distance from the audience, determined by the size and structure of the performance space. Edward T. Hall, the founding father of the discipline of proxemics, proposes a continuum of four phases that define the spatial relationship between two people, ranging from "intimate distance" to "personal distance," "social distance," and "public distance."[27] Thus, in a small venue such as London's Poetry Café, a substantial proportion of the audience will be sitting within the 'social distance' range, partaking in a friendly, familiar atmosphere that can be one of the strengths of small spaces. In large spaces like the Queen Elizabeth Hall (Southbank Centre), by contrast, the poet-performer is positioned at 'public distance' to even the first row: beyond the front rows, audience members will barely recognise his/her face and s/he would hardly be heard at all if it were not for the microphone. Live poetry events in large spaces can therefore seem more formal and 'cold' in character. If a poet is reading "high up on a stage with an enormous gap between poet and audience," James Schevill remarks, "the result is often a cold, impersonal distance and an increasingly uncomfortable reading" (142). Schevill recalls a reading by Robert Frost in such an environment, where the poet complained, "The bastards are killing me"

---

[26] Following Abercrombie (42) and Van Leeuwen (24-28) I am using the term "social distance" to signify the degree of intimacy with others that a person's communicative behaviour signals. In Edward T. Hall's proxemic continuum, "social distance" also refers to one particular range of spatial distance (4-12ft).

[27] In Hall's continuum, "intimate distance" denotes "physical contact or touching distance" (117), "personal distance" (1.5-4ft) is common in interaction among close family, or as a way of "keeping someone 'at arm's length'" (120), "social distance" (4-12ft) is maintained for "impersonal business" interactions that occur at a "normal" voice level (121), while "public distance" (12-25ft) finally requires a "loud voice" (122). Hall notes that people's "perception of space is dynamic because it is related to action – what can be done in a given space – rather than what is seen by passive viewing" (115) and that proxemic patterns are culturally specific (116). He points out that the patterns he identifies have been developed on the basis of data from North American test persons (116).

(Schevill 142). However, if an event in a large space is sold out and the performance takes place in front of a full auditorium, the atmosphere may also be more solemn, befitting a 'grand' occasion.

Participants in a live poetry performance are not completely at the mercy of the shape and arrangement of the performance space. The perceived social distance between poet-performer and audience is also related to the performer's use of voice, as Van Leeuwen points out: the microphone, for instance, enables a person to whisper to the audience and still be heard from a great distance (Van Leeuwen 27), allowing the performer to suggest physical closeness, and thus, intimacy. Furthermore, poets have various means of loosening up 'confrontational' spatial arrangements that suggest separation and distance. When an audience member shouted out "Simple Lyric!" at the 2008 Vienna Lit Festival, willing Brian Patten to read that particular poem, Patten responded, "oh, I could but … ok … anyway. I'll do a poem called 'A Blade of Grass' first." The beginning of the poem – "You ask for a poem. I offer you a blade of grass" – apparently struck Patten as an amusing comment on the interaction: he had indeed been asked for a poem and offered "A Blade of Grass" instead. So, after reciting the first phrase Patten suddenly stopped, looked into the audience and exclaimed: "there's no reference though," provoking audience laughter. As he inserted this clarifying comment his right arm reached towards the audience, in the direction where the demand for "Simple Lyric" had come from, and he made a gesture that looked as though he wanted to wipe away the idea that he had intentionally been making a meta-comment on his little dialogue with the audience. His kinetographic gesture was significant with regard to the arrangement of the performance space. Patten was standing on a slightly raised platform; he was facing the audience out of a confrontational spatial arrangement that was based on a clear, linear division of stage space and audience space, and which – in the theatre – is associated with the notion of a 'fourth wall,' an invisible barrier that cuts the stage off from the auditorium. While the naturalistic performance practices of 'fourth wall theatre' have the actors talk to each other, pretending that no audience is present, poet-performers will usually be facing the audience to talk at them directly. Patten's gesture can be understood as reinforcing this acknowledgement that an audience is present: he reached out into the audi-

Fig. 21: Brian Patten, Vienna Lit Festival 2008.

ence space and thus breached whatever imaginary barrier was felt to separate him from his listeners.

As such, social distance is not necessarily a direct result of spatial arrangements: it also depends on the poet-performer's willingness to interact with the audience, and on his/her *use of space*. Brian Patten's gesture offers one example of how spatial relations can be actively shaped. Another aspect is the direction from which a poet-performer enters the stage space. If s/he emerges from a backstage area, from what Ric Knowles calls a "space of production," which "the audience rarely sees" (66), the idea that performer and audience inhabit separate worlds is reinforced by their spatial segregation. By contrast, poets at open mics usually mount the stage from out of the audience space, as 'one of the audience turned performer,' which decreases the social distance between stage and auditorium. Furthermore, a poet-performer may consciously manipulate the performance space not only for social but also for aesthetic reasons. British performance poet Phenzwaan often declaims his poetry from behind the audience, standing at the back of the room (Tutu 161), which results in the impression of a disembodied voice reaching the audience, testifying to a presence deprived of a visual dimension. Similarly, Anne Waldman sometimes performs poems walking about the performance space. During an event at the Vienna Poetry Academy in 2007, she began reciting a poem while she was still in the anteroom, invisible to the audience, before progressing through the audience space into the stage space. Her performance challenged the conventional conception of live poetry performances as static, adding a compelling forward drive, a kind of marching quality, especially to her political poetry.

The audience's relation to performance space also plays a role in live poetry. The potential effect of a full auditorium has already been mentioned: not only does it improve spectator-spectator communication, increasing the audience's confidence "to respond to the performance" as a group (Bennett 131), it also impacts, in turn, on the poet's performance: as a motivational factor. Patience Agbabi notes: "you do get a special energy when something sold out and people are much more excited as an audience" (Agbabi interview). Apart from the effect of audience numbers, audience behaviour is also regulated by the seating arrangements and function of the auditorium. When seats are aligned in straight parallel rows, emphasis is placed on concentration, on sitting still and mentally cancelling out one's body: on not letting oneself be distracted from the performance that is taking place at the front. However, live poetry events are sometimes held in bar spaces which are designed for a specific use: the audience are seated around tables and are allowed to consume drinks as well as food during the performance. "The incorporation of eating and drinking facilitates audience activity and community," as Susan Bennett remarks (121), though it may also distract from the poet's performance. For the audience, the emphasis here is on enjoying themselves. Finally, there are venues without seating arrangements, or where only parts of the audience are seated and the rest are standing. This is often the case in pubs, for instance, where allowing the audience to stand around with their drinks results in a club atmosphere that allows for an energised state that a sitting position often reduces.

Two more aspects of space that ought to be examined are the roles of light and soundscape. In comparison to the theatre, *light* appears to play a minor role in live poetry and is often paid little attention to, as demonstrated by the following account of a 2003 Canadian theatre festival by spoken-word artist T. L. Cowan:

> When I arrived for my tech run-through – which, up until that point in my spoken-word career, I'd thought of as the sound-check – I stood onstage while the stage manager called questions from the booth at the top of the theatre. Where did I want my light? What colour of light did I want? Did I want to walk into my light or should it come on once I was already on stage? (7)

Although live poetry, with its strong focus on the spoken word, may not often deal with light design,[28] as Cowan's amazement at the stage manager's questions underlines, it cannot be denied that the way in which a performance space is illuminated creates particular effects. Performance artist Anthony Howell summarises the effects of different sources of light:

> The spotlight pins the performer down, as if he were a specimen in a butterfly cabinet: the footlight foreshortens him, and stares up his nostrils, aggrandizing him even so: the backlight makes a silhouette of him, or gives him a halo. The gaslamp is a pool, however, rather than a gaze – similar to the embers of a fire […]. (200)

Not only the stage space but also the auditorium is of interest in this respect: "What the darkness does for the audience is to lessen self-consciousness," as Howell points out: "No one can look at them looking" (200). Similarly, Bennett notes that a dark auditorium "assures anonymity" (133), adding that subdued lights "encourage a subdued atmosphere in the auditorium at large, and prepare the audience for interpretive activity" (135), while "a well-lit auditorium continues the element of social display encouraged by the theatre foyer" (135).

---

[28] There are exceptions to this rule: British poet Lemn Sissay's 2006 spoken-word show "Something Dark" worked extensively with light effects as the contrast of light and dark (black and white) was a major theme.

A venue's *soundscape* is an aspect that is particular to a performance space but can, at the same time, be influenced by the participants in a live poetry performance. Reminiscing about the poetry readings at the Blue Unicorn coffeehouse in 1964, Stephen Vincent notes, "unlike the Orphic atmosphere and precise set-up of the Gallery Lounge, the Blue Unicorn was in many ways an extension of the street. (A motorcycle might be warming up outside during your first poem, or a drunk might come in off the sidewalk [...])" (26). At the Bath Literature Festival in March 2007, the weather was so warm that the organisers opened the windows of the Guildhall, immersing various poetry readings in birdsong. Thus, each venue has its own soundscape within which a live poetry performance is embedded. Sometimes this may be to the detriment of the poetry – for instance when beer pumps and coffee machines, or inattentive audiences, are making so much noise that one can hardly hear the poet – but it may also add an interesting 'sound effect' to the audiotext, as in the case of the Bath birds.

6.3.3 Place of Performance and Fictive Space

An analysis of the performance space will be most important for the researcher of live poetry as it constitutes the site of the live encounter between poet-performer and audience and adds to its unique character by way of its spatial arrangement, light, and soundscape. However, there are two other aspects of space in live poetry that should be given due consideration: the "place of performance," which designates the location of an event in its "wider civic or other environment" (Balme 49) and the 'fictive space' that a poem evokes, and which is on a level with its fictive speaker and addressee.

"The generation of meaning in the theatre is not just restricted to factors within the enclosed space of the building (if a building is indeed where it takes place). Of equal importance is the positioning of theatre space in the wider cultural, usually urban, environment," as Christopher Balme notes (58). The building or site where a live poetry performance takes place is located in a certain street, quarter, area etc. that frames it, influencing our perception of it. Susan Bennett also stresses the importance of a venue's "milieu" (125) – what Balme calls the *place of performance* –, pointing out that the experience of visiting London's National Theatre, for instance, is enhanced by its position on the South Bank. The beautiful view of the river Thames and the Houses of Parliament, and the numerous nearby trendy pubs, coffeehouses, and galleries all contribute to the sense of "cultural activity" (Bennett 125). The close connection between place of performance and programming strategy can be seen at the Theatre Royal Stratford East, which is situated in the London Borough of Newham, in an area with a high black population. One of the theatre's key aims is to "lead in the development of shows which reflect both specific ethnic identity and multiculturalism" ("Mission Statement"). They run a series of spoken-word events and classes led by four black resident artists, and the theatre draws a diverse audience, matching its multicultural staffing and casting strategies.

While the concept of 'performance space' revolves around the particular shape, and use, of the stage space and the auditorium, 'place of performance' also refers to the *function* of a performance site within its wider environment. This is especially relevant with regard to the notion of the 'borrowed' space, as live poetry performances often take place in venues that usually serve some other purpose, be it a theatre, lecture hall, or bar. When interviewed about his weekly spoken-word event "Shortfuse," host Nathan Penlington explains, "we're trying to get an audience in that will enjoy themselves and see poetry as a sort of … as not very difficult sometimes … and the way to do this in this country is kind of place it in a pub, or a bar or something" (Penlington interview). Penlington's statement points towards the close connection between place and aims of a performance. "Shortfuse" is at home at The Camden Head, which is a traditional British pub off Upper Street, a trendy shopping street in Islington (London N1). Besides numerous shops, there are many bars and restaurants around, making this a popular area for leisure activities. The Camden Head runs comedy nights for most of the week and has acquired a reputation for comic entertainment (Penlington interview). Consequently, "Shortfuse" profits from the fact that it takes place in a pub in an area renowned for its night-life where people know they will be able to drink and enjoy themselves in a relaxed atmosphere, as well as from the fact that The Camden Head has made a name for itself as a comedy venue and is associated with a particular kind of evening entertainment. The place of performance thus provides poet-performer and audience with a frame of reference and shapes their expectations of a live poetry event.

While an examination of the 'place of performance' amounts to a broadening of the researcher's range of observation, the concept of *fictive space* demands a kind of 'zooming in': a close focus on the poetic text and the ideas of space it evokes. In theatre studies, this is sometimes called "virtual space" (Elam 60), and Peter Middleton in his essay on "The Contemporary Poetry Reading" (271) refers to it as "projected space." It is "generated from within the person," Middleton explains, as "an abstract space similar to that used in the theatre, but much more raggedly, so that the actual site constantly shows through the rips in the fabric of the reading [i.e. the performance]" (271). A poem's fictive space(s) – the space in which fictive speaker and fictive addressee are located, and/or the space that the fictive speaker refers to – is a product of the text, dependent on the inclusion of spatial references (such as "I will arise and go now, and go to Innisfree / And a small cabin build there, of clay and wattles made," in Yeats's "The Lake Isle of Innisfree").

The concept of fictive space as such is not, of course, restricted to live poetry but can just as well be found in a written poem. What is interesting for an analysis of fictive space in a live poem, however, is its relation to the actual performance space and place of performance. Deictic expressions can be significant in this regard, as they root the fictive speaker, who emerges via the physical body of the poet-performer, in a more or less defined space, which may then perceptually overlap, or jar, with the performance space. A telling example is once more offered by Patricia Smith's monologic poem "Skinhead," which explicitly mentions "America" and also refers to it as "right here" ("Skinhead"). In a US performance, the irony of Smith's poem will come across as a critique of her own society that produces self-righteous supremacists like the eponymous skinhead. In a performance abroad, on the other hand, her critique will be felt to be less 'close to home.'

Ultimately, one must not forget, however, that a poetic text may contain very little or no spatial information, and that the performance space is never transformed into a fictive space in live poetry to the same degree as this is possible in (illusionist) theatre. The aesthetic illusion that poetry yields is comparatively weak, as Müller-Zettelmann (125ff) notes, which is what Middleton means when he claims that the fictive space of live poetry is generated "raggedly, so that the actual site constantly shows through" ("The Contemporary Poetry Reading" 271).

6.3.4 Time of Performance and Act Sequence

Temporal aspects play a crucial role in live poetry to distinguish it in various ways from the printed poem. The very phenomenon of sound – and, by extension, audiotextual parameters such as pitch, rhythm, and pauses – depend for their occurrence on the passing of time (i.e. regular rhythm being defined as so many 'beats *per minute*'). A live poetry performance has a certain duration; its beginning and end are tied to specific points in time. While a book may lie around unread for decades before someone picks it up to read it, live poetry exists only within the temporal limits defined by the poet's performance. Due to our definition of live poetry as work performed by the author, live poetry performances are also bound to the poet's 'biographical time,' which means that they are closely tied to specific historical periods in terms of their production *and* reception, both of which are happening simultaneously.

Thus, for the researcher of live poetry it is important to record the *time of performance*. This may include not only the year, and time of year, but also the time of day, which may add additional significance to an event. For instance, with regard to the theatre, Susan Bennett observes that "[t]he traditional evening performance is in many ways a central aspect of the mainstream theatrical event. This [...] emphasizes the work/leisure split and thus promotes a sense of passivity in audiences" (120-1). While audience passivity or activity is certainly dependent on other factors beside the time of day, the work/leisure split that Bennett mentions does play a role in live performances, for instance in terms of the composition of the audience. An afternoon performance will most likely not be attended by people who are working full time, for instance. Conversely, a late-night performance will quite definitely not be attended by children. If a poetry performance takes place out in the street in the middle of the day it will thus signal a disregard for the convention of setting artistic events apart from everyday life by staging them during after-work hours, perhaps as an implicit statement on the relevance of art irrespective of time and setting.

A crucial difference between printed poetry and live poetry becomes apparent with regard to the "*act sequence*" of a performance, whose importance to the researcher is stressed, for instance, by Elizabeth Fine (159). At first sight, the order of a poet-performer's pieces, or the order of appearance of several poet-performers, could be compared to the composition of a poet's published collection or an anthology of poetry. However, whereas a reader can always read at his/her own leisurely tempo, or at breathtaking speed, and skip a poem in an anthology or read the last poems first, the audience's experience of live poetry is sequential and time-bound. Poet and/or producer have control over the act sequence of a live poetry event,[29] while the order of poems in a book will, at best, be understood as a suggestion. Producers often make conscious use of the curative potential this affords, as Russell Thompson's account of the "Apples & Snakes in Soho" event (London, 20 February 2007), which featured several poet-performers, demonstrates:

---

[29] Occasionally it may happen, of course, that a famous poet responds to audience requests for a particular poem or that a poet changes the order of poems originally decided on in order to respond to the previous performer's poem with one of his/her own, but even then s/he has control over the act sequence and can decide whether or not to yield to a request or change plans.

> I tried to alternate different styles of performance. I got Fran doing her quite full-on thing and then I had Abraham doing more storytelling, Andy doing his very loud, right-in-your-face stuff and then Patience doing the more sort of considered, subtle style, so I tried to alternate like that. (Thompson interview 2007)

Thompson also notes that he deliberately programmed the evening's star poet Jean 'Binta' Breeze at the end of the set so as to create a build-up and finish on a "celebratory" note (Thompson interview 2007), befitting the event's aims of celebrating the work of "Apples & Snakes" on the occasion of the organisation's 25th birthday and of raising the profile of the spoken word as an art form.

That the time of performance and act sequence of a live poetry event can have a strong impact on individual performances is most clearly demonstrated by Peter Whitehead's filmed record of one of the most notorious live poetry events of the 20th century: the "International Poetry Incarnation" at the Royal Albert Hall on 11 June 1965. This international poets' get-together is referred to by William Fowler as an "enormously significant countercultural birthing event 'headlined' by Allen Ginsberg" which "brought together and, for a day, unified various London scenes: cultural, creative and drug-taking" (1). Adrian Mitchell performed his anti-war poem "To Whom It May Concern," the chorus of which – "Tell me lies about Vietnam" – reverberated in the enthusiastic applause of a large, responsive audience. When Austrian poet Ernst Jandl mounted the stage a little later and read out his "ode auf N" – an experimental sound poem playing with, and taking apart, the name of 'Napoleon' – the audience joined in with the poet's rhythmic dismantling of the famous dictator's name, obviously edging Jandl on to perform with even greater energy, and afterwards rewarded his performance with a storm of applause and cheers that did not dissipate for a long time. Fowler notes that "many in the proto-hippy audience felt a sense of entitlement toward getting involved, no doubt helped by the fact that many had also taken drugs" (2). Be that as it may, the audience's exceptionally strong reaction must have been motivated by other factors as well. The historical context certainly played a role, as the Vietnam War had begun to escalate only months prior to the Royal Albert Hall event, and as such it took place amid a period of acute political debate and strong anti-war sentiment. Moreover, Jandl scholar Frieder von Ammon points out that the act sequence – Jandl going on after Adrian Mitchell – was significant in this respect:

> prior to Jandl's performance, Adrian Mitchell had read his famous Anti-Vietnam poem To Whom it May Concern, and was greatly acclaimed for it. If one takes this into consideration, the excitement of the audience during the performance

of the Ode to N makes sense: it was easy to transfer Jandl's "sounds of surfeit, aversion" etc. from the Napoleonic Wars to the Vietnam War, and from the French Emperor to the President of the United States. (von Ammon)

As these examples demonstrate, it is often not sufficient to study individual performances in isolation. As constituent elements of a larger temporal process, the proceeding and succeeding performances can serve as powerful contextual determiners and shapers of the meaning and connotations of an individual reading.

7. Jackie Hagan's "Coffee or Tea?": A Sample Analysis

The following sections constitute a sample analysis of a poem entitled "Coffee or Tea?" and composed by British poet Jackie Hagan, who performed it at the "Seconds Out" poetry slam in Manchester's Contact Theatre on the evening of 6 March 2007. While so far the brief analytical passages on a range of poems have served to exemplify individual aspects of live poetry performances, the purpose of this chapter is to demonstrate how various critical criteria introduced in this study can be integrated in a more comprehensive analysis of one particular text. Moreover, the sample analysis of "Coffee or Tea?" will underline the interdependence of verbal, paralinguistic, kinesic and contextual performance aspects and make clear once more how remarkably live poetry differs from print publication as a mode of poetic communication.

Jackie Hagan's performance of "Coffee or Tea?" has been chosen for a number of reasons: on an imagined continuum ranging from quiet, static poetry 'readings' to flashy, theatrical performances Hagan roughly occupies a middle position, not tending towards extremes. That said, she does employ paralinguistic and body communication in a distinctive manner and her performance is well suited for a demonstration of the critical 'toolkit' introduced in this study. Furthermore, as a self-declared 'performance poet' she provides a fine counter-example to the cliché of performance poetry being the exclusive domain of black poets. And finally, "Coffee or Tea?" has been published in print and thus allows for a comparison of printed and performed versions.

"Seconds Out" was produced by Segun Lee-French for the poetry organisation "Apples & Snakes," for whom he acted as North West Regional Coordinator. It was conceived as a series of slam events that would provide a focal point for spoken-word activity in Manchester. In addition, the series presented featured performers so as to "show the slam contestants that there were many ways to present oneself as a performance poet," to "provide an opportunity for Manchester people to see poets from outside Manchester, who might otherwise not often get the chance to perform here" as well as "an opportunity for emerging local poets" (Lee-French interview). This outline of the aims of the "Seconds Out" series also establishes a definite connection of "Seconds Out" slams with performance poetry. Jackie Hagan, a young poet of 25 who at that time to Lee-French seemed "raw, but very promising," was booked as support act to the better-known Mark Gwynne Jones. Predictably, the event sequence was dictated by the poets' reputation: Hagan was featured at the beginning of the first half of the event, Jones, as headliner, in the second half (Lee-French interview). The choice of performers also reflected the producer's aim to "book a male and female poet for Seconds Out Slams" so as to maintain the gender balance (Lee-French interview). The slam proper was open to anyone who chose to register for a slot to present their work, thus keeping in line with the tradition of the poetry slam as an open, accessible format.

The Contact Theatre had close ties with "Apples & Snakes" and was chosen because it fitted the profile of "funky, raw, in your face" that the producer had envisaged for the "Seconds Out" series. The Contact has a focus on New Writing, participative work and youth work and often puts on spoken word as it well matches the theatre's programming strategy. Situated in an ethnically diverse area in a university quarter with many student bars, the theatre thus seemed a more than suitable 'borrowed space' for poetry slams (Lee-French interview).

The performance space itself was a dark room with black walls, a dark floor and black chairs that could hold an audience of 75 people. The seating arrangement was confrontational – the chairs being aligned in straight rows that faced the stage space – but without creating a great social distance as there was no raised platform for the performers and a few coffee tables with loose chairs were placed in front of the first row. This "cabaret format" was embraced by producer Lee-French because it "establishes a relaxed informal vibe and democratic link to the audience on the same level" (Lee-French interview). The informal atmosphere was supported by the Contact's policy of allowing drinks into the theatre. On entering the performance space one was greeted by the loud music of DJ Masta Wong, whom Segun Lee-French had chosen for his "strong hiphop credentials" (Lee-French interview) and who added to the event's "relaxed informal vibe" by shaping the theatre's soundscape.

The audience of about 45 seemed roughly to match the producer's description of his usual audiences as "age 18-50, gender split even, 10-20% non-white, politically liberal or leftwing, students & yes some poets" (Lee-French interview). The majority that night was rather young – people in their mid-twenties – with many young men dressed casually in jeans and hoodies, and among them were, of course, a number of poets who were going to take part in the slam.

When Segun Lee-French took up the microphone to open the event he stood in the spotlight in a triple function as producer, MC, and poet-performer. After briefly explaining the rules of slam and mentioning the two featured poets, he performed an erotic poem that involved some heavy breathing into the microphone and a comic piece called "Xmas Kisses" with extensive dynamic variations, singing, shouting, and gesturing. His own live poetry set the tone for the rest of the night, signalling clearly that "Seconds

Out" was not meant to be an ordinary, 'well-behaved' poetry 'reading' but that performative skills were in demand, and his efforts were rewarded with enthusiastic applause. Finally, he announced Jackie Hagan with the following words:

> I would like to welcome our very special first guest, a fantastic poet whom I've seen, oh, many times and I'm always excited when I see her – [*points at Hagan*] don't get that the wrong way! [*audience laughs*], excited poetically when I see her – [*shouts:*] Jackie Hagan! (*Seconds Out*)

Thus, Lee-French desisted from listing Hagan's credentials as a writer – she had recently had her first collection published (*Shut Your Eyes and Put Out Your Hand*) and won the Poetry Kit award for Best Emerging Poet in 2006 – except for mentioning that he had been impressed by her previous performances. He obviously wanted her performance to 'speak for itself.'

"Coffee or Tea?"

Even as Hagan walks towards the microphone in her baggy T-shirt and casual cardigan to adjust the height of the stand her relaxed posture gives an impression of calm confidence. A mental health worker by profession, she has performed her poetry around the North West and is "well known in poetry circles in the region" (Lee-French interview). She begins her set with a poem called "I managed to annoy you in ten new ways," introducing it as follows: "I thought I'd start you off with something that isn't quite a poem, called a poem-ish, and this is about when I made that decision to move in with my girl-friend" (*Seconds Out*). Thus, she addresses her audience directly, acting upon her conviction that the task of performance poets is "to try to connect with your audience while they are there in front of you" (Hagan interview). Her strong Scouse accent, which she keeps in performance, sounds melodious, with a characteristic rising pitch at the end of many phrases. Her typical performance style – confident and calm, though also lively – is already apparent in the first poem and there is little difference between her delivery of her poems and the ad lib (paratext) in between them.[1] This can be said to reflect her attitude towards, and aim for, per-

---

[1] In an interview, Hagan cites Manchester poet Gerry Potter – "another working-class Scouser" – and Conor A – "because he seemed so in control and confident" (Hagan interview) – as two poets who have had an influence on her performance style. Potter's performances are similarly naturalistic, often sounding like slightly exaggerated everyday speech.

formance, which is "to have a laugh and hang out" (Hagan interview): for Hagan, poetry is not a 'high art' to be separated from mundane everyday concerns. Segun Lee-French therefore calls her performance style "naturalistic," remarking that Hagan provides an interesting contrast to headliner Mark Gwynne Jones's "very theatrical" style (Lee-French interview). Hagan's mentioning of her "girl-friend" furthermore identifies her poetry as, to some degree, confessional and reveals her sexual orientation, which is also the theme of the following poem, "Coffee or Tea?". In her introduction, Hagan already gives her audience the key to the poem's theme:

> Er, the … eagle-eyed, eagle-eared … can you be eagle-eared? The eagle-eared amongst you will have noticed that I'm not gay or not straight. Bloody hell, how can I exist? It's like trying to get a flyer made that isn't quite A4 or A5. [*audience laughs*] It confuses people. So … although I think it's relatively straightforward, I thought I'd write a poem to explain it to everyone, and I thought I'd use the metaphor of hot beverages. It's called "Coffee or Tea." (*Seconds Out*)

While Hagan's explanation contains important information about the poem's imagery it also foregrounds the social function of paratext to "connect with your audience" (Hagan interview): Hagan addresses her audience and makes them laugh. The poem itself contains humorous elements. However, it traces the speaker's negotiation of her sexual identity in the face of social pressure to conform to certain group standards, which is not necessarily a comic issue. In that sense Hagan's humorous introduction can perhaps be seen as embracing Brian Patten's idea that humour "is a way of attracting the audience's attention. If you can make an audience laugh, they will more readily listen to your more serious work. They feel you have earned the right to be taken seriously!" (Patten interview). Another remarkable point to observe during Hagan's introduction is that she puts her book down – she read the first poem from the book though she occasionally looked up at the audience – and she takes the microphone from the stand so as to be able to move more freely. Abandoning the book also means relinquishing a barrier between herself and the audience.

The theme of the individual struggling against conformist social pressures is underscored repeatedly by Hagan's subtle use of paralinguistic and body communication, as can already be noticed at the very beginning of the poem: "I was born and they said 'I bet she'll like coffee.' The right chromosomes you see" ("Coffee or Tea?"). In the audiotext, this prophecy is realised as

I ^{bet} she'll like cof$_{fee.}$

Each syllable is distinctly articulated, with a falling pitch to the end of the phrase, signalling finality. The tone is one of absolute certainty: the baby's sex – "the right chromosomes" – makes it unthinkable that she could like anything else but coffee, i.e. heterosexual love. This is borne out by the poet's accompanying hand movements, which are motor gestures in the rhythm of her speech, suggesting that whoever "they" are, they are hammering in an undisputable fact rather than offering a guess. Later, in her teenage years, the speaker "saw the tea my father chain drank, the coffee my mother savoured" and "figured either would do to douse my thirst" ("Coffee or Tea?"). However, her sexual interest is forcefully channelled when she "looked up with childish glee and saw tall faces: You will drink coffee. You will admire coffee. You will fall in love with coffee, settle down with coffee." The emphatic articulation of "will" with its subsequent pause, which gives the word more room in "You **will**… drink coffee," renders this utterance a definite command. Hagan's body behaviour makes it clear that there is a change of speaker at this point in the poem. While she looks up and even points upwards with her index finger at "looked up with childish glee" [22a] she slightly bends forward and looks down during "You will drink coffee" [22b]:

Fig. 22a & 22b. Jackie Hagan, "Seconds Out" slam 2007.

This change of posture reinforces the paralinguistic colouring of the following utterances: the young girl is being 'talked down to' from an authoritative position. The last of this series of utterances introduces an element of open aggression:

You will serve coffee all your god-damn life.

The swearing, the renewed motor gestures and the final falling pitch indicate that the girl is, or feels, coerced into serving coffee. 'Serve,' in this context, is an ingenious word choice as traditionally, both serving coffee and being servile to a male partner are typically seen as woman's duties. The adversarial speaker in the poem is thus identified as the representative of a traditional order.

Interestingly, the print publication of the poem includes an additional line "you will do what coffee says" which is not realised by Hagan in performance. This is one of several instances where the live performance contradicts the written poem, the most notable of which is the title itself: while Hagan announces the poem as "Coffee or Tea," its title in her printed collection is "Tea or Coffee?". The absolute verbal identity of a poem is, apparently, not a crucial requirement for Hagan. Her texts are permitted slight variations in performance, thus embracing the flexibility that the medium of live poetry affords.

"So I did drink coffee," Hagan continues, "I drank it by the gallon: tried instant coffee against the back walls of clubs, tried espresso, found it was over too soon, tried filter coffee, who just told me to lose weight, tried latte which was just too phlegmy" ("Coffee or Tea?"). The humour of this passage arises not only from the potential parallels between coffee drinking and sexual experience but also from the poet-performer's facial expressions and the shape of her audiotext. Right after "tried espresso" Hagan pulls her face into a grimace that expresses discomfort [22c] and is accompanied by a slight shaking of the head. This symbolic gesture of negation is made before she pronounces her negative judgement of heterosexual 'espresso sex' ("found it was over too soon"), thus anticipating information contained in the verbal text. After "tried latte which was just …" Hagan pauses for a moment as though she were struggling for words before she utters "too phlegmy." This phrasing makes her speech appear hesitant, spontaneous and authentic, and earns her some laughter from the audience. This apparent authenticity also forges a stronger connection between Hagan's performance self and the experiences of her fictive speaker, who thus appears not quite as fictive after all. The identification of the poem's author and its speaker was already provoked in the introductory paratext, when Hagan explained that she was "not gay or not straight" and had decided to "write a poem to explain it to everyone" (*Seconds Out*). Thus, the audience is invited to 'read' the poem as auto-

Fig. 22c. Jackie Hagan.

biographical and confessional, which obviously adds yet another layer of humour to the passage discussed: the promiscuity of the poem's adventurous coffee drinker can now be attributed to Hagan herself.[2]

Subsequently, the poem outlines the difficulties experienced with coffee, for instance that "coffee wanted me to wank it off in the middle of the night" ("Coffee or Tea?"), which again provokes laughter. This must be the point in the poem where the verbal text renders it plainly obvious what 'coffee' actually stands for,[3] which demonstrates once more the crucial role of paratext in performance: if Jackie Hagan had not explained the central metaphor of her poem right at the beginning her audience would perhaps only now, after about one third, realise that "Coffee or Tea?" revolves around the speaker's sexual orientation. The print publication provides no such enlightening introduction, as it is not necessary there. A silent perusal of the poem will always offer the reader a chance to pause and rethink earlier passages in this new light or to re-read them so as to fully appreciate the ingenuity of the extended comparison between sexual orientation and hot beverages. It may even be more enjoyable to discover the poem's 'encoded' references gradually if one has the time to ponder on earlier phrases from this new perspective. In performance, however, the tempo is mostly dictated by the poet and leaves little time for reflections on past utterances if one wants to keep following the poet, which is probably why Hagan thought it necessary to inform her readers about the poem's theme right at the start.

When the speaker exclaims "It's alright this coffee, but have you got anything else?", she is answered "oh yes my dear but it's not for you," and, "you like coffee, remember?" ("Coffee or Tea?"). What appears to be, on the surface, the reply of a coffee vendor can again be understood as the authoritative voice of normative heterosexuality and is similarly realised by Hagan as in the two previous instances ("I bet she'll like coffee" and "You will drink coffee"). At "but it's not for you"

Fig. 22d: Jackie Hagan.

---

2   While Jackie Hagan explained in an interview that "Coffee or Tea" was autobiographical, though "exaggerated and embellished," she placed no such limitation on the interpretation of her performance in Manchester.

3   Incidentally, the use of drinking coffee as a metaphor for sexual intercourse can be found as early as in Jonathan Swift's correspondence with "Vanessa" (Esther Vanhomrigh). See for example Ann Cline Kelly's *Jonathan Swift and Popular Culture: Myth, Media, and the Man*. Basingstoke: Palgrave Macmillan, 2002. 121.

she lifts up her left index finger in a forbidding, teacherly gesture and noticeably leans her torso back as though the authoritative speaker were trying to increase the distance to his/her girl addressee: to keep her at bay [22d]. The same raised index finger is then used to perform motor gestures in the rhythm of "you like coffee," creating again the impression of an undisputable fact being 'hammered in.'

The girl speaker responds by claiming "But that we're told we mustn't do becomes just that which we pursue" ("Coffee or Tea?") to introduce the passage that relates her first homosexual experiences. This aphorism, which recurs later in the poem, is interesting for the fact that the word 'we' is addressed to an actual audience in performance. The audience are thus implicated in this assumed collective consent that the 'we' suggests and, by extension, in Hagan's ideological position. Their political orientation – "liberal or leftwing," according to Lee French (interview) – is therefore not insignificant, especially in view of the socially and politically contested issue that Hagan's poem addresses. The audience's approving laughter at the poet's initial revelation of her sexual orientation and the poem's central metaphor can in this sense be understood as a signal of toleration and consent.

When the speaker notes that she "was surrounded without censor by sweet, curvy, sexy cups of tea" and is once more told "It's not for you" she bursts out,

But my father loved tea!

Fig. 22e: Jackie Hagan.

This utterance stands out from the surrounding ones: its pitch curve peaks at 'loved' as the poet closes her eyes and performs a hand-to-heart gesture [22e], which suggests emotional involvement, extreme longing, something the printed page would hardly be able to convey. Its emotive expansion is noticeable all the more as Hagan's pitch range is usually rather contained, her tone being one of understatement.

"So under the pretence of seeking a university degree," she continues, "came to chester, in ravenous search for tea" ("Coffee or Tea?"). When she then utters "And tea leaks out of Manchester's walls," pointing behind her [22f], the audience responds once

Fig. 22f: Jackie Hagan

more with laughter. She is performing in the very place she has referred to, after all. Her deictic gesture roots the poem in the present location and adds a sense of immediacy, a connection with 'real life.'

"University life is filled with tea," the speaker observes and begins to list the kinds of tea she encountered: "Crusty, dreadlocked, herbal tea, Daddy prada earl grey tea, enthusiastic new found tea with asymmetric hairdos" ("Coffee or Tea?"). While so far Hagan's performance has followed the irregularities of everyday speech, she now delivers these varieties of tea in a regular rhythm in 4/4 time, the evenly distributed beats being matched with a regular up-and-down pitch movement (Hagan slides from a lower to a higher pitch within one syllable, on the first, second and third beats of the phrase):

Cr^{usty}, dr_{ea}dlocked, h_erbal tea

Da^{ddy} pr^a_{da} _{ea}rl grey tea

The regular rhythm reinforces the 'cataloguing' quality of Hagan's utterance. In musical notation, it can be represented thus:

Crusty, dreadlocked, herbal tea,

Daddy prada earl grey tea, en-

thusiastic   new found tea with [...]

Due to the rhythm's regularity and the recurrence of "tea" in the same position in both measures, the virtual offbeat at the end of the first measure would be expected also at the end of the next one. However, Hagan immediately sets in with the next item on her list, beginning "enthusiastic new found tea" on the last offbeat of the previous measure. This adds an urgent quality to her speech, reinforced by a slight increase of tempo on "enthusiastic" when she also moves on to a slightly higher pitch. Thus, while the regular rhythm marks this passage as a 'listing,' this sudden increase of energy points to the speaker's excitement in the face of the sheer wealth of 'tea brands' found in Manchester. "And tea took me, nourished me, let me be me," she reports contentedly: "let me be me" is uttered in the falling pitch of finality and relief, of the speaker having finally attained a fulfilment of sorts.

However, after a brief account of the advantages of tea-drinking ("Tea fucked me like tea does," … "Didn't shriek at menstruation," … "Didn't moan about my breasts, for tea has breasts too") she notes in a breathy timbre, "But the world of tea it seems is not itself without constriction," explaining that "tea drinkers can't help but force the conviction I must drink only tea" ("Coffee or Tea?"). The breathiness of Hagan's voice seems like a sigh that pervades her utterance, adding a note of disappointment. "They said coffee was against us," she continues, "and that coffee was the enemy," delivering both utterances with the exact same exaggerated rising pitch curve that drops on the last two syllables, making it clear that she is not simply repeating what tea-drinkers told her but that she is, in fact, mocking them with her tone of voice:

They said cof^fee was a^gainst us

and that cof^fee was the ene^my.

The speaker is again experiencing the pressure of a group to conform to its norms and is quite obviously irritated by "this dichotomy of just what it is I must not do" ("Coffee or Tea?"). She notes, "And remember, that we must not do becomes just that which we pursue," repeating her aphorism from the first half of the poem and thus establishing a symmetry that is borne out by the following utterance, "and coffee leeks out of Manchester's walls." Her renewed enjoyment of coffee thus echoes her discovery of the delights of tea-drinking, as well as her determination to confront imposed taboos and 'have her way,' albeit with greater wisdom: "I learnt to avoid the phlegmy coffee, the coffee that just wanted to watch me drink tea." At this point the audience breaks into hysterical laughter that continues for some time. Spectator-performer communication has become manifest earlier in the form of laughter, but this time it spreads across the room and continues long enough for Hagan to have to pause. Consequently, Hagan slightly turns away from the audience to give them a little time to recover, thus regulating their interaction through her body behaviour.

Eventually, the speaker notices that "the world was rife with those who want their coffee **and** their tea, drink one in public, the other secretively," strongly emphasising the word 'and' to insist once more that there is no obligation to choose. Significantly, at "those who want their coffee and their tea," Hagan performs the same motor gesture with her left hand – index finger raised – that she employed when speaking in the forbidding voice of authoritative heterosexuality. The poem's youthful speaker has, in a sense, taken over the baton: it is now she who is 'hammering in' a fact and talking back at society in the magisterial tone of her newly-won self-confidence. The speaker concludes in a quiet, self-assured tone, "And now when I drink tea they call me a tea drinker. When I drink coffee, a coffee drinker. But they know I do both, I drink tea, I drink coffee, because they both wet my whistle" ("Coffee or Tea?").

In summary, Jackie Hagan's performance of "Coffee or Tea?" at the "Seconds Out" slam is delivered by the poet in a seemingly spontaneous and authentic manner that reinforces the autobiographical connection she established in her introductory paratext. Hagan explains the poem's central metaphor at the start, addresses her audience and reacts to their manifest responses, thus enacting her view of live performance as a direct encounter of poet-performer and audience. She develops the poem's theme of a young woman's struggle against conformist social pressures by adopting the voice and body communication of different adversarial speakers in opposition to hers. The utterances of the poem's various fictive speakers are frequently assigned distinct tones of voice or emotional colouring, thus adding information that the printed page could hardly convey. The strange symmetry of "Coffee or Tea?" points to the artificial nature of social restrictions on sexual orientation, which are eventually overcome by the speaker. It is not only through her choice of words but also through Hagan's subtle employment of paralinguistic features and body communication that the poem traces the speaker's development from shame and despair to irritation and finally to a self-confident assertion of her own needs.

8. Checklist for the Analysis of Live Poetry Performances

The following list of criteria is intended as an analytical grid for live poetry performances. It was inspired by Patrice Pavis' widely used questionnaire for the analysis of theatrical performances, developed in "Theatre Analysis: Some Questions and a Questionnaire." The criteria below are based on aspects of live poetry performance as discussed in Chapters 3 to 6 of this study. They are intended as prompts to help the researcher structure his/her perception of a performance by breaking it down into different components. However, it should be remembered that this deconstruction of the performance experience is artificial in so far as the isolated elements are closely interrelated in a live performance, and as such the relationships between them ought also to be taken into account in a full analysis.

Arguably, an analysis of a live poem need not necessarily comprise all the aspects addressed by the checklist proposed here. Depending on the researcher's particular interest and the information available, it may be useful to focus on a few selected questions so as to develop a consistent analysis and interpretation; indeed, the live performance itself may suggest a particular focus or render certain criteria irrelevant if the related features are not conspicuous in performance. Furthermore, the checklist – and thus the approach to live poetry presented in this study – does not cover those aspects of poetry that traditionally have been dealt with in literary studies, such as theme, imagery, or rhetorical tropes. These may, of course, be of interest to the researcher as they apply to live poetry, too, and may be included in the analysis.

1. General information concerning the event

- Time and location/place of performance
- Aims and format of event
- Series or larger scheme of which event is a part
- Participants
- Order of poets/pieces presented (act sequence)

2. Performance space

- Usual function of performance space ('borrowed space')
- Structure of performance space/relationship between stage space and auditorium
- Soundscape and lighting

3. Poet's performance
3a. Information on the poet-performer

- Biographical information, age, gender, ethnicity, etc.
- Position in the literary field
- Performance tradition

3b. Audiotext

- Poet's voice set and original accent
- Other accents employed
- How the poet works with the following articulatory parameters:
    - rhythm
    - pitch
    - volume
    - articulation
    - timbre
- Conspicuous use of certain tones of voice
- Non-verbal sounds
- Position and function of paratext in performance
- Relation between audiotext and written version

3c. Body communication

- Poet's body set
- How body communication is employed in order to
    - express emotions
    - regulate interpersonal interaction
    - present the poet's performance self or the fictive speaker's personality
    - convey attitudes towards the addressee or topic of speech
    - replace, accompany, or modify speech
- Postures and gestures
- Facial and artefactual communication

3d. Relation of actual to fictive speech situation

- Relationship established between poet and fictive speaker in performance
- Relationship of the actual spatio-temporal situation and audience to the fictive spatio-temporal situation and addressee evoked by the poetic text

4. Audience

- Audience numbers and composition: age, gender, ethnicity, political orientation, etc.
- Development of spectator-performer communication/spectator-spectator communication

5. Other participants

- Role of MC in event
- Role of producer in event

Conclusion

The last decades have seen a boom in live-poetry events in much of the English-speaking world. The rise of literary festivals, open mics, and poetry slams has given a fresh impetus to poetry's oral realisation mode and has raised awareness for the aesthetic and social potential of live performances. This revaluation of oral performance has been noticeable to the extent that its practitioners have regularly proclaimed 'spoken word' – incorporating performances of prose and poetry, storytelling, and certain forms of comedy – an art form in its own right.

The examples of live poetry introduced in this study have demonstrated the multifaceted nature of meaning-making in live performance and revealed the performed poem to provide a vastly different experience from a silent reading of printed poetry. Yet, academia has barely responded to these recent developments in poetry. The lack of historical documentation of live poetry performances is aggravated by the deployment of quasi-acoustic terminology in literary studies to discuss the 'evoked' sound of (written) poetry, which masks the absence of a coherent approach to the actual, physical sounds of live poetry as well as other performance-related characteristics.

The approach to live poetry presented in this thesis conceives of its subject as an art that is brought forth through the physical body, operating in the acoustic and visual dimensions, and which is created in a live encounter of poet-performer and audience. Its methodology does not follow the distinction, frequently drawn in critical literature, of live poetry into a popular form and a 'literary' form, a distinction which has proved rather impracticable in view of the active exchange between two allegedly separate 'scenes.' Instead, the concept of 'live poetry' characterises a broad variety of poetry performances in front of a physically present audience, 'performance' thus being understood as including more traditional poetry 'readings' as well as 'theatrical' recitations by 'performance poets' or 'spoken word artists.' Consequently, the analytical criteria proposed are applicable also to a broad variety of live-poetry manifestations.

Although literary studies, the academic discipline that is most obviously concerned with the study of poetry, has little to offer in the way of an analytical 'toolkit' with which to address the distinctive characteristics of live poetry as an artistic medium, other disciplines have been shown to provide useful methods and sensible points of departure. Paralinguistics has developed ways of classifying and interpreting non-verbal acoustic elements of speech, while musicology can be drawn on for describing and notating aspects such as speech melody (pitch) and regular rhythms. The work conducted on body behaviour in the field of kinesics helps to account for the part the visible body plays in speech communication. Theatre studies, performance studies, and folklore studies have variously theorised the spatio-temporal aspects of verbal performance as well as the social dimension and the dynamics of interaction entailed in a live encounter of performer and audience. Literary theory, finally, proposes a concept of 'paratext' that is essentially geared towards writing but which has proved to be adaptable to live poetry.

The present study thus closes a methodological gap by combining and integrating approaches from different disciplines in order to provide a 'toolkit' for the analysis of live poetry. In this way, the study is intended as a contribution to the revaluation of live poetry as a subject worthy of academic research and literary criticism. It is designed to facilitate comparisons of a poet's print publications and performance practice, for instance, and to determine the role of either in relation to the entirety of his/her work and career. It will equally be of use in examining the differences, similarities, and mutual influences of individuals or groups of poets in terms of their live performances, as well as the role of particular event series or producers in the emergence of local live poetry practices. Thus, it also provides a basis for future investigations into the historical development of live poetry.

Moreover, this study lays the foundation for enquiries into the function of music in conjunction with live poetry, as the two media are often paired together in performance. It paves the way for comparative studies of live poetry and other speech-based art forms, such as spoken word theatre or storytelling, and the analytical tools proposed in the audiotext chapter are, in fact, applicable also to the study of audio poetry and audiobooks. A rewarding field of enquiry, which often yields very different results from the study of printed poetry, live poetry offers many points of entry.

Finally, it should not be forgotten that scholarly engagement with live poetry touches upon an important question concerning poetry in general: that of the future development, and survival, of the genre in contemporary media cultures. While poetry is often declared a dying literary genre in terms of the publishing industry, a shift in perspective may reveal the possibilities for the genre to appear in different media in changing proportions. There is then ample space for long-ranging enquiries into the ways in which live poetry, audio poetry, hyper poetry or poetry films, for instance, are changing the face of poetic composition and publication in particular and the shape of the literary field in general. The present study is a contribution to this area of investigation and hopes to spark off future research into poetry and its media.

Bibliography

Primary Sources:

Agbabi, Patience. "Josephine Baker Finds Herself." *Apples & Snakes in Soho.* London, 28 Feb. 2007. <www.livepoetry.net>.
Published in print: Patience Agbabi. *Bloodshot Monochrome.* Edinburgh: Canongate, 2008. 24.

-----. "Ufo Woman." video from the Literature Online "Poets on Screen" collection ProQuest 2002. 28 Dec. 2008
<rtsp://multimedia.chadwyck.co.uk:554/video/optic-nerve/on0716.rm?cloakport=80%2c554%2c7070>.
Published in print: Patience Agbabi. *Transformatrix.* Edinburgh: Canongate 2000. 15-17.

Andrade, Suzanne. "Goring-by-Sea." *Thousands of Men and Women Running.* Self-published audio CD. 2005.

[*A&S in Soho*] *Apples & Snakes in Soho.* London, 28 Feb. 2007. Unpublished video recording.

Baraka, Amiri. "Somebody Blew Up America." *Somebody Blew Up America & Other Poems.* Phillipsburg: House of Nehesi, 2003. 41-50.

Bernard, Jeneece. "Underground." *Vienna Lit Festival 2006.* Vienna, 14 Oct. 2006. <www.livepoetry.net>.

Brooks, Gwendolyn. "The Pool Players: Seven at the Golden Shovel." Audio recording. 3 May 1983, Guggenheim Museum. *The Academy Audio Archive.* 17 Mar. 2009
<http://www.poets.org/viewmedia.php/prmMID/15433>.
Published in print: Gwendolyn Brooks. *The Bean Eaters.* New York: Harper, 1960. 17.

Cope, Wendy. "Spared." *Life Lines.* Audio CD. Ed. Todd Swift. London: Oxfam, 2006.
Text published: *BBC Home page.* 28 Dec. 2009
<http://news.bbc.co.uk/2/hi/entertainment/5052786.stm>.

Craven-Griffiths, Andy. "Lottery Mentality." *Apples & Snakes in Soho*. London, 28 Feb. 2007. <www.livepoetry.net>.

English, Lucy. "Family Prayers." *Family Prayers*. Self-published audio CD. 2004. <www.livepoetry.net>.

-----. "I want to be a bitch." *Apples & Snakes in Soho*. London, 28 Feb. 2007. <www.livepoetry.net>.

-----. "Temple Cloud." *Apples & Snakes in Soho*. London, 28 Feb. 2007. <www.livepoetry.net>.

Finch, Peter. "Damage." *Peter Finch Archive*. 20 Apr. 2009 <http://www.peterfinch.co.uk/sound/damage.mp3>.
Published in print: Peter Finch. *The Welsh Poems*. Exeter: Shearsman Books, 2006. 61.

Foster, Patricia. "Lips." *Spit Lit Festival 2007*. London, 9 Mar. 2007. <www.livepoetry.net>.
Published in print: *Brown Eyes: A Selection of Creative Expressions by Black and Mixed-Race Women*. Ed. Nicole Moore. Leicester: Troubador, 2005. 75-76.

Francois, Kat. "Anything." *Blessed by Words*. Self-published audio CD. London, 2005. <www.livepoetry.net>.

Gibson, Abraham. "Nancy and Reeva." *Apples & Snakes in Soho*. London, 28 Feb. 2007. <www.livepoetry.net>.

-----. "Margaret Thatcher and her African Lover." *Apples & Snakes in Soho*. London, 28 Feb. 2007. <www.livepoetry.net>.

Hagan, Jackie. "Coffee or Tea?" *Seconds Out Slam*. Manchester, 6 Mar. 2007. <www.livepoetry.net>.
Published in print: Jackie Hagan. *Shut Your Eyes and Put Out Your Hand*. Manchester, Citizen32 Publications, 2006.

Hardi, Choman. "Journey Through the Dead Villages." *Poetry in Performance* Vol. 2. Audio CD. London: 57 Productions, 2003.
Published in print: Choman Hardi. *Life for Us*. Newcastle upon Tyne: Bloodaxe Books, 2004. 10.

Hegley, John. "Not Waving." *Poetry in Performance* Vol. 1. Audio CD. London: 57 Productions, 2002.
Published in print: John Hegley. *Glad to Wear Glasses*. London: André Deutsch, 1990. 48.

Jandl, Ernst. "Ode auf N." *Peter Whitehead And the Sixties*. [Compilation DVD consisting of the Peter Whitehead films Wholly Communion (1965) and Benefit of the Doubt (1967)]. Dir. Peter Whitehead. DVD. BFI Video, 2007.
Published in print: Ernst Jandl. *Poetische Werke*. Vol. 2. Ed. Klaus Siblewski. Munich: Luchterhand, 1997. 41-43.

Jones, Mark Gwynne. "Mumblemumblewoeisme." *Seconds Out Slam*. Manchester, 6 Mar. 2007. <www.livepoetry.net>.

-----. "The Yorkshire Rapper." *Seconds Out Slam*. Manchester, 6 Mar. 2007. <www.livepoetry.net>.

Joseph, Anthony. "Aranguez." *Vienna Lit Festival 2006*. Vienna, 13 Oct. 2006. Unpublished video recording.
Published in print: Anthony Joseph. *Excerpts from The African Origins of UFOs*. London: Poison Engine Press, 2005. 19-20.

-----. "Kneedeepnditchdiggerniggersweat." *Vienna Lit Festival 2006*. Vienna, 13 Oct. 2006. Unpublished video recording.
Published in print: Anthony Joseph. *Excerpts from The African Origins of UFOs*. London: Poison Engine Press, 2005. 5-6.

-----. *The African Origins of UFOs*. London: Salt, 2006.

Kane, Denizen. "Patriot Act." *Russell Simmons' Def Poetry*, Season 5, Episode 10. 2005. 30 Mar. 2009
<http://www.youtube.com/watch?v=PYFhUJUj5Kg>.
Text published: *HBO Home page*. 30 Mar. 2009
<http://www.hbo.com/defpoetry/excerpts/season5/episode10.html>.

Kay, Jackie. "My Grandmother." *Poetry in Performance* Vol. 2. Audio CD. London: 57 Productions, 2003.
Published in print: Jackie Kay. *Darling: New & Selected Poems*. Tarset: Bloodaxe, 2007. 12.

Landesman, Fran. "The Last Smoker." *Apples & Snakes in Soho*. London, 28 Feb. 2007. Unpublished video recording.

Lee-French, Segun. "Xmas Kisses." *Seconds Out Slam*. Manchester, 6 Mar. 2007. <www.livepoetry.net>.

Lip Up Fatty!. Shortfuse, London, 1 Mar. 2007. Unpublished video recording.

Mannix, Aoife. "Marked." Video. *Welcome Collection* Home page. 13 Mar. 2008. 28 Dec. 2009 <http://www.wellcomecollection.org/whatson/events/the-meat-of-the-tongue-series/disfigurement.aspx>.

McGough, Roger. "Bees Cannot Fly." *Poetry in Performance* Vol. 2. Audio CD. London: 57 Productions, 2003.
Published in print: Roger McGough. *Selected Poems*. London: Penguin, 2006. 137.

Mendelssohn, Felix de. "Kyoto Conversation." *Vienna Lit Festival 2008*. Vienna, 17 Apr. 2008. <www.livepoetry.net>.

Mitchell, Adrian. "To Whom It May Concern." *Peter Whitehead And the Sixties*. [Compilation DVD consisting of the Peter Whitehead films Wholly Communion (1965) and Benefit of the Doubt (1967)]. Dir. Peter Whitehead. DVD. BFI Video, 2007.
Published in print: Adrian Mitchell. *Out Loud*. London: Cape Goliard, 1968.

Patten, Brian. "Angel Wings." *Poetry in Performance* Vol. 2. Audio CD. London: 57 Productions, 2003.
Published in print: Brian Patten. *Collected Love Poems*. London: Harper Perennial, 2007. 53-55.

-----. "Hair Today, No Her Tomorrow." *Vienna Lit Festival 2008*. Vienna, 17 Apr. 2008. <www.livepoetry.net>.
Published in print: Brian Patten. *Storm Damage*. London: Flamingo, 1995. 55-57.

Peter Whitehead And the Sixties. [Compilation DVD consisting of the Peter Whitehead films Wholly Communion (1965) and Benefit of the Doubt (1967)]. Dir. Peter Whitehead. DVD. BFI Video, 2007.

Pötscher, Gabriele. "OK." *Vienna Lit Festival 2008*. Vienna, 18 Apr. 2008. <www.livepoetry.net>.
Published in print: Walter W. Hölbling and Gabriele Pötscher. *Love Lust Loss*. Graz: Steirische Verlagsgesellschaft, 2003. 94.

[*Seconds Out*] *Seconds Out Slam*. Manchester, 6 Mar. 2007. Unpublished video recording.

Shortman. "Beautifully Hectic." Video. *Platform 21* Home page. 29 Dec. 2009 <http://www.platform21.co.uk/Profiles/shortMAN.html>.
Published in print: Shortman. *shortMAFRICAN*. London: OnRoom, 2005. 40-42.

Siddique, John. "90 Day Theory." *Vienna Lit Festival 2006*. Vienna, 14 Oct. 2006. <www.livepoetry.net>.
Published in print: John Siddique. *The Prize*. Norwich: The Rialto, 2005. 14.

-----. "Yes." *Vienna Lit Festival 2006*. Vienna, 14 Oct. 2006. <www.livepoetry.net>.
Published in print: John Siddique. *The Prize*. Norwich: The Rialto, 2005. 55.

-----. "Neckgrip." *The Prize*. Norwich: The Rialto, 2005. 21.

Smith, Patricia. "Skinhead." *Russell Simmons' Def Poetry*, Season 2, Episode 2. 2002. 30 Dec. 2009 <http://www.youtube.com/watch?v=5LswzRttYVw>.
Published in print: Patricia Smith. *Big Towns, Big Talk*. Cambridge, Mass.: Zoland Books, 1992. 67-68.

Spit-Lit Festival 2007. London, 2-10 Mar. 2007. Unpublished video recording.

UK Poetry Slam Championships. London, 11 Mar. 2006. Unpublished audio recording.

[*VLF 2006*] *Vienna Lit Festival 2006.* Vienna, 12-14 Oct. 2006. Unpublished video recording.

[*VLF 2008*] *Vienna Lit Festival 2008.* Vienna, 17-19 Apr. 2008. Unpublished video recording.

Yeats, W. B. "The Lake Isle of Innisfree." Audio recording. *The Poetry Archive.* 28 Feb. 1935. 16 Nov 2009 <www.poetryarchive.org/poetryarchive/singlePoet.do?poetId=1688>.
Published in print: *The Variorum Edition of the Poems of W. B. Yeats.* Ed. Peter Allt and Russell K. Alspach. New York: Macmillan, 1966. 117.

Zephaniah, Benjamin. "Rong Radio Station." *Poetry in Performance* Vol. 2. Audio CD. London: 57 Productions, 2003.
Published in print: "De Rong Radio." *You're History! How People Make the Difference.* Ed. Michelle P. Brown and Richard J. Kelly. London: Continuum, 2005. xi-xiv.

Secondary Sources:

Abercrombie, Nicholas, and Brian Longhurst. *Audiences: A Social Theory of Performance and Imagination.* London: Sage, 1998.

"About." *Apples & Snakes* Home page. 29 Jan. 2010 <http://www.applesandsnakes.org/about.php>.

"About Renaissance One." *Renaissance One* Home page. 11 Jan. 2010 <http://www.renaissanceone.co.uk/?location_id=31>.

Abrahams, Melanie. Telephone interview. 26 Nov. 2009.

"Accent." *Longman Dictionary of Contemporary English.* 3rd ed. Harlow: Longman, 1995.

Agbabi, Patience. Personal interview. 9 Mar. 2007.

Alberts, David. *The Expressive Body: Physical Characterization for the Actor.* Portsmouth, NH: Heinemann, 1997.

Ammon, Frieder von. "How to Do Things with Words and Music: The Performative Poetry of Ernst Jandl." *Proceedings of the Seventh International Conference on Word and Music Studies at Vienna, 2009.* Word and Music Studies. Amsterdam: Rodopi, 2011. Forthcoming.

Anderson, Fortner. "All the Voices." *Canadian Theatre Review* 130 (spring 2007): 43-46.

Antin, David. *Talking at the Boundaries.* New York, NY: New Directions, 1976.

Argyle, Michael. *Bodily Communication.* London: Methuen, 1975.

Armitage, Simon, and Robert Crawford, eds. *The Penguin Book of Poetry from Britain and Ireland Since 1945.* New York: Viking, 1998.

Astley, Neil. "Give Poetry Back to People." *New Statesman* 23 Oct. 2006. 14 Jan. 2010 <http://www.newstatesman.com/200610230043>.

Athanases, Steven Z. "When Print Alone Fails Poetry: Performance as a Contingency of Literary Value." *Text and Performance Quarterly* 11 (1991): 116-127.

Attridge, Derek. *Poetic Rhythm: An Introduction.* Cambridge: CUP, 1995.

Auslander, Philip. *Liveness: Performance in a Mediatized Culture.* 2nd ed. London: Routledge, 2008.

Austin, J. L. *How to Do Things with Words.* 2nd ed. Cambridge, Mass.: Harvard Univ. Press, 1975.

Bakker, Egbert J. *Poetry in Speech. Orality and Homeric Discourse.* London: Cornell University Press, 1997.

Baldick, Chris. *The Concise Oxford Dictionary of Literary Terms.* Oxford: OUP, 1990. *Literature Online.* Vienna University Library. 14 June 2008 <http://lion.chadwyck.co.uk/>.

Balme, Christopher B. *The Cambridge Introduction to Theatre Studies*. Cambridge: CUP, 2008.

Barnet, Sylvan et al. *An Introduction to Literature: Fiction, Poetry, Drama*. 11th ed. New York: Longman, 1997.

Barthes, Roland. "The Death of the Author." *Image, Music, Text*. Trans. Stephen Heath. London: Fontana, 1977. 142-148.

Bauman, Richard, and Charles Briggs. "Poetics and Performance as Critical Perspectives on Language and Social Life." *Annual Review of Anthropology* 19 (1990): 59-88.

Bauman, Richard. *Story, Performance, and Event: Contextual Studies of Oral Narrative*. Cambridge: CUP, 1986.

-----. *Verbal Art as Performance*. 1977. Prospect Heights, Illinois: Waveland Press, 1984.

Bennett, Susan. *Theatre Audiences: A Theory of Production and Reception*. 2nd ed. London: Routledge, 1997.

Bernstein, Charles, ed. *Close Listening: Poetry and the Performed Word*. New York: OUP, 1998.

Berry, Francis. *Poetry and the Physical Voice*. London: Routledge & Kegan Paul, 1962.

Birdwhistell, Ray L. *Introduction to Kinesics: An Annotation System for Analysis of Body Motion and Gesture*. Louisville: University of Louisville, 1952.

-----. *Kinesics and Context: Essays on Body Motion Communication*. Philadelphia: University of Pennsylvania Press, 1970.

Bode, Christoph. *Einführung in die Lyrikanalyse*. Trier: WVT, 2001.

Boenisch, Peter M. "Aesthetic Art to Aisthetic Act: Theatre, Media, Intermedial Performance." *Intermediality in Theatre and Performance*. Ed. Freda Chapple and Chiel Kattenbelt. Amsterdam: Rodopi, 2006. 103-116.

-----. *körPERformance 1.0: Theorie und Analyse von Körper- und Bewegungsdarstellungen im zeitgenössischen Theater.* München: ePODIUM Verlag, 2002.

Booth, Wayne C. *The Rhetoric of Fiction.* Chicago: Univ. of Chicago Press, 1961.

Bourdieu, Pierre. *Rules of Art: Genesis and Structure of the Literary Field.* Trans. Susan Emanuel. Stanford: Stanford UP, 1996.

-----. "The Field of Cultural Production, or: The Economic World Reversed." *Poetics* 12 (1983): 311-356.

Bråten, Stein, ed. *On Being Moved: From Mirror Neurons to Empathy.* Amsterdam: Benjamins, 2007.

Brazil, D., Coulthard, M., and Johns, C. *Discourse Intonation and Language Teaching.* London: Longman, 1981.

Breeze, Jean Binta, Patience Agbabi, Jillian Tipene, Ruth Harrison, and Vicki Bertram. "A Round-Table Discussion on Poetry in Performance." *Feminist Review* 62 (Summer 1999): 24-54.

Brogan, T. V. F. "Poetry." *The New Princeton Encyclopedia of Poetry and Poetics.* Princeton, New Jersey: Princeton UP, 1993. 940-43.

Brogan, T. V. F., and Fabian Gudas. "Tone." *The New Princeton Encyclopedia of Poetry and Poetics.* Princeton, New Jersey: Princeton UP, 1993. 1293-4.

Brooks, Cleanth. *The Well Wrought Urn: Studies in the Structure of Poetry.* New York: Harcourt, 1947.

Brooks, Cleanth, and Robert P. Warren. *Understanding Poetry.* 3rd ed. New York: Holt, Rinehart and Winston, 1960.

Büscher-Ulbrich, Dennis. "The Poet/Poem as *Agent Provocateur*: Sounding the Performative Dimension of Amiri Baraka's 'Somebody Blew Up America.'" *State(s) of the Art: Considering Poetry Today.* Ed. Klaus Martens. Würzburg: Königshausen & Neumann, 2010. 86-101.

Butler, Judith. *Gender Trouble: Feminism and the Subversion of Identity.* 1990. New York: Routledge, 2006.

Caddel, Richard. "Developmental Thoughts on Poetry in Performance." *Words Out Loud: Ten Essays about Poetry Readings*. Ed. Mark Robinson. Exeter: Stride Publications, 2002.

Campbell, Murray. "Timbre." The Oxford Dictionary of Music. 2nd ed. Ed. Michael Kennedy. Oxford: Oxford University Press, 2007. 14 Apr. 2009 <http://www.oxfordmusiconline.com/subscriber/article/grove/music/27973?q=timbre&search=quick&pos=7&_start=1#firsthit>.

Carlson, Marvin. "Histoires des codes." *Théâtre: Modes d'approche*. Ed. André Helbo and Marvin Carlson. Brussels: Labor, 1987. 65-75.

Chivers, Tom. Personal interview. 21 Sep. 2006.

Chovil, Nicole. "Facing Others: A Social Communicative Perspective on Facial Displays." *The Psychology of Facial Expression*. Ed. James A. Russell and José Miguel Fernández-Dols. Cambridge: CUP, 1997. 321-333.

Colebrook, Claire. *Irony*. The New Critical Idiom. London: Routledge, 2004.

Collinge, Geraldine. Personal interview. 10 Mar. 2006.

"Context." *Macmillan Dictionary for Advanced Learners*. 2nd ed. Oxford: Macmillan, 2007.

Cowan, T. L. "An Emerging Discourse." *Canadian Theatre Review* 130 (spring 2007): 7-9.

Crystal, David. *A Dictionary of Linguistics and Phonetics*. 6th ed. Malden, Mass.: Blackwell, 2008.

Cuddon, John A. *The Penguin Dictionary of Literary Terms and Literary Theory*. 4th ed. London: Penguin, 1999.

Culler, Jonathan. *Literary Theory: A Very Short Introduction*. Oxford: OUP, 1997.

Cusic, Don. *The Poet As Performer*. Lanham: University of America Press, 1991.

Damon, Maria. "Was That 'Different,' 'Dissident' or 'Dissonant'? Poetry (n) the Public Spear: Slams, Open Readings, and Dissident Traditions." *Close Listening: Poetry and the Performed Word*. Ed. Charles Bernstein. New York: OUP, 1998. 324-342.

Davidson, Ian. "Occasions For Additional Apparitions: Performing Poets & The Performed Poem." *Additional Apparitions: Poetry, Performance & Site Specificity*. Ed. David Kennedy and Keith Tuma. Sheffield: The Cherry On The Top Press, 2002. 129-144.

Davidson, William, and Shai Goldstein. "ADL Writes to the Governor of New Jersey about Amiri Baraka." Online posting. 27 Sept. 2002. 19 Oct. 2009 <http://www.adl.org/anti_semitism/ltr_mcgreevy.asp>.

Derrida, Jacques. *Of Grammatology*. Trans. Gayatri Chakravorty Spivak. Baltimore, MD: Johns Hopkins University Press, 1976.

Diderot, Denis. *Oeuvres de théâtre de M. Diderot: avec un discours sur la poésie dramatique*. Vol 2. Amsterdam: M. M. Rey, 1772.

Diehl, Joanne F. "Poetry and Literary Theory." *A Companion to Twentieth-Century Poetry*. Ed. Neil Roberts. Oxford: Blackwell, 2001. 89-100.

Dillard, Scott. "The Art of Performing Poetry: Festivals, Slams, and Americans' Favorite Poem Project Events." *Text and Performance Quarterly* 22.3 (July 2002): 217-227.

Dube, Pamela. *Contemporary English Performance Poetry in Canada and South Africa: A Comparative Study of the Main Motifs and Poetic Techniques*. Heidelberg: Universitätsverlag C. Winter, 1997.

Eagleton, Terry. *How to Read a Poem*. Oxford: Blackwell, 2007.

Eckstein, Lars. *Reading Song Lyrics*. Internationale Forschungen zur Allgemeinen und Vergleichenden Literaturwissenschaft 137. Amsterdam: Rodopi, 2010.

Eco, Umberto. "Semiotik der Theateraufführung." *Performanz: Zwischen Sprachphilosophie und Kulturwissenschaften*. Ed. Uwe Wirth. Frankfurt a. M.: Suhrkamp, 2002. 262-276.

Egbert, Marie-Luise. "Audiobooks and Reception Aesthetics." *Intermedialities*. Ed. Werner Huber. Trier: WVT, 2007. 59-68.

Eisenberg, Barry. "Getting There a Little Late: A Review of the *Kuksu* Benefit Poetry Reading." *The Poetry Reading: A Contemporary Compendium on Language & Performance*. Ed. Stephen Vincent and Ellen Zweig. San Francisco: Momo's Press, 1981. 64-67.

Ekman, Paul, and Wallace V. Friesen. *The Repertoire of Nonverbal Behavior: Categories, Origins, Usage, and Coding*. Semiotica 1. Den Haag: 1969.

Elam, Keir. *The Semiotics of Theatre and Drama*. 2nd ed. London: Routledge, 2002.

Eleveld, Mark. *The Spoken Word Revolution: Redux*. Naperville, Illinois: Sourcebooks, Inc., 2007.

Engler, Balz. *Reading and Listening: The Modes of Communicating Poetry and their Influence on the Texts*. Bern: Francke, 1982.

English, Lucy. Personal interview. 20 Sep. 2006.

Erlich, Victor. "Russion Formalism." *The New Princeton Encyclopedia of Poetry and Poetics*. Princeton, New Jersey: Princeton UP, 1993. 1101-1102.

Evaristo, Bernardine, and Neil Astley. "Head to Head." *Free Verse: Publishing Opportunities for Black and Asian Poets*. London: Spread the Word, 2007. 14-17.

Eversmann, Peter. "The Experience of the Theatrical Event." *Theatrical Events: Borders, Dynamics, Frames*. Ed. Cremona, V. et al. Amsterdam: Rodopi, 2004. 139-174.

Ferrier, Ian. "Tools of Poetry in Performance in Canada." *Canadian Theatre Review* 130 (spring 2007): 32-37.

Finch, Peter. "Sound Poetry in the UK." *57 Productions* home page. 1 July 2003. 10 Mar. 2009
<http://www.57productions.com/article_reader.php?id=11>.

Fine, Elizabeth. C. *The Folklore Text: From Performance to Print*. 1984. Bloomington: Indiana University Press, 1994.

Finnegan, Ruth. *Oral Poetry: Its Nature, Significance and Social Context.* 1977. Bloomington: Indiana University Press, 1992.

-----. *Oral Traditions and the Verbal Arts: A Guide to Research Practices.* London: Routledge, 1992.

-----. "The How of Literature." *Oral Tradition* 20.2 (2005): 164-187.

Fischer-Lichte, Erika. *Ästhetik des Performativen.* Frankfurt am Main: Suhrkamp, 2004.

-----. "Die Zeichensprache des Theaters: Zum Problem theatralischer Bedeutungsgenerierung." *Theaterwissenschaft Heute: Eine Einführung.* Ed. Renate Möhrmann. Berlin: Dietrich Reimer, 1990. 233-259.

-----. "Grenzgänge und Tauschhandel: Auf dem Wege zu einer performativen Kultur." *Performanz: Zwischen Sprachphilosophie und Kulturwissenschaften.* Ed. Uwe Wirth. Frankfurt a. Main: Suhrkamp, 2002. 277-300.

Fish, Stanley. *Is There A Text in This Class?.* Cambridge, Mass.: Harvard Univ. Press, 1980.

Foley, John Miles. *How to Read an Oral Poem.* Urbana: University of Illinois Press, 2002.

Foster, Patricia. E-mail interview. 11 – 16 Oct. 2009.

Fowler, William. "One Plus One, or Two Films by Peter Whitehead." DVD brochure: *Peter Whitehead And the Sixties.* [Compilation DVD consisting of the Peter Whitehead films Wholly Communion (1965) and Benefit of the Doubt (1967)]. Dir. Peter Whitehead. DVD. BFI Video, 2007.

Furniss, Graham. *Orality: The Power of the Spoken Word.* Basingstoke: Macmillan, 2004.

Furniss, Tom, and Michael Bath. *Reading Poetry: An Introduction.* London: Prentice-Hall, 1996.

Geertz, Clifford. "Thick Description." *The Interpretation of Cultures: Selected Essays.* New York: Basic Books, 2001.

Genette, Gérard. *Paratexts: Thresholds of Interpretation*. Trans. Jane E. Lewin. Ed. Richard Macksey. Cambridge: CUP, 1997.

Gibson, Abraham. Personal interview. 4 Mar. 2007.

Ginsberg, Allen. *Poets on Stage: The Some Symposium on Poetry Readings*. New York: Release Press, 1978.

Gioia, Dana. *Disappearing Ink: Poetry at the End of Print Culture*. Saint Paul, Minnesota: Graywolf Press, 2004.

-----. "The New Oral Poetry: An Excerpt from the Essay 'Disappearing Ink: Poetry at the End of Print Culture.'" *The Spoken Word Revolution Redux*. Ed. Mark Eleveld. Naperville, Ill.: Sourcebooks Inc., 2007. 242-245

Glazner, Gary M., ed. *Poetry Slam: The Competitive Art of Performance Poetry*. San Francisco: Manic D Press, 2000.

Goffman, Erving. *The Presentation of Self in Everyday Life*. New York: Doubleday, 1959.

Groff, David. "The Peril of the Poetry Reading: The Page Versus the Performance." 26 Jan. 2005. 24 Nov. 2008 <http://www.poets.org/viewmedia.php/prmMID/5913>.

Grotowski, Jerzy. "Towards a Poor Theatre." 1968. *The Routledge Reader in Politics and Performance*. Ed. Lizbeth Goodman and Jane de Gay. London: Routledge, 2000. 21-27.

Gudas, Fabian. "Explication." *The New Princeton Encyclopedia of Poetry and Poetics*. Princeton, New Jersey: Princeton UP, 1993. 395-396.

Habekost, Christian. *Verbal Riddim: The Politics and Aesthetics of African-Caribbean Dub Poetry*. Amsterdam: Rodopi, 1993.

Hagan, Jackie. E-mail interview. 3 – 10 Jan. 2010.

Hall, Donald. "The Poetry Reading: Public Performance/Private Art." *American Scholar* 54 (1985): 63-77.

Hall, Edward T. *The Hidden Dimension*. 1966. New York: Anchor Books, 1990.

Hardy, Jane. "Now He's Sixty Five: Adrian Mitchell in Conversation with Jane Hardy." *Poetry Review* 87.3 (1997): 4-8.

Hart, Josephine. "The Visionary Company of Love." *Guardian*, 9 June 2007. 15 Sep. 2008 <http://www.guardian.co.uk/books/2007/jun/09/featuresreviews.guardianreview1>.

Hawthorn, Jeremy. "Orality." *A Concise Glossary of Contemporary Literary Theory*. 2nd ed. London: Arnold, 1994.

Hays, K. Michael. *The Public and Performance: Essays in the History of French and German Theater 1871-1900*. Ann Arbor, Mich.: UMI Research Press, 1981.

Hiebler, Heinz. "Medienorientierte Literaturinterpretation." *Metzler Lexikon Literatur- und Kulturtheorie*. 4th ed. Stuttgart: Metzler, 2008. 474-476.

Higgins, Dick. "Sound Poetry." *The New Princeton Encyclopedia of Poetry and Poetics*. Princeton, New Jersey: Princeton UP, 1993. 1182-1183.

Hiß, Guido. *Der theatralische Blick: Einführung in die Aufführungsanalyse*. Berlin: Reimer, 1993.

Hobsbaum, Philip. *Metre, Rhythm and Verse Form*. New Critical Idiom. London: Routledge, 1996.

Holland, Jane. "Speed Poetry at Short-Fuse Tomorrow." *Poets on Fire* Blog. 26 Nov. 2009 <http://poetsonfire.blogspot.com/2006/02/speed-poetry-at-short-fuse-tomorrow.html>.

Howell, Anthony. *The Analysis of Performance Art: A Guide to its Theory and Practice*. Amsterdam: Harwood, 1999.

Hoyles, Asher, and Martin Hoyles. *Moving Voices: Black Performance Poetry*. London: Hansib, 2002.

Jakobson, Roman. "Closing Statements: Linguistics and Poetics." *Style in Language*. Ed. Thomas A. Sebeok. Cambridge, Mass.: MIT Press, 1960. 350-377.

Jauß, Hans Robert. *Toward an Aesthetic of Reception*. Trans. Timothy Bahti. Minneapolis: Univ. of Minnesota Press, 1982.

Jebb, Keith. "Hitherandthithering." *Poetry Review* 87.3 (autumn 1997): 17.

Joseph, Anthony. E-mail interview. 19 June – 3 July 2009.

-----. Home page. 28 Dec. 2009 <http://www.anthonyjoseph.co.uk>.

-----. Personal interview. 10 Mar. 2006.

Kattenbelt, Chiel. "Theatre as the art of the performer and the stage of intermediality." *Intermediality in Theatre and Performance*. Ed. Freda Chapple and Chiel Kattenbelt. Amsterdam: Rodopi, 2006. 29-39.

Kendon, Adam. "Language and Gesture: Unity or Duality?" *Language and Gesture*. Ed. David McNeill. Language, Culture and Cognition 2. Cambridge: CUP, 2000. 47-63.

Kennedy, David, and Keith Tuma. *Additional Apparitions: Poetry, Performance & Site Specificity*. Sheffield: The Cherry On The Top Press, 2002.

Klarer, Mario. *An Introduction to Literary Studies*. London: Routledge, 1999.

Knowles, Ric. *Reading the Material Theatre*. Cambridge: CUP, 2004.

Krämer, Sybille. "Sprache – Stimme – Schrift: Sieben Gedanken über Performativität als Medialität." *Performanz: Zwischen Sprachphilosophie und Kulturwissenschaften*. Ed. Uwe Wirth. Frankfurt a. M.: Suhrkamp, 2002. 323-346.

Krauss, Robert M., Yihsiu Chen, and Rebecca F. Gottesman. "Lexical Gestures and Lexical Access: A Process Model." *Language and Gesture*. Ed. David McNeill. Language, Culture and Cognition 2. Cambridge: CUP, 2000. 261-283.

Kress, Gunther, and Theo Van Leeuwen. *Multimodal Discourse: The Modes and Media of Contemporary Communication*. London: Hodder Arnold, 2001.

Kühn, Christine. *Körper – Sprache: Elemente einer sprachwissenschaftlichen Explikation non-verbaler Kommunikation.* Frankfurt a. M.: Peter Lang, 2002.

LaBelle, Brandon, and Christof Migone, eds. *Writing Aloud: The Sonics of Language.* Los Angeles: Errant Bodies Press, 2001.

Leech, Geoffrey. "Metre." *The Language and Literature Reader.* Ed. Ronald Carter and Peter Stockwell. London: Routledge, 2008. 60-69.

Lee-French, Segun. E-mail interview. 27 Nov. 2009 – 7 Jan. 2010.

Lejeune, Philippe. *Le Pacte autobiographique.* Paris: Seuil, 1974.

Lennard, John. *The Poetry Handbook: A Guide to Reading Poetry for Pleasure and Practical Criticism.* 2nd ed. Oxford: OUP, 2005.

Levertov, Denise. *Light Up the Cave.* New York: New Directions Publishing, 1981.

Lewis, Harry. "The Circuit / New York City Public Readings: A Short History." *The Poetry Reading: A Contemporary Compendium on Language & Performance.* Ed. Stephen Vincent and Ellen Zweig. San Francisco: Momo's Press, 1981. 85-90.

"Lip Up Fatty." *Shortfuse* Home page. 5 Mar. 2007. 19 Dec. 2009 <http://shortfuse.20six.co.uk/shortfuse/cat/80865/3>.

Literature North East, "Events – Being Alive." 11 Sep. 2008 <http://www.literaturenortheast.co.uk/events/EventDetail-828>.

"live." *Collins Cobuild English Dictionary.* London: Harper Collins, 1998.

Lord, Albert Bates. "Oral Poetry." *The New Princeton Encyclopedia of Poetry and Poetics.* Princeton, New Jersey: Princeton UP, 1993. 863-866.

Mackey, Nathaniel. "Sight-Specific, Sound-Specific…" *Additional Apparitions: Poetry, Performance & Site Specificity.* Ed. David Kennedy and Keith Tuma. Sheffield: The Cherry On The Top Press, 2002. 95-105.

Mae, Naila Keleta. "Introduction to No Knowledge College: Spoken Word vis-à-vis Theatre." *Canadian Theatre Review* 130 (spring 2007): 102-107.

Marsh, Nicky, Peter Middleton, and Victoria Sheppard. "'Blasts of Language': Changes in Oral Poetics in Britain since 1965." *Oral Tradition* 21.1 (2006): 44-67.

Masefield, John. *With the Living Voice: An Address given at the First General Meeting of The Scottish Association For the Speaking of Verse, 24th October 1924.* London: Heinemann, 1925.

Matterson, Stephen, and Darryl Jones. *Studying Poetry.* London: Arnold, 2000.

McDaniel, Jeffrey. "Slam and the Academy." *Poetry Slam: The Competitive Art of Performance Poetry.* Ed. Gary Glazner. San Francisco: Manic D Press, 2000. 35-37.

McLuhan, Marshall. *Understanding Media: The Extensions of Man.* 1964. London: Routledge, 2001.

McNeill, David. Introduction. *Language and Gesture.* Language, Culture and Cognition 2. Ed. David McNeill. Cambridge: CUP, 2000. 1-10.

Merleau-Ponty, Maurice. *Phenomenology of Perception.* 1962. Trans. Colin Smith. London: Routledge, 2002.

Meyer, Michael. *English and American Literatures.* 3rd ed. Tübingen: Francke, 2008.

Middleton, Peter. *Distant Reading: Performance, Readership, and Consumption in Contemporary Poetry.* Tuscaloosa: University of Alabama Press, 2005.

-----. "How to Read a Reading of a Written Poem." *Oral Tradition* 20.1 (2005): 7-34.

-----. "Performing an Experiment, Performing a Poem: Allen Fisher and Bruce Andrews." *Additional Apparitions: Poetry, Performance & Site Specificity.* Ed. David Kennedy and Keith Tuma. Sheffield: The Cherry On The Top Press, 2002. 29-55.

-----. "Recognition." *Poetry Review* 94.1 (Spring 2004): 48-56.

-----. "The Contemporary Poetry Reading." *Close Listening: Poetry and the Performed Word*. Ed. Charles Bernstein. New York: OUP, 1998. 262-299.

Millum, Trevor. "Performance Poetry: What's in it for the Kids?" *Reading the Applause: Reflections on Performance Poetry by Various Artists*. Ed. Stephen Wade and Paul Munden. York: Talking Shop, 1999. 83-85.

"Mission Statement." *Theatre Royal Stratford East* Home page. 8 Dec. 2009 <http://www.stratfordeast.com/our_work/mission_statement.shtml>.

Möhrmann, Malte. "Über das Flüchtige und das Fixieren: Die Sprache der Theaterkritik." *Theaterwissenschaft Heute: Eine Einführung*. Ed. Renate Möhrmann. Berlin: Dietrich Reimer, 1990. 165-186.

Müller-Zettelmann, Eva. *Lyrik und Metalyrik: Theorie einer Gattung und ihrer Selbstbespiegelung anhand von Beispielen aus der englisch- und deutschsprachigen Dichtkunst*. Heidelberg: Universitätsverlag C. Winter, 2000.

Nünning, Vera, and Ansgar Nünning. *An Introduction to the Study of English and American Literature*. Trans. Jane Dewhurst. Barcelona: Klett, 2004.

Oliver, Douglas. *Poetry and Narrative in Performance*. Basingstoke: Macmillan, 1989.

Olson, Charles. "Projective Verse." *Human Universe and Other Essays*. Ed. Donald Allen. New York, NY: Grove Press, 1967. 51-62.

Ong, Walter J. *Orality and Literacy: The Technologizing of the Word*. London: Methuen, 1982.

"Paralanguage." *The Concise Oxford Dictionary of Linguistics*. Ed. P. H. Matthews. Oxford University Press, 2007. *Oxford Reference Online*. Oxford University Press Universitatsbibliothek Wien. 26 Feb. 2009 <http://www.oxfordreference.com/views/ENTRY.html?subview=Main&entry=t36.e2427>.

Patten, Brian. E-mail interview. 8 Jan. 2010.

Pavis, Patrice. "Theatre Analysis: Some Questions and a Questionnaire." *New Theatre Quarterly* 1.2 (1985): 208-12.

Penlington, Nathan. *Don't Need English Lessons to Learn our Lines: The Unspoken History of Performance Poetry*. Unpublished MA thesis, Guildhall School of Music & Drama, London, 2000.

-----. Personal interview. 6 Mar. 2006.

Perelman, Bob. "Speech Effects: The Talk as a Genre." *Close Listening: Poetry and the Performed Word*. Ed. Charles Bernstein. New York: OUP, 1998. 200-216.

Perrine, Laurence. *Sound and Sense: An Introduction to Poetry*. 6th ed. New York: Harcourt, 1982.

Pfeiler, Martina. *Poetry Goes Intermedia: US-amerikanische Lyrik des 20. und 21. Jahrhunderts aus kultur- und medienwissenschaftlicher Perspektive*. Tübingen: Francke, 2010.

-----. *Sounds of Poetry: Contemporary American Performance Poets*. Tübingen: Narr, 2003.

"phrase." *The Concise Oxford Dictionary of Music*. Eds. Michael Kennedy and Joyce Kennedy. Oxford: Oxford University Press, 2007. *Oxford Reference Online*. Oxford University Press. Universitatsbibliothek Wien. 9 Apr. 2009 <http://www.oxfordreference.com/views/ENTRY.html?subview=Main&entry=t76.e7025>.

Poets Against War Home page. 2009. 28 Dec. 2009. <http://www.poetsagainstthewar.org>.

Poyatos, Fernando. *Paralanguage: A Linguistic and Interdisciplinary Approach to Interactive Speech and Sound*. Amsterdam Studies in the Theory and History of Linguistic Science. Amsterdam: Benjamins, 1993.

Quartermain, Peter. "Sound Reading." *Close Listening: Poetry and the Performed Word*. Ed. Charles Bernstein. New York: OUP, 1998. 217-230.

Quirk, Randolph, Sidney Greenbaum, Geoffrey Leech, and Jan Svartvik, eds. *A Comprehensive Grammar of the English Language*. London: Longman, 1985.

Rasula, Jed. "Understanding the Sound of Not Understanding." *Close Listening: Poetry and the Performed Word*. Ed. Charles Bernstein. New York: OUP, 1998. 233-261.

Reynolds, Joshua. *Discourses on Art*. New York: Collier Books, 1966.

Robinson, Mark, ed. *Words Out Loud: Ten Essays About Poetry Readings*. Exeter: Stride Publications, 2002.

-----. "In the Familiar Space of the Voice." *Words Out Loud: Ten Essays About Poetry Readings*. Ed. Mark Robinson. Exeter: Stride Publications, 2002. 37-42.

Rodríguez-Vázquez, Rosalía. *The Rhythm of Speech, Verse, and Vocal Music: A New Theory*. Linguistic Insights 110. Bern: Peter Lang, 2010.

Russell, James A., and José Miguel Fernández-Dols. "What does a facial expression mean?" *The Psychology of Facial Expression*. Ed. James A. Russell and José Miguel Fernández-Dols. Cambridge: CUP, 1997. 3-30.

Ruthrof, Horst. *The Body in Language*. London: Cassell, 2000.

Salah, Trish. "What's All the Yap? Reading Mirha-Soleil Ross's Performance of Activist Pedagogy." *Canadian Theatre Review* 130 (spring 2007): 64-71.

Saussure, Ferdinand de. *Course in General Linguistics*. Ed. Charles Bally. New York, NY: Philos. Library, 1959.

Sauter, Willmar. "Introducing the Theatrical Event." *Theatrical Events: Borders, Dynamics, Frames*. Ed. Vicky Ann Cremona, Peter Eversmann, Hans van Maanen, Willmar Sauter and John Tulloch. Amsterdam: Rodopi, 2004. 4-14.

Scannell, Vernon. *How to Enjoy Poetry*. London: Piatkus, 1983.

Schechner, Richard. *Performance Studies: An Introduction*. 2nd ed. New York: Routledge, 2006.

Schevill, James. "Notes on the Performance Poem." *The Poetry Reading: A Contemporary Compendium on Language & Performance*. Ed. Stephen Vincent and Ellen Zweig. San Francisco: Momo's Press, 1981. 142-146.

Schmidt, Tom. "The Poetry Performance." *The Poetry Reading: A Contemporary Compendium on Language & Performance*. Ed. Vincent, Stephen, and Ellen Zweig. San Francisco: Momo's Press, 1981. 134-137.

Schneider, Dan. "This Old Poem #36." 11 Sep. 2002. 24 Nov. 2008 <http://www.cosmoetica.com/TOP36-DES33.htm>.

Schwarz, Aljoscha A., and Ronald P. Schweppe. *Das Lexikon der Körpersprache*. Rastatt: Moewig, 1998.

Severin, Laura. *Poetry Off the Page: Twentieth-Century British Women Poets in Performance.*
Aldershot, Hants: Ashgate, 2004.

Shakespeare, William. *Macbeth*. Ed. G. K. Hunter. London: Penguin, 1995.

Sherwood, Kenneth. "Elaborate Versionings: Characteristics of Emergent Performance in three Print/Oral/Aural Poets." *Oral Tradition* 21.1 (2006): 119-147.

Shortfuse Home page. 19 Dec. 2009
<http://shortfuse.20six.co.uk/shortfuse/cat/80865/0>.

Shot from the Lip Home page. 22 Mar. 2008 <http://sftl.metaroar.com/>.

Siddique, John. "Of You and I and Depressing Ducks." Interview with Julia Novak. *Poetry Salzburg Review* 11 (Spring 2007): 180-85.

-----. Personal interview. 11 Oct. 2006.

Smith, Rommi. Personal interview. 21 Apr. 2008.

Somers-Willett, Susan. *Authenticating Voices: Performance, Black Identity, and Slam Poetry*. Unpublished dissertation, University of Texas, Austin, 2003. 12 Dec. 2008
<http://repositories.lib.utexas.edu/handle/2152/960>.

Stein, Deborah, and Robert Spillman. *Poetry into Song: Performance and Analysis of Lieder*. New York: Oxford Univ. Press, 1996.

Stern, Frederick. "The Formal Poetry Reading." *The Drama Review* 35.3 (Fall 1991): 67-84.

Stewart, Garrett. *Reading Voices: Literature and the Phonotext*. Berkeley, Calif.: Univ. of California Press,1990.

Tedlock, Dennis. *The Spoken Word and the Work of Interpretation*. Philadelphia: University of Pennsylvania Press, 1983.

Thompson, Russell. Personal interview. 7 Mar. 2006.

-----. Personal interview. 1 Mar. 2007.

"timbre." *The Concise Oxford Dictionary of Music*. Eds. Michael Kennedy and Joyce Kennedy. Oxford: Oxford University Press, 2007. *Oxford Reference Online*. Oxford University Press. Universitatsbibliothek Wien. 14 Apr. 2009 <http://www.oxfordreference.com/views/ENTRY.html?subview=Main&entry=t76.e9115>.

Toro, Fernando de. *Theatre Semiotics: Text and Staging in Modern Theatre*. Trans. John Lewis. Frankfurt: Vervuert, 1995.

Trager, George L. "Paralanguage: A First Approximation." 1958. *Language in Culture and Society*. Ed. Dell Hymes. New York: Harper and Row, 1966. 274-88.

Tuma, Keith. "Midnight at the Oasis: Performing Poetry inside the Spectacle." *Modernism/Modernity* 6.1 (1999): 153-162.

Tutu, Samera Owusu. "The Resounding Underground: Performance Poetry in the U.K. Today." *"Black" British Aesthetics Today*. Ed. R. Victoria Arana, R.V. Newcastle: Cambridge Scholars Publishing, 2007.

Ubersfeld, Anne. "The Pleasure of the Spectator." Trans. Pierre Bouillaguet and Charles Jose. *Modern Drama* 25.1 (March): 12-39.

Van Leeuwen, Theo. *Speech, Music, Sound*. Basingstoke: Macmillan, 1999.

Vincent, Stephen. "Poetry Readings / Reading Poetry: San Francisco Bay Area, 1958-1980." *The Poetry Reading: A Contemporary Compendium on Language*

& *Performance*. Ed. Stephen Vincent, and Ellen Zweig. San Francisco: Momo's Press, 1981. 19-54.

Vincent, Stephen, and Ellen Zweig, eds. *The Poetry Reading: A Contemporary Compendium on Language & Performance*. San Francisco: Momo's Press, 1981.

Wade, Stephen, and Paul Munden, eds. *Reading the Applause: Reflections on Performance Poetry by Various Artists*. York: Talking Shop, 1999.

Watzlawick, Paul, Janet H. Beavin, und Don D. Jackson. 1971. *Menschliche Kommunikation: Formen, Störungen, Paradoxien*. Bern: Hans Huber, 1990.

Wennerstrom, Ann. *The Music of Everyday Speech: Prosody and Discourse Analysis*. Oxford: OUP, 2001.

"What is Live Literature?" LitUp Conference Debate with Jonathan Davidson, Sarah Jane Albury and Segun Lee-French. Kendal, 22 Sep. 2006. Unpublished audio recording.

Wheeler, Lesley. *Voicing American Poetry: Sound and Performance from the 1920s to the Present*. Ithaca, N.Y.: Cornell University Press, 2008.

Whitworth, John. "Vox Po – Vox Pop?" *Poetry Review* 87.3 (1997): 18-20.

Winters, Yvor. "The Audible Reading of Poetry." *Hudson Review* 4.3 (1951): 433-447.

Wojahn, David. "A Kind of Vaudeville: Appraising the Age of the Poetry Reading." *New England Quarterly and Bread Loaf Quarterly* 8.2 (1985): 265-282.

Wolf, Werner. "Illusion, ästhetische." *Metzler Lexikon Literatur- und Kulturtheorie*. 4th ed. Stuttgart: Metzler 2008. 310-311.

-----. "Intermediality." *The Routledge Encyclopedia of Narrative Theory*. Ed. David Herman, Manfred Jahn and Marie-Laure Ryan. London: Routledge, 2005. 252-256.

Table of Figures

Cover image: Rommi Smith, Vienna Lit Festival 2008. © Glen Sweeney.
Figure 1:   The mediality of poetry.
Figure 2:   Surprise pitch curve (Van Leeuwen 96).
Figure 3:   Transcription of "In the Funk World" (Sherwood 125).
Figure 4a & 4b: Segun Lee-French, "Seconds Out" slam" 2007.
Figure 5a-5c: Mark Gwynne Jones, "Seconds Out" slam" 2007.
Figure 6a-6e: Lucy English, "Apples & Snakes in Soho" 2007.
Figure 7a-7d: Andy Craven-Griffiths, "Apples & Snakes in Soho" 2007.
Figure 8a & 8b: Abraham Gibson, "Apples & Snakes in Soho" 2007.
Figure 9:   Mark Gwynne Jones, "Seconds Out" slam 2007.
Figure 10a-10c: Posture: Anthony Joseph, John Siddique, Abraham Gibson.
Figure 11:   Anthony Joseph, Vienna Lit Festival 2006.
Figure 12:   Brian Patten, Vienna Lit Festival 2008.
Figure 13a & 13b: Abraham Gibson, "Apples & Snakes in Soho" 2007.
Figure 14a-14d: Felix de Mendelssohn, Vienna Lit Festival 2008.
Figure 15:   A communication model for poetry (Nünning & Nünning 53).
Figure 16:   A communication model for live poetry.
Figure 17a & 17b: Patricia Smith, "Def Poetry" 2002.
Figure 18:   Patricia Foster, Spit-Lit Festival 2007.
Figure 19:   Kat Francois, UK Poetry Slam Championships 2006.
Figure 20:   Poetry Idol logo, 12 Dec 2009
                 <http://shortfuse.20six.co.uk/shortfuse/cat/80860/0>.
Figure 21:   Brian Patten, Vienna Lit Festival 2008.
Figure 22a-22f: Jackie Hagan, "Seconds Out" Slam 2007.

Index

Abercrombie, Nicholas, 194, 207-10
Abrahams, Melanie, 5, 203-4
accent, 79, 105, 119, 132, 135-7, 223, 234
Agard, John, 45
Agbabi, Patience, 20-1, 31-32, 47, 67, 70, 117, 127, 168-9, 212
Alberts, David, 148, 151, 157-9
alternants, 81
Amis, Martin, 26, 181
Ammon, Frieder von, 218-9
amplitude graph, 113, 116, 130-2
Anderson, Fortner, 18, 47, 206
Andrade, Suzanne, 197-8
Antin, David, 58
Apples & Snakes, 30, 43, 45, 67, 81, 152-6, 163, 204-6, 217-8, 221-2
Argyle, Michael, 147, 158, 164, 167
artefactual communication, 13, 151, 158, 168-9, 235
articulation, 13, 85, 115-6, 118-9
Astley, Neil, 11, 28-9, 31
Athanases, Steven Z., 26, 40
Attila the Stockbroker, 16
Attridge, Derek, 86-7, 90, 95, 110
audience interaction, 41, 52, 55, 151, 153-4, 157, 167-8, 201-2, 211-2, 230, 235, 238
audio poetry, 50, 75, 145, 238
audiotext, 13, 34, 38, 42, 65-7, 71-3, 75, 80-2, 84, 85, 98-9, 100, 109, 114, 119, 125-6, 132-3, 136, 138, 141, 145, 147-8, 150, 157, 167, 170, 182, 214, 216, 224, 226, 234, 238
Auslander, Philip, 49

Austin, John Langshaw, 17, 185
Bakker, Egbert, 24
Baldick, Chris, 51
Balme, Christopher B., 208-9, 214
Baraka, Amiri, 139, 193-4
Barnet, Sylvan, 53
Barthes, Roland, 25-6
Bauman, Richard, 34-6, 125, 174-5, 177, 185
beat, 49, 82-4, 88-91, 94-9, 128-9, 149, 216, 229
Beat Poets, 15-6, 46-7
Bennett, Susan, 195, 197, 212-4, 217
Bernard, Jeneece, 110-1, 127, 142
Bernstein, Charles, 11, 19, 24, 42, 56, 60, 75, 80-1, 84, 87, 95
Berry, Francis, 36, 120
Birdwhistell, Ray L., 145-7, 160, 164
Bode, Christoph, 54
body action, 119, 147, 156-7
body communication, 120, 145-9, 150-3, 156-8, 160, 163, 167-8, 170, 182, 221, 224, 231, 235
body set, 147, 235
Boenisch, Peter M., 25, 150-1, 158, 170
Booth, Wayne C., 176
Bourdieu, Pierre, 180-1
Bråten, Stein, 78
Brazil, David, 103
breathiness, 76, 122-3, 125, 191, 230
Breeze, Jean Binta, 17, 47, 218
Briggs, Charles, 174-5, 177, 185
Brogan, T. V. F., 51, 56, 133

Brooks, Cleanth, 17, 133
Brooks, Gwendolyn, 26-7, 39, 40, 93-5, 128
Büscher-Ulbrich, Dennis, 193-4
Butler, Judith, 187-8

Campbell, Murray, 120
Carlson, Marvin, 209
Cheek, Cris, 47
Chivers, Tom, 18
Chovil, Nicole, 164
Cobbing, Bob, 113-4
Colebrook, Claire, 134
Collinge, Geraldine, 206
Cooper-Clarke, John, 16, 47, 140, 184
Cope, Wendy, 107
Cowan, T. L., 213
Craven-Griffiths, Andy, 153-5
crescendo, 114-5
Crystal, David, 76
Cuddon, John A, 76
Culler, Jonathan, 54
Cusic, Don, 15, 19, 46

Damon, Maria, 42
Davidson, Ian, 69
Davidson, Jonathan, 60-1
decrescendo, 114-5
Def Poetry, 88, 189
Derrida, Jacques, 24-5
Diderot, Denis, 58, 209
Diehl, Joanne F, 188
Dillard, Scott, 186
Dube, Pamela, 45-6
dub poetry, 16-7, 20, 45, 53, 90, 182, 184, 196
duration, 37, 90, 95, 98, 105, 110, 115, 128-30, 137, 159, 160, 163, 216
dynamics, 38, 69, 111, 113-5, 130, 133, 197, 222

Eagleton, Terry, 37, 54
Eckstein, Lars, 55
Eco, Umberto, 185
Edwards, Zena, 31
Egbert, Marie-Luise, 28
Eisenberg, Barry, 41
Ekman, Paul, 154, 160-2
Elam, Keir, 57, 145-6, 184, 194, 196-7, 209, 215
Eleveld, Mark, 45
embodiment, 55, 59, 66, 78, 188, 191-3
emotive confinement, 105
emotive expansion, 105, 228
Engler, Balz, 25, 37, 39, 65-71, 183
English, Lucy, 20, 30, 102, 124, 131, 133, 151-3, 157, 161
Erlich, Victor, 25
Evaristo, Bernardine, 29-31
Eversmann, Peter, 59
evoked sound, 12, 36, 39, 53, 75, 87, 89, 182, 237

facial expression, 13, 52, 55, 60, 73, 78, 135, 148-9, 151, 154, 158, 164-7, 226, 235
Ferrier, Ian, 17, 47
Finch, Peter, 47, 113-4, 116, 131
Fine, Elizabeth C., 34-5, 41, 63-4, 97, 125-7, 131-2, 146-7, 168, 170, 175, 178, 198, 204, 217
Finnegan, Ruth, 17, 20, 23, 35-6, 72, 125-6
Fischer-Lichte, Erika, 17, 56, 58, 145, 173-5, 195-7
Fish, Stanley, 195
Fisher, Allen, 21, 47
Foley, John Miles, 19, 24, 35-6, 63, 126
Foster, Patricia, 190-2
Fowler, William, 218

Francois, Kat, 122-3, 201-2
Frost, Robert, 46, 210
Furniss, Graham, 19, 24, 28
Furniss, Tom, 54

Geertz, Clifford, 175
Genette, Gérard, 13, 138-41
gesture, 11, 13, 39, 52, 56, 60, 78, 145-51, 154, 157-64, 166-9, 190, 211-2, 222, 225-6, 228-9, 231, 235
deictic g., 160-1, 164, 190, 229
motor g., 160-2, 164, 225-6, 231
spatial g., 162-4
symbolic g., 147-8, 160, 162, 164, 226
Gibson, Abraham, 60, 81, 118-9, 128, 132, 136-7, 155-6, 158-9, 163, 169
Ginsberg, Allen, 46, 195, 199, 218
Gioia, Dana, 16, 29, 43, 45, 89
Glazner, Gary M., 45
Goffman, Erving, 187-8
griot, 34
Groff, David, 27
Grotowski, Jerzy, 56
Gudas, Fabian, 25, 133

Habekost, Christian, 45-6, 136, 184, 196
Hagan, Jackie, 63, 221, 223-31
Hall, Donald, 40
Hall, Edward T., 210
Hardi, Choman, 45, 134-6
Hardy, Jane, 20, 67
Harrison, Ruth, 17
Harrison, Tony, 136
Hawthorn, Jeremy, 23
Hays, K. Michael, 208
Hegley, John, 16, 92-3, 109, 140-1, 204
Hiebler, Heinz, 16

Higgins, Dick, 113
Hirshfield, Jane, 186
Hiß, Guido, 64, 150
Hobsbaum, Philip, 87
Horovitz, Michael, 31
Howell, Anthony, 169, 187, 213
Hoyles, Asher, 47
hyper poetry, 50-1, 238

illusion, aesthetic, 58, 61, 185, 188, 216
intonation, 27, 72, 76, 105, 107, 136, 183
isochrony, 95, 98

Jakobson, Roman, 176
Jandl, Ernst, 218-9
Jauß, Hans Robert, 195
Jebb, Keith, 31
Jones, Mark Gwynne, 140, 149-50, 156, 167, 221, 224
Jonzi D, 16
Joseph, Anthony, 20-2, 32, 83-5, 97-9, 109-10, 126, 128, 141-2, 158, 160, 181, 195, 203

Kane, Denizen, 88
Kattenbelt, Chiel, 56
Kay, Jackie, 28, 41, 68, 112, 117-8, 130, 201
Kendon, Adam, 148
Kennedy, David, 41
kinesics, 13, 34, 64, 76, 119, 131-2, 145-7, 158, 160, 164, 170, 221, 238
kinetograph, 162-4, 211
Klarer, Mario, 51, 54
Knowles, Ric, 208, 212
Krämer, Sybille, 192, 194
Krauss, Robert M., 160-2
Kress, Gunther, 77, 79
Kühn, Christine, 146, 167

LaBelle, Brandon, 42
Landesman, Fran, 140-1
L=A=N=G=U=A=G=E poetry, 188
Leech, Geoffrey, 87, 90, 95
Lee-French, Segun, 148-9, 221-4
legato, 115-6, 120
Lejeune, Philippe, 188
Lennard, John, 86, 136
Levertov, Denise, 9, 11, 46, 199
Lewis, Harry, 15
Lindsay, Vachel, 46
live literature, 5, 13, 16, 60-1, 138, 168, 208
Liverpool Poets, 16, 47
Lord, Albert Bates, 23, 27
Lorde, Audre, 46

Mackey, Nathaniel, 72
Mae, Naila Keleta, 59
Mannix, Aoife, 121
Marsh, Nicky, 15, 17, 21, 44, 47, 182
Masefield, John, 24-5
Matterson, Stephen, 37, 53
MC, 13, 18, 140, 144, 179, 200-2, 204, 207, 222, 235
McDaniel, Jeffrey, 45, 181
McGough, Roger, 95-7, 105-6
McLuhan, Marshall, 51
McNeill, David, 145, 162
measure, 90-1, 94-5, 98, 128, 130, 229
melody, 11, 49, 69, 72, 77, 93, 95, 105-6, 237
Mendelssohn, Felix de, 162, 165-7
Merleau-Ponty, Maurice, 78
metre, 13, 49, 69, 76, 86-7, 89-90
Meyer, Michael, 52-5, 188-9

Middleton, Peter, 15, 17, 21, 24, 40-4, 47, 66, 68, 117, 178-9, 182, 186, 215-6
Millum, Trevor, 45
Mitchell, Adrian, 20, 67, 103-6, 111-2, 118, 129, 218
Möhrmann, Malte, 196
Müller-Zettelmann, Eva, 5, 49, 58, 61, 216
Muldoon, Paul, 27, 70
Myspace, 28

Nagra, Daljit, 45
New Criticism, 16, 25-6
non-verbal sounds, 13, 73, 76, 80-2, 84-6, 126, 128, 234
notation, integrated verbal, 126-9
Nünning, Ansgar, 176-7
Nünning, Vera, 176-7

offbeat, 90, 94, 98, 229
Oliver, Douglas, 69
Olson, Charles, 15
Ong, Walter J., 23, 28
open mic, 11, 18, 62, 66, 198, 205-7, 212, 237
orality, medial, 24
-----, conceptional, 24
-----, secondary, 28
oral poetry, 23-4, 33-6, 43, 45, 58, 63
orature, 23, 27, 52

page poetry, 33, 50
paralanguage, 13, 34, 43, 64, 75-6, 79-81, 85-6, 97, 105, 113-4, 116, 119, 126-7, 130-1, 134, 146-8, 170, 221, 224-5, 231, 237
paratext, 13, 35, 43, 75, 107, 113, 138-44, 157, 179, 193, 223-4, 226-7, 231, 234, 238

Patten, Brian, 91-3, 123, 129, 139, 161, 211-2, 224
pause, 39, 43, 54, 68, 76, 92-3, 96, 98, 103, 113, 115, 117-20, 127, 130, 133, 139, 153-4, 191, 216, 225-6, 230
Pavis, Patrice, 233
Penlington, Nathan, 31-2, 44, 46, 138, 179, 184, 199, 205, 206, 215
Perelman, Bob, 58
performability, 32, 57, 70-1
performance poetry, 16, 19, 21, 29-34, 38-9, 43-7, 57, 62, 136, 157, 181, 184, 212, 222-3, 237
performance record, 35, 63
performance report, 35, 41, 63
performance self, 155, 187-8, 201, 226, 235
performance space, 39, 41, 204, 208-9, 210-6, 222, 234
Perrine, Laurence, 37, 52
Pfeiler, Martina, 27, 38-9, 51, 99, 118-9
phonocentrism, 24, 40
phrasing, 43, 77, 86, 93, 96, 98, 101, 103-10, 116-8, 120, 127, 133-5, 142, 152, 161, 164, 202, 211, 223, 225-7, 229
pictograph, 162, 164
pitch, 13, 34, 37, 54, 72, 76-82, 84-6, 90, 92-4, 96-113, 115-6, 118-20, 122, 124-30, 132-5, 137, 143, 165, 167, 183, 197, 202-3, 216, 223, 225-6, 228-30, 234, 237
poetry film, 238
poetry reading, 11, 15, 17, 26, 27, 29, 32, 40-6, 56-7, 62, 69, 107, 179-81, 186, 202, 208, 214-6
Poets Against War, 204
Pötscher, Gabriele, 107-8, 143

posture, 13, 28, 78, 119, 132, 155-6, 158-9, 163-4, 167, 170, 183, 187, 223, 225, 235
Poyatos, Fernando, 76, 81, 85, 93, 99, 102, 109, 118-9, 124, 146-7, 159-60
producer, 13, 32, 44, 93, 173, 175-6, 178-9, 199, 202-5, 207, 217, 222, 235, 238
prosody, 76, 86-7, 90, 95
provenance, 38, 75, 77, 79-80, 149

Quartermain, Peter, 72, 133, 187
Quirk, Randolph, 90, 105, 110

rap poetry, 45, 87, 89-90, 98, 150
Rasula, Jed, 182-4
resonance, 123-5, 131, 135, 183
Reynolds, Joshua, 183
rhythm, 11, 13, 20, 37-8, 45, 49, 61, 66, 71, 76, 80, 82, 84-99, 109-10, 115, 128, 130, 132, 134, 136-7, 149, 150, 152, 161-2, 164, 182, 184, 216, 218, 225, 228-9, 234, 237
Robinson, Mark, 26, 41, 187
Rodríguez-Vázquez, Rosalía, 95
Russell, James A., 164, 204, 217
Ruthrof, Horst, 146

Salah, Trish, 199, 200
Saussure, Ferdinand de, 24-5
Sauter, Willmar, 139, 178
Scannell, Vernon, 26
Schechner, Richard, 174-5, 177, 179, 200
Schevill, James, 210-1
Schmidt, Tom, 21
Schneider, Dan, 27
Schwarz, Aljoscha A., 146
score, 37, 56, 65, 67-70

Severin, Laura, 41
Sheppard, Victoria, 15, 17, 21, 44, 47, 182
Sherwood, Kenneth, 17, 42-4, 125-6, 132, 139
Shortfuse, 179, 205-6, 215
Shortman, 66, 82, 85
Siddique, John, 31-2, 100-1, 116, 142-4, 158-9, 191-2
slam, 11, 15, 16, 26, 28-9, 34, 36, 38, 43-8, 52, 62, 100-1, 140-1, 148-50, 156, 181-2, 189, 196, 201-2, 205-7, 221-2, 225, 231, 237
Smith, Patricia, 189-90, 193, 196, 200, 216
Smith, Rommi, 21, 28, 32, 60, 169, 182
Somers-Willett, Susan, 46
sound poetry, 113-4
soundscape, 38, 213-4, 222, 234
speech act, 116, 185, 200
spoken word, 11, 16, 18, 21, 25, 28, 33-4, 38, 43, 44-5, 47, 55, 59, 60, 62, 66, 96, 116, 138, 179, 181, 192, 194, 199, 201-5, 207, 213, 215, 218, 221-2, 237
staccato, 115-6, 118, 120, 131
Stein, Deborah, 37, 114-5
Stern, Frederick, 41, 179-80
Stevens, Wallace, 26
Stewart, Garrett, 53, 75, 87

Tedlock, Dennis, 34-5, 96-7, 126
tempo, 69, 76, 82, 93, 99, 115, 127-8, 161, 173, 217, 227, 229
Tennyson, Lord Alfred, 183
tense, 77-8, 120-1, 125, 189
Thomas, Dylan, 15, 46
Thompson, Russell, 30-2, 60, 70, 76, 204, 217-8

timbre, 13, 37-8, 80, 85, 120-5, 133, 230, 234
tone, 13, 52-4, 67-8, 72, 76, 84, 93, 97, 99, 107-11, 113, 115, 118, 120, 122-3, 132-6, 141, 144, 150, 152, 162, 166, 183, 197, 202, 222, 225, 228, 230-1, 234
Toro, Fernando de, 185, 188
Trager, George L., 80-1
transcription, 82, 83, 90, 92-3, 96-7, 111, 113-4, 125-8, 130-2, 139-40, 164-5
Tuma, Keith, 41
Tutu, Samera Owusu, 136, 210, 212

Ubersfeld, Anne, 197

Van Leeuwen, Theo, 38, 77-80, 85, 90, 99-107, 115-7, 120-4, 129, 148-50, 210-1
verbal art, 23, 27, 33-6, 38, 125-7, 156, 174-5
vibrato, 123, 125, 183
video poetry, 50-1
Vienna Lit, 83, 91, 97, 100, 101, 107, 110, 139, 141-4, 160-1, 165-6, 201, 211
Vincent, Stephen, 41, 214
vocal segregates, 81
voice action, 75, 80, 99, 102, 109, 147
voice set, 75, 80, 99, 102, 109, 147, 234
volume, 13, 34, 37, 77-8, 82, 85, 92, 98, 104, 109-15, 118, 120, 125-8, 130, 133, 165, 189, 202, 234

Wade, Stephen, 45

Index 271

Watzlawick, Paul, 196
Wennerstrom, Ann, 76-7, 89, 105
Wheeler, Lesley, 47, 182, 187
Whitworth, John, 60
Winters, Yvor, 26, 37, 40
Wojahn, David, 22, 40
Wolf, Werner, 50, 58-9

Yeats, William Butler, 183, 216
YouTube, 28

Zephaniah, Benjamin, 134, 184

www.ingramcontent.com/pod-product-compliance
Lightning Source LLC
Chambersburg PA
CBHW021358290426
44108CB00010B/294